The Writings of Teresa de Cartagena

Library of Medieval Women   ISSN 1369–9652

Series Editor: Jane Chance

The Writings of Teresa de Cartagena

Translated with
Introduction, Notes, and Interpretive Essay

Dayle Seidenspinner-Núñez
University of Notre Dame

D.S. BREWER

First published 1998
D. S. Brewer, Cambridge

ISBN 0 85991 446 1

D.S. Brewer is an imprint of Boydell & Brewer Ltd
PO Box 9, Woodbridge, Suffolk IP12 3DF, UK
and of Boydell & Brewer Inc.
PO Box 41026, Rochester, NY 14604–4126, USA

A catalogue record for this book is available
from the British Library

Library of Congress Cataloging-in-Publication Data
Teresa, de Cartagena, 15th cent.
    [Selections. English. 1998]
    The writings of Teresa de Cartagena / translated with
introduction, notes, and interpretive essay [by] Dayle Seidenspinner-Núñez.
        p.   cm. – (Library of medieval women)
    This book presents two prose works written by Teresa de Cartagena :
Grove of the infirm (Arbolea de los enfermos) and Wonder at the
works of God (Admiración operum Dey).
    Includes bibliographical references and index.
    ISBN 0–85991–446–1 (pbk. : alk. paper)
    1. Spiritual life – Catholic Church – Early works to 1800.
2. Spirituality – Spain – Early works to 1800.   3. Women – Spain –
History – Middle Ages, 500–1500.   4. Teresa, de Cartagena, 15th
cent.   I. Seidenspinner-Núñez, Dayle.   II. Teresa, de Cartagena,
15th cent.   Grove of the infirm.   III. Teresa, de Cartagena, 15th
cent.   Wonder at the works of God.   IV. Title.   V. Series.
BX2186.T47213   1998
248.4'82–dc21   97–37484

This publication is printed on acid-free paper

Printed in Great Britain by
Athenæum Press Ltd, Gateshead, Tyne & Wear

Contents

The publishers gratefully acknowledge the generous
subvension from the Program for Cultural Co-operation
between Spain's Ministry of Education and Culture
and United States Universities
in aid of publication for this volume.

To Jay, Kate, and Mia

Preface

Teresa de Cartagena's two prose works survive in a unique manuscript in the Escorial library copied by Pero López del Trigo after 1481. Sitting at a heavy wooden desk in the reading room of the Escorial on a warm July morning, lulled by strains of music from a boys' choir rehearsing at the Augustinian school below, and leafing through the waxen folios of MS. III.h.24, I was hauntingly reminded how fragile and incomplete our knowledge is of the Middle Ages and how contingent on circumstance. I cannot explain why Pero López del Trigo copied what Teresa describes as a sheaf of rough draft papers written in her hand, but he did, and his copy – an invaluable window into the world of women in fifteenth-century Spain – has survived. And so, fortunately, we can recover, if only in part, Teresa's remarkable struggle, first to give meaning to her misfortune and definition to her self through writing, and later to confront her detractors and defend the divine inspiration for her texts and her life and her own right to write.

My translation is based on the text of *Arboleda de los enfermos* and *Admiraçión operum Dey* in the Escorial manuscript and on Lewis J. Hutton's critical edition. The unique manuscript of Teresa's writings presents a text that is challenging, often obscure, and occasionally badly garbled in its transmission. In translating *Grove of the Infirm* and *Wonder at the Works of God* I opted to produce a readable text rather than a slavishly literal translation; on rare occasions, therefore, I have simplified some of Teresa's repetitive language or filler phrases that, in my view, compromised the readability of the translation but did not affect the sense of her text.

References to the Vulgate Bible are generally rendered by means of the Douay-Rheims translation, and I have identified biblical quotations in brackets; since Teresa often translates her biblical authorities, in tagged instances I have substituted my own translations for the Douay-Rheims.to accord with her readings. When Teresa provides a partial or truncated biblical citation, the missing portion has been supplied within brackets. I have left in Teresa's Latin quotes because, as I argue in the interpretive essay, these are part of her strategy to establish a female authority in her texts. Translations of other texts in Spanish and Latin are mine.

x *Preface*

The following abbreviations have been used:

PL *Patrologia cursus completus: Series latina*, ed. J.P. Migne, 221 vols. Paris: Migne, etc., 1841–64. References are to volume and column.

Hutton Teresa de Cartagena, *Arboleda de los enfermos y Admiraçión operum Dey*, ed. Lewis J. Hutton. Anejos del Boletín de la Real Academia Española, 16. Madrid: Real Academia Española, 1967.

It is a pleasure to acknowledge the various sources of support for this project. A generous grant from the Academic Senate of the University of California at Irvine enabled me to initiate my research at the Escorial library; a grant from the Program for Cultural Co-operation between Spain's Ministry of Education and Culture and United States Universities has contributed to its publication here. Parts of the interpretive essay were presented previously as discrete papers and benefitted considerably from audience commentary at Queen Mary and Westfield College, Emory University, the University of Colorado at Boulder, and Western Michigan University. An earlier study, " 'El solo me leyó': Gendered Hermeneutics and Subversive Poetics in the *Admiraçión operum Dey* of Teresa de Cartagena," has been revised and expanded in the interpretive essay; my thanks to the editors of *Medievalia* for permission to include parts of that article. Intellectual and theoretical debts have been recorded in the footnotes, but I consulted with several generous and responsive colleagues at different stages of research and writing: Dwayne E. Carpenter, Alan Deyermond, Deborah S. Ellis, Charles B. Faulhaber, María Eugenia Lacarra, Louise Mirrer, and Madeline Sutherland-Meier. I am particularly indebted to Joseph T. Snow, Ronald E. Surtz, and Jane Whetnall for their meticulous critical reading of the typescript and numerous suggestions which have greatly improved my rendering of Teresa's text. Special thanks are due to Father Teodoro Alonso Turienzo of the Escorial library; to Mark Rose, Debra Massey, Christine Aschan, and Rosemary Humphreys for providing research and computer support at the University of California Humanities Research Institute; to Jane Chance for her encouragement and help in negotiating several years of prepublication delays and frustrations; and to Caroline Palmer and Pru Harrison for bringing the project to press so expeditiously at Boydell & Brewer.

Finally, because they are never separate from anything I do, I thank my husband, José Luis, and our children, to whom I dedicate what has become for me a labor of love.

Introduction

> And I would have willingly endured this suf-
> fering from birth, so that no words that may
> have offended or disserved God could ever
> enter the cloisters of my ears.
>
> Teresa de Cartagena, *Grove of the Infirm*

"More than One Teresa"[1]

This book presents two prose works written by Teresa de Cartagena.[2] Her first text, *Grove of the Infirm* (*Arboleda de los enfermos*), was written after 1450; its theme is the spiritual benefits of illness, and Teresa's own deafness serves as an autobiographical exemplum. Apparently Teresa's authorship of *Grove of the Infirm* occasioned some controversy, and she wrote her second work, *Wonder at the Works of God* (*Admiración operum Dey*), to counter the incredulity (*admiración*) of her detractors

---

[1] The heading is from Electa Arenal and Stacey Schlau, *Untold Sisters: Hispanic Nuns in Their Own Works* (Albuquerque: University of New Mexico Press, 1989), and refers to convent writing by Hispanic nuns after St. Teresa de Avila (1515–82), the great mystic, writer, and reformer of the Carmelite Order. Arenal and Schlau recover and make available materials for a fuller understanding of women's social, cultural, and intellectual history in Teresian and post-Teresian Spain and Latin America. Relatively little attention has focused on the tradition of nuns' writing prior to the saint of Avila; see, however, Ronald E. Surtz, *Writing Women in Late Medieval and Early Modern Spain: The Mothers of Saint Teresa of Avila* (Philadelphia: University of Pennsylvania Press, 1995).

[2] In medieval Spain, there are only a few women writers – all from the fifteenth century – whose work is known to us: Leonor López de Córdoba (*Memorias*), several poets (Florencia Pinar, Mayor Arias, María Sarmiento, Isabel González, Tecla de Borja), Sor Constanza de Castilla (*Devocionario*), Sor Isabel de Villena (*Vita Christi*), and Teresa de Cartagena. On women writers in medieval Spain, see Alan Deyermond, "Spain's First Women Writers," in *Women in Hispanic Literature: Icons and Fallen Idols*, ed. Beth Miller (Berkeley: University of California Press, 1983), 27–52; Francisco López Estrada, "Las mujeres escritoras en la Edad Media castellana," in *La condición de la mujer en la edad media, Actas del Coloquio celebrado en la Casa de Velázquez del 5 al 7 de noviembre de 1984* (Madrid: Editorial de la Universidad Complutense, 1986), 9–38; the biobibliography of Manuel Serrano y Sanz, *Apuntes para una biblioteca de escritoras españolas desde el año 1401 al 1833*, 2 vols. (Madrid: Sucesores de Rivadeneyra, 1903–5); and Ronald E. Surtz, *Writing Women in Late Medieval and Early Modern Spain*. For an overview, see Louise Mirrer, "Feminist Approaches to Medieval Spanish History and Literature," *Medieval Feminist Newsletter* 7 (Spring 1989): 2–7; and Deyermond's update, "Las autoras medievales castellanas a la luz de las últimas investigaciones," in *Medioevo y Literatura: Actas del V Congreso de la Asociación Hispánica de Literatura Medieval*, ed. Juan Paredes (Granada: Universidad de Granada, 1995), I: 31–52.

who contended that a woman – and particularly a handicapped woman – had nothing of value to teach.

Teresa's writings merit serious and sustained critical attention on several counts.[3] First, they constitute remarkable documents in the context of the intellectual, literary, and social landscape of fifteenth-century Spain, for both Teresa's family and her texts are deeply rooted in the literary culture of her times. *Grove of the Infirm* is an excellent example of the consolatory treatises cultivated widely in the fifteenth century and is the only extant *consolatio* written from a woman's position. Moreover, throughout the *cuatrocientos* in Spain pro-versus antifeminist debates were waged in *cancionero* poetry, moralist commentary, and the sentimental romances. The participants were male clerics, poets, moralists, and writers of prose fiction: the *Corbacho* by Alfonso Martínez de Toledo, *Repetiçión de amores* by Luis de Lucena, *Jardín de nobles doncellas* by Fray Martín de Córdoba, *Tratado en defensa de las mujeres* by Mosén Diego de Valera, *Cárcel de amor* by Diego de San Pedro, *Grisel y Mirabella* by Juan de Flores, *Coplas en vituperio delas malas hembras y en loor delas buenas mugeres* by Fray Yñigo de Mendoza, and *Coplas de las calidades de las donas* by Pero Torrellas. Pro- and antifeminist *images* of women are perpetuated by these male authors, but Teresa, in *Wonder at the Works of God*, represents the only authentic female *voice*.

3   In 1967, Lewis J. Hutton published a scholarly edition of the two works (*Anejos del Boletín de la Real Academia Española*, 16 [Madrid: Real Academia Española]), and in 1976, Alan Deyermond wrote an important study, " 'El convento de dolençias': The Works of Teresa de Cartagena," *Journal of Hispanic Philology* 1 (1976–77): 19–29, revised and slightly reworked in "Spain's First Women Writers." Studies since then include: Deborah S. Ellis, "The Image of the Home in Early English and Spanish Literature," Diss. University of California at Berkeley, 1981, Chapter 2, and "Unifying Imagery in the Works of Teresa de Cartagena: Home and the Dispossessed" (forthcoming, *Journal of Hispanic Philology*); Ronald E. Surtz, "Image Patterns in Teresa de Cartagena's *Arboleda de los enfermos*," *La Chispa '87: Selected Proceedings*, ed. Gilbert Paolini (New Orleans: Tulane University, 1987), 297–304; Luis Miguel Vicente García, "La defensa de la mujer como intelectual en Teresa de Cartagena y Sor Juana Inés de la Cruz," *Mester* 18:2 (Fall 1989): 95–103; Irene Alejandra Molina, "La *Arboleda de los enfermos* de Teresa de Cartagena: Un sermón consolatorio olvidado," M.A. Thesis, University of Texas, Austin, December 1990; Carmen Marimón Llorca, *Prosistas castellanas medievales* (Alicante: Caja de Ahorros Provincial, 1990), 102–40; Gregorio Rodríguez Rivas, "La *Arboleda de los enfermos* de Teresa de Cartagena, literatura ascética en el siglo XV," *Entemu* (Centro Asociado de Asturias) 3 (1992): 117–30; Dayle Seidenspinner–Núñez, " 'El solo me leyó': Gendered Hermeneutics and Subversive Poetics in *Admiraçión operum Dey* of Teresa de Cartagena," *Medievalia* 15 (1993): 14–23; Surtz, "The New Judith: Teresa de Cartagena," in *Writing Women*, 21–40; Rocío Quispe, "El espacio medieval feminino entre la escritura y el silencio: *Admiraçión operum Dey* de Teresa de Cartagena," *Lexis* 19 (1995): 85–101; Elizabeth Teresa Howe, "Sor Teresa de Cartagena and *Entendimiento*," *Romanische Forschungen* 108 (1996): 133–45; and Seidenspinner–Núñez, " 'But I Suffer Not a Woman to Teach': Two Women Writers in Late Medieval Spain," in *Hers Ancient and Modern: Women Writing in Spain and Brazil*, ed. Catherine Davies and Jane Whetnall (London: Department of Hispanic Studies, Queen Mary and Westfield College, in press).

Secondly, Teresa's work is of considerable interest in the overall context of women writers in medieval Europe. Even a cursory glance at recent bibliography indicates how much work has been accomplished toward the definition of this context (Dhuoda, Hrotsvit of Gandersheim, Marie de France, Heloise, Hildegard of Bingen, Castelloza, Mechthild of Magdeburg, Hadewijch, Marguerite Porete, Margaret of Oingt, Catherine of Siena, Julian of Norwich, Margery Kempe, Christine de Pizan). Of particular relevance to Teresa de Cartagena are the numerous recent studies on women's spirituality; from the twelfth century on, nuns in England, France, Germany, and Italy contributed significantly to the literature of devotion, mysticism, and auto-biography. In Hispanic literature, Teresa de Cartagena is the spiritual precursor of both St. Teresa de Avila in the sixteenth century and Sor Juana Inés de la Cruz in the seventeenth in combining devotional writing with an autobiographical focus and a defense against male detractors.

Finally, Teresa's writings represent a unique example of marginalized discourse; *Grove of the Infirm* and *Wonder at the Works of God* are compelling as records of personal suffering and religious experience. In effect, as a writer, Teresa is thrice marginalized – by her gender, by her deafness, and by her status as a conversa. She writes at a time when anti-Jewish and anti-converso riots were common and the worst of these – the Toledo uprising of 1449 – occurred just before the composition of *Grove of the Infirm*.[4]

---

[4] Deyermond (" 'El convento de dolençias,' " 27) suggests that the social unrest and hostility toward conversos inspired Teresa's transformation of the traditional Christian image of the city as a secure place under God's rule (Augustine's *City of God*) to "the city of our conscience," a place of danger and of fear.

  The 1449 uprising – the first outbreak of violence and discrimination against judeoconversos – marked an irreversible shift from "the Jewish problem" (the anti-Semitic pogroms, preaching, and disputations of the first half of the century) to "the converso problem," an obsession with lineage, Old Christian "cleanliness of blood," and converso impurity which would last for centuries. Attempts to justify this fixation with origins with accusations against the conversos of judaizing, heterodoxy, and sacrilege culminated in the establishment of the Inquisition. See Eloy Benito Ruano, "Del problema judío al problema converso," in *Los orígenes del problema converso* (Barcelona: El Albir, 1976), 15–37; José Faur, *In the Shadow of History: Jews and Conversos at the Dawn of Modernity* (Albany: State University of New York Press, 1992); Stephen Gilman, *The Spain of Fernando de Rojas: The Intellectual and Social Landscape of "La Celestina"* (Princeton: Princeton University Press, 1972); Francisco Márquez Villanueva, "El problema de los conversos: Cuatro puntos cardinales," in *Hispania Judaica: Studies on the History, Language, and Literature of the Jews in the Hispanic World*, ed. Josep Solà-Solé, Samuel G. Armistead, and Joseph H. Silverman, 3 vols. (Barcelona: Puvill, 1980–84), 1:51–75; Norman Roth, *Conversos, Inquisition, and the Expulsion of the Jews from Spain* (Madison: University of Wisconsin Press, 1995); Benzion Netanyahu, *The Origins of the Inquisition in Fifteenth Century Spain* (New York: Random House, 1995); and David M. Gitlitz, *Secrecy and Deceit: The Religion of the Crypto-Jews* (Philadelphia: The Jewish Publication Society, 1996).

The Cartagena/Santa María Family

Teresa de Cartagena belonged to the most influential and powerful judeoconverso clan in late medieval Spain; throughout the fifteenth and well into the sixteenth century, the Cartagena/Santa María family was pivotal in the political, religious, economic, and literary culture of the late Middle Ages and the Renaissance.[5] A brief overview of her family will help us to contextualize Teresa and her works and to understand the possibility of her writing.

In Burgos, Rabbi Šelomó ha-Levi (ca. 1350–1435), Teresa's grandfather, presided over Spain's largest community of Jews and established the foremost school of rabbinical studies in the Iberian Peninsula.[6] On 21 July 1390, along with his children and brothers, he converted to Christianity.[7] Baptized Pablo de Santa María,[8] he departed for Paris to complete his theological studies; in Avignon he became friends with Pedro de Luna, later (1394) Pope Benedict XIII.[9] Santa María advanced rapidly both within the ranks of the church (he became bishop of Cartagena in 1402 – hence the derivation of his family name – and bishop of Burgos in 1412) and in the courts of Enrique III and Juan II, where he served as royal chancellor of Castile and as tutor of Juan II during his minority.[10] He wrote

---

5   Francisco Cantera Burgos's exhaustive history of the Cartagena/Santa María family, *Alvar García de Santa María y su familia de conversos: Historia de la Judería de Burgos y de sus conversos más egregios* (Madrid: Instituto Arias Montano, 1952), includes and corrects previous works and is still the standard reference work for the subject. He notes: "It can be said that there was no important aspect of the civil, religious, literary, military, political, diplomatic or economic life of the fifteenth and sixteenth centuries that did not involve some member of this illustrious family from Burgos" (6).

6   See M. Jean Sconza, "A Reevaluation of the *Siete Edades del Mundo*," *La Corónica* 16 (1987–88): 94–112.

7   Whether his conversion took place in July 1390 or 1391 has been the subject of scholarly debate. The later date advanced by his critics would be after the rash of pogroms and massacres against the Jews of Burgos and would confer a measure of convenience to his conversion; Cantera Burgos argues in favor of the earlier date (*Alvar García de Santa María*, 304–5).

8   A document from 1604 conferring the *beneficio de limpieza de sangre* (benefit of purity of blood) to the Patriarch Pablo de Santa María and his descendants speaks of his "miraculous conversion" and states that he assumed the name Santa María because the Virgin appeared to him shortly before his conversion. He was also known as Pablo de Burgos and Pablo de Cartagena. The Cartagena family coat of arms consisted of a white fleur de lis on a green background, symbolizing their descent from the Virgin.

9   One of the main sources for Teresa's *Grove of the Infirm* is the *Libro de las consolaciones de la vida humana* (*Book of Consolations for Human Life*) by her grandfather's friend, Pedro de Luna, written after he renounced the Avignon papacy.

10 The 1604 document praises his "many ecclesiastical and civil titles and offices; the importance and multitude of services that he performed for the Church, the Crown, and the republic with his example, doctrine, and good conduct, having been bishop of Cartagena and Burgos and patriarch of Aquileya, delegate to the Apostolic Sede, High Chancellor of the kingdom, executor for King Enrique, tutor to King Juan II during his minority, and

exegetical and theological tracts, polemical treatises against the Jews, historical works, and an extended poem, *Siete edades del mundo (Seven Ages of the World)*, a compendium of universal and national history designed for the instruction of Castile's future monarch, Juan II.[11]

Two of Pablo de Santa María's five children were also ecclesiastics. The oldest, Gonzalo García de Santa María (1379/80–1448), was a professor at the University of Salamanca and subsequently bishop of Plasencia; he also served on diplomatic and ecclesiastical missions for the Spanish court. The second son, Alonso de Cartagena (1385–1456), was bishop of Palencia before succeeding his father as bishop of Burgos; he was named judge of the Royal Tribunal of Juan II and with his brother Gonzalo attended the Council of Basel. Cantera Burgos lists twenty-six works written by Alonso de Cartagena and classifies them into works of law, history, and moral philosophy.

The third son, Pedro de Cartagena (1387–1478), had a distinguished and picturesque career as a knight in the court of Juan II. He was one of the *regidores* (aldermen) of Burgos, a guard de corps of Juan II, and counselor to Enrique IV and to the Catholic Monarchs, Fernando and Isabel. In 1440, Juan II granted the right of primogeniture to him and his descendants.[12] Pedro de Cartagena had first married Doña María de Sarabia, with whom he had five children (Alonso de Cartagena [d. 1467], Alvaro de Cartagena [d. 1471], Juana de Cartagena, Teresa de Cartagena, and María Sarabia) and later married Doña Mencía de Rojas, with whom he had two children (Elvira de Rojas and Lope de Rojas [1444–77]); in addition, he recognized three illegitimate sons (Paulo de Cartagena, Gonzalo Pérez de Cartagena [d. 1519], and Pedro de Cartagena).

---

ambassador to popes, councils, and kings; the important works he wrote, the conversion of 40,000 Jews through his preaching, as well as everything his sons (legitimate because he was married prior to his conversion) and descendants did in times of peace and of war which fill our books of history" (Cantera Burgos, *Alvar García de Santa María*, 281).

[11] Among Teresa's other relatives and literary connections was Pablo de Santa María's brother, Alvar García de Santa María, an influential political figure and historian during the first half of the fifteenth century, who served as royal scribe and secretary and royal chronicler of the court of Juan II; he is the principal subject of Cantera Burgos's family history.

[12] The fourth son, Doctor Alvar Sánchez de Santa María (ca. 1488–?), was disinherited by his father in his will (1431) for having incurred Juan II's wrath because of his *error*, which is not specified ("quia propter errorem suum regiam indignacionem incurrit"). At the same time, Pablo de Santa María requested royal clemency for his son and concluded that when and if pardon were granted, then the errant Alvar should receive the same share as his three older brothers. Finally, little or nothing is known about Pablo's daughter, María de Cartagena, who was probably born between Gonzalo and Alonso around 1383; Cantera Burgos speculates that she may have married Alonso Alvarez de Toledo, chief auditor for Juan II, but Faur, following Américo Castro, claims that she was the grandmother of Fernando de Aragón, who expelled the Jews from Spain in 1492 (*In the Shadow of History*, 48).

I have discussed in some detail the Cartagena/Santa María clan because they were so clearly a product of their times: they came into being as a response to the surge of anti-Semitism in the late fourteenth century[13] and their trajectory as a leading converso family ironically culminated in 1604, when the patriarch Pablo de Santa María and his descendants were granted *limpieza de sangre*.[14] They figured prominently and often decisively in the major historical events of the fifteenth century. In the early part of the century, the Cartagenas were involved in Benedict XIII's renunciation of the Avignon papacy, in the Council of Constance (1414–18) that ended the papal schism, and in the subsequent election of Pope Martin V. Pablo de Santa María's conversion deeply troubled the Jewish community of Burgos, and while the claim that he converted more than 40,000 Jews through his proselytizing is probably inflated, his example inspired many prominent Jewish intellectuals to follow suit, most notably Yehošu'a ha-Lorqí, later the Christian activist Jerónimo de Santa Fe. Santa María's own *Scrutinium Scriptuararum* promoted the Christian cause and impugned the Jews, "ad fidelium eruditionem et infidelium impugnationem"; his son, Gonzalo García de Santa María, was appointed as the pope's representative to implement in Spain papal statutes regarding Jews. Pablo de Santa María, Gonzalo García de Santa María, and Alonso de Cartagena must have been instrumental in defining Juan II's anti-Jewish policies, but whether their voices were fired by fanatic anti-Semitism or tempered by moderation has not been established. Critics of the Cartagena family (José Amador de los Ríos, Yitzhak Baer, Américo Castro) see their conversion as opportunistic and their allegedly aggressive persecution of Jews as a mask for their own lack of religious conviction and as a means to insinuate themselves into the power structures of church and state. Cantera Burgos argues that no historical documents substantiate such a negative interpretation and that the Cartagenas were characteristically moderate and judicious in their political and social interventions.

This same controversy colors interpretations of the Cartagenas' political conduct. Pablo de Santa María, Alvar García de Santa María, Gonzalo

---

13 This is not to call into question the sincerity of the 1390/91 conversion but rather to suggest that conversion might never have become an issue without the violence of the pogroms of 1369 and 1391, the proselytizing of the mendicant orders, the theological disputations, etc.

14 *Limpieza de sangre* – purity of blood – certified an Old Christian bloodline necessary for obtaining membership in semi-official social institutions such as the military orders, for receiving titles of nobility, and for holding ecclesiastical and political office. The first of many statutes exclusionary of conversos, or New Christians, was the *sentençia estatuto* (statute of exclusion) promulgated by Pero Sarmiento, mayor of Toledo, in 1449, which ousted some thirteen city councillors, notaries, and judges from office because of the impurity of their bloodline. Alonso de Cartagena provided an immediate and influential theological refutation in 1450, *Defensorium Unitatis Christianae* (*A Defense of Christian Unity*).

García de Santa María, Alonso de Cartagena, and Pedro de Cartagena were highly visible, as we have seen, in the royal court, particularly during the tumultuous first half of the fifteenth century. Pablo de Santa María served as tutor for the young Juan II during the co-regency of Fernando de Antequera (Juan II's uncle) and Catherine of Lancaster (the queen mother). While the family allied with Fernando de Antequera during his regency and after he became king of Aragon, their relationship to his controversial sons, the Infantes de Aragón, is unclear. Equally undefined is their position with regard to the Condestable Alvaro de Luna, Juan II's favorite and the key political figure of his court. The Condestable was ultimately placed under house arrest in 1453 while staying at Pedro de Cartagena's family residence in Burgos, and when Juan II pronounced his death sentence, Alonso de Cartagena stood at the monarch's side. To their detractors, the Cartagenas participated in a variety of political intrigues to first secure and then promote their influential positions in the court. Cantera Burgos, however, refutes this judgement as arbitrary and argues that their political interventions were motivated, above all, by an unswerving loyalty to the king rather than their own personal interest.[15] Most recently, Netanyahu proposes that Don Alvaro's downfall was engineered by Alonso de Cartagena and Fernán Díaz de Toledo (the converso Relator) because of the Condestable's ultimately anti-converso resolution of the Toledan rebellion (*The Origins of the Inquisition*, 681–702).

While the Cartagenas were active agents of history, they were more importantly *writers* of history, and their most significant impact was on fifteenth-century culture. Alonso de Cartagena was the leading humanist of his day;[16] he spent much of his adult life outside Spain as a representative of the Castilian king and acquired a circle of acquaintances among the Italian humanists. He translated several classical and Italian authors (including Seneca, Cicero, and Boccaccio) and wrote a commentary on Aristotle's *Ethics* critiquing Leonardo Bruni's Latin version, *A*

---

[15] Extreme monarchism and self-interest are, of course, not mutually exclusive. Márquez Villanueva notes that while conversos failed to establish any political identity in the fifteenth century (their best defense was to assimilate as much as possible to Christian society and not to stand out), converso intellectuals – like the Cartagena/Santa Marías, Juan de Mena, Juan de Lucena, Diego de San Pedro, Fernando de la Torre – allied themselves with a powerful antifeudal monarch as protection against popular unrest ("El problema de los conversos," 54–55).

[16] Faur describes him as the most prestigious converso in Spain, "the founder of religious humanism in Europe, and the one who introduced the study of the humanities in Spain" (*In the Shadow of History*, 31); see also Ottavio di Camillo, "La contribución de Alonso de Cartagena al humanismo castellano," in *El humanismo castellano del siglo XV* (Valer Fernando Torres, 1976), 135–93.

Defense of Christian Unity in favor of the conversos, *Doctrinal for Knights*, and *Genealogy of the Kings of Spain*, an influential reinterpretation of Spanish history defending the superiority of Castile by demonstrating its antiquity and comparing its chronology to that of other nations. His most famous political work was the Latin speech he delivered before the Council of Basel in 1434 where he argued Castile's precedence over England because of the greater antiquity of the Castilian monarchy (according to the Cartagenas' own rewriting of early Spanish history) and because of the Castilian king's ongoing war against the Moslems in Granada which proved his superior obedience to divine will.

Alonso de Cartagena's disciples and colleagues included Alonso de Palencia, Rodrigo Sánchez de Arévalo, Juan de Lucena, the Marqués de Santillana, Juan de Mena, Fernán Pérez de Guzmán, and Diego Rodríguez de Almella, an intellectual elite composed primarily of conversos. Alonso de Cartagena, his father, and his students introduced a political theory, a literary style, and a theological approach new to fifteenth-century Castile and associated with the *letrados*,[17] an incipient humanism heavily modified by medieval scholasticism that prevailed in the court of the Catholic Monarchs and determined the nature and development of the Renaissance in Trastámara Castile.

The Life and Writings of Teresa de Cartagena

Teresa's affiliation with the Cartagena family was not definitively established until 1952, when, sifting through the hundreds of documents pertaining to the Cartagena/Santa María clan, Cantera Burgos finally uncovered a specific mention of Teresa de Cartagena in the testament of her uncle. In Santa Olalla on 6 July 1453, Alonso de Cartagena be-

---

17 On the *letrados*, see Helen Nader, *The Mendoza Family in the Spanish Renaissance, 1350–1550* (New Brunswick: Rutgers University Press, 1979). The first Trastámaran king, Enrique II, divided political power between two groups, the *caballeros*, or knights, who controlled the military and the *letrados* (university graduates with advanced degrees in canon or civil law) who controlled the judiciary. The *caballeros* saw themselves and the king as partners in a secular, aristocratic, and particularist government, while the *letrados* developed a theory of monarchy that placed the king at the apex of a divinely ordained and immutable hierarchy:

> These two definitions of the Spanish monarchy were developed by intellectuals whose educational backgrounds and professions were so divergent that their most basic assumptions – about the relationship between the past and the present, the nature of historical sources, the validity of universal models derived from philosophy, and the worth of man's rational and irrational natures – were equally divergent (Nader, 20).

At the end of the fifteenth century, changing political circumstances made the extreme monarchism of the *letrados* attractive to the Catholic Monarchs and it prevailed through the Golden Age.

queathed certain sums of money to the children of his brother, Pedro de Cartagena:

For Alfonso, the firstborn, 300 florines . . .

For Alvaro, his brother, 500 florines . . .

For Lope de Rojas, their brother, 600 florines . . .

For Juana, their sister, 200 florines . . .

For Teresa, a nun, 100 florines . . .

For María Sarabia, 100 florines . . .

For Elvira de Rojas, 600 florines . . .[18]

The little else we know about Teresa de Cartagena may be culled from the scattered details of her manuscript and reconstructed from our knowledge of her family. Her name is revealed in the introductory rubrics to both her works: "This treatise is called *Grove of the Infirm*, which Teresa de Cartagena composed . . ." (23; see also 86); she was deaf: "afflicted with grave ailments and, in particular, having lost completely her sense of hearing" (23), and had been deaf for twenty years: "for it is now twenty years since this bridle first constrained the jaws of my vanities" (36); she was a nun: "Teresa de Cartagena, a nun of the order of [. . .], composed [*Wonder at the Works of God*]" (86); she was in constant poor health: "the illnesses and physical sufferings that I have continually for companions" (86); prior to her deafness she had studied in Salamanca: "the few years that I was at the University of Salamanca" (80); and after her deafness she spent much time alone reading and meditating: "I must recur to my books which have wondrous graftings from healthful groves" (24).

Teresa was either the third or fourth child of Pedro de Cartagena and María de Sarabia.[19] She probably was born around 1415–20 and grew up

---

[18] Cantera Burgos, *Alvar García de Santa María*, 440–41; on the will, see M. Martínez Burgos, "Don Alonso de Cartagena, Obispo de Burgos: su testamento," *Revista de Archivos, Bibiliotecas y Museos* 63 (1957): 81–110. Alonso de Cartagena explained that Alfonso received less than his brothers because as firstborn he would inherit more from his father; Juana and María Sarabia married well and therefore received less; Lope de Rojas, being the youngest, received 600 florines as did his sister Elvira de Rojas to provide for her dowry.

This is the only historical document that refers to Teresa. As daughter and nun, Teresa is absent from other official documents pertaining to her family. Her married or marriageable sisters are mentioned in the primogeniture document prepared by Pedro de Cartagena (see Cantera Burgos, 471–73) and in marriage documents.

[19] Family documents – like Alonso de Cartagena's will or Pedro de Cartagena's right of primogeniture – list first the male children in order of birth and then the female children, so it is difficult to establish a relative chronology. Cantera Burgos (*Alvar García de Santa María*, 470–71) cites a document (Biblioteca Nacional de Madrid 18192) that states that in 1424 Pedro de Cartagena killed Juan Hurtado de Mendoza in a duel and to re-establish peace between the two families he married his oldest son, Alonso de Cartagena, to the deceased's daughter María and his own daughter, Juana de Cartagena, to Diego Hurtado, the deceased's son. Presumably either Alvaro or Teresa would be the next child.

in the family home on Calle de Cantarranas la Menor in Burgos, a center for social, political, and cultural activity.[20] In the Cartagena tradition, Teresa and her brothers and sisters must have received an excellent education and would have had available the appreciable resources of the various family libraries.[21] Teresa herself tells us that she attended the University of Salamanca before succumbing to deafness, although it is difficult for us to gauge the nature of her studies. In all likelihood, she would have been tutored at home and then sent to Salamanca to study in a convent, for in the late Middle Ages religious houses trained not only their own novitiates but also the sons or daughters of the nobility and the wealthy bourgeoise.[22] Her privileged position as a Cartagena must have afforded her an exceptional foundation in religion and moral philosophy (which she later deepened and expanded with her own solitary readings), access to the books that she incorporated in her text, and a tradition of writing – firmly established in the Cartagena men – which she acted upon when twenty years later she wrote *The Grove of the Infirm.*

The single most important event in Teresa's life was her affliction with deafness.[23] At the opening of *Grove of the Infirm,* she allegorizes her grief and confusion as she is cut off from the world and enveloped in silence and solitude: "[T]he cloud of temporal and human sadness covered the borders of my life and with a thick whirlwind of anguished sufferings carried me off to an island called 'Oprobrium hominum et abiecio plebis' ['The Scorn of Mankind and Outcast of the People']" (23). With the sorrow and pain that subtends the entire treatise, she describes her exile

---

[20] In Burgos, the Cartagena home must have been a frequent political and social meeting place and a stopover for visiting national and international dignitaries. In the summer of 1440 Princess Blanche of Navarre lodged there on her way to Valladolid to marry Crown Prince Enrique; and in 1453 the Condestable Alvaro de Luna was staying at the Cartagena home when he was arrested (see Cantera Burgos, *Alvar García de Santa María,* 175, 432, 471).

[21] Cantera Burgos (*Alvar García de Santa María,* 198–202) examines the inventory of Alvar García's personal library, which at one point lists "another copy of Boethius that I had in Latin and in Castilian, all on parchment, which I loaned to my niece, Doña Juana de Cartagena [Teresa's sister], and she hasn't returned" (200). Although no inventory exists of Alonso de Cartagena's famous library, Rodríguez de Almella praises his "many books of diverse theological sciences and of philosophy, law, and canon law; and also many histories and chronicles about Holy Scriptures as well as emperors, kings, and princes, particularly those from Spain" (Cantera Burgos, 443).

[22] For an important overview of educational opportunities for women, see Joan M. Ferrante, "The Education of Women in the Middle Ages in Theory, Fact, and Fantasy," in *Beyond Their Sex: Learned Women of the European Past,* ed. Patricia H. Labalme (New York: New York University Press, 1980), 9–42. As with women's history in the Middle Ages in general, the task is primarily reconstructive: "[W]e must piece together allusions in letters and lives and romances with passages from monastic rules, and supplement them with the writings of the women whose work is extant, in order to deduce what they must have been taught and where" (9).

[23] Teresa obliquely dates her sickness in her discussion of the vanity of youth; see 37–38 n. 34.

from a world to which she was deeply attached – "thus enmeshed in the confusion of worldly chatter, with my understanding disordered and bound up in worldly cares" (26) – and her subsequent estrangement from her own family: "Worldly pleasures despise us, health forsakes us, friends forget us, relatives get angry, and even one's own mother gets annoyed with her sickly daughter, and one's father despises the son who with chronic afflictions dwells in his home" (46). At this time Teresa must have entered the convent.

Either accidentally or intentionally the name of Teresa's religious order was omitted by the copyist, Pero López de Trigo, in 1481, but it is generally believed that she belonged to the Franciscan Order and probably lived in a convent house in Burgos, possibly the monastery of Santa Clara.[24] Carmen Marimón Llorca notes that Teresa's convent must have been one of those for daughters of wealthy families where a certain degree of social life was permitted (*Prosistas castellanas*, 111). Teresa speaks of social visits paid to her and complains of requests that she visit others (27–28); clearly she maintains contact with the outside world: "[W]hen I find myself in the company of others, I am completely forsaken, for I cannot profit from the joy of companionship nor from the speech of those around me nor from myself" (25). Marimón Llorca, however, remarks that "there is not even one mention in the two treatises of Teresa's convent sisters or the tranquility of convent life, which leads us to believe that the convent was simply the space where Teresa endured her own isolation from the world, lived her profound inner life in communication with God, and occasionally met with her contemporaries" (*Prosistas castellanas*, 112). To escape her idleness, Teresa explains, she composed *Grove of the Infirm*: "Thus, for these reasons, and because my experience lends them credence, you can well believe how very lonely I am; and since I cannot rid myself of this unsparing and lasting loneliness, I want to combat my idleness by busying myself with this little treatise . . ." (25). In her work, she addresses a community of fellow sufferers– the convent of the infirm – with whom she pledges her sisterhood and for whom she finally breaks her silence.[25]

---

24 Serrano y Sanz believed that Teresa belonged to a convent in Toledo or Calabazanos, the latter patronized by Gómez Manrique, husband of Juana de Mendoza, to whom Teresa directs her second work. Cantera Burgos notes Teresa's frequent citing of St. Augustine, which might indicate an Augustinian house, but adds, however, that her reference to "our glorious father St. Francis" (*Alvar García de Santa María*, 106) suggests a Franciscan convent. Hutton traces certain Franciscan features in Teresa's works, especially the influence of Ramon Llull and Teresa's use of light.

25 At the time she wrote her first treatise, Teresa would have been about forty years old. When she died and where she was buried are unknown, as is frequently the case with women in the Middle Ages. In Cantera Burgos's genealogical survey, information regarding dates of

Grove of the Infirm

In the prologue, Teresa addresses a "virtuous lady" (commonly thought to be Juana de Mendoza) and embarks on a lengthy allegorical description of the isolation and suffering imposed by her deafness. She enumerates her reasons for writing her treatise: to combat her idleness, to share her experience with others so they may learn from it, and to give praise and thanks to God. Her prologue concludes with the biblical verses her treatise will gloss: "With bit and bridle bind fast their jaws, who come not near unto thee" (Psalm 31:9).

Teresa regards her deafness as a well-deserved punishment inflicted upon her by a stern, authoritative but loving God in order to cut her off from the distractions of worldly noise. While her suffering is painful and anguished on a physical or material plane, from a spiritual perspective it imposes "a kind solitude, a blessed solitude, a solitude that isolates me from dangerous sins and surrounds me with sure blessings, a solitude that removes me from things harmful and dangerous to both my body and soul" (26). The other spiritual benefit of her deafness is the physical silence it enforces, for Teresa interprets her lack of hearing as a divine prohibition from speaking as well: "And since God has placed such cloisters on my hearing, it is clear that with equal seriousness he prohibits my speech; thus with His second sign of His finger to His lips our sovereign Lord commands me to keep silent, showing me clearly by increasing my suffering that it is His will that I avoid any worldly chatter and maintain complete silence in order to better understand what with the din of worldly distractions I would not be able to hear" (28). Enveloped in silence, Teresa listens, instead, to "the voices of holy doctrine that Scriptures teach us" (26); *Grove of the Infirm* is the result of a prolonged and profoundly personal dialogue between Teresa and her texts.

Her experience is invested with meaning when she appropriates Psalm 31:9: "For indeed I can repeat, and even take as my own, David's most gracious and truthful song, which I cited as the beginning and foundation of this simple treatise: 'With bit and bridle bind fast their jaws, who come not near unto thee . . .' " (32–33). A bit and bridle, Teresa writes, are designed for dumb animals who lack reason, in order to bring them by

birth or death for any of the Cartagena women is lacking; their only mention is in documents pertaining to marriage or primogeniture, from which Teresa is predictably absent. Even when women are named in documents, their identities are unfixed: Teresa's older sister Juana is misnamed Leonor de Cartagena in a document about her marriage to Diego Hurtado and in her father's primogeniture document she appears as María de Cartagena.

force where their master desires. Rational animals are naturally provided with the bit of reason and the bridle of temperance and discretion, and when human beings properly exercise their reason and discretion they avoid sin and live virtuously and honestly. When, however, we are not guided by our reason and discretion, we act like dumb animals and must be provided with the bit and bridle of affliction. The purpose of Teresa's suffering and physical ailments is to constrain her worldly desires and to lead her to God: "And this is the reason that in worldly things that lead me to sin, He causes my good suffering and inflicts pain; but in spiritual things that direct us to God, He never punishes me but rather invites me to them, and He even pulls at my mantle to lead me to a rich supper" (39). The supper, Teresa explains, is the marriage supper of the Lamb (Apocalypse 19:9) and, led to the supper by their afflictions, the infirm must call for admission with the door-knocker of humble and devout prayer (40). Yet Teresa positions herself in the coterie of sufferers who remain outside because of their stubborn attachment to "the streets of this world": "But what shall I say of us sick who with our suffering could partake of such a rich supper but choose instead because of our sins to remain in the street?" (40). Nevertheless, a recent revelation has convinced her of her error,[26] she determines to rejoice in her sufferings so that Christ's virtue may dwell in her and exhorts her fellow sufferers to join her:

> I address and admonish only the sick, sad and sorrowful with their ailments and suffering, so that, indeed, we may all use our tribulation and human sadness to procure spiritual joy with devout and healthy intention, and we may say with the Apostle: 'Gladly, therefore, will I glory in my infirmities' . . . Therefore, let us postpone our pleasure for another time, for the end of this brief journey, and let us sow with our tears our future exultation and joy; may we deserve to harvest healthful fruit, and we shall glory generously and willingly in our sickness so that Christ's virtue may dwell in our souls (45).

The second half of *Grove of the Infirm* is a lengthy discussion of Patience who presides as abbess over the convent of afflictions. Teresa begins by explaining that the etymology of *paçiença* (paz [suffer] + çiença [wisdom, knowledge]) indicates that patience means to suffer with

---

[26] "However, it has pleased God's mercy to show this sign of new life in me: I now realize that my willfulness and obstinacy are as dangerous as they are enduring. I now recognize the great good in my misfortune and the mercy God has shown me in making me suffer for so long" (41).

prudence. She speaks of the three purposes of affliction (to test, to correct, to condemn) and the two degrees of patience, and offers an exegesis of the parable of the five talents to demonstrate the economy of deriving spiritual profit from affliction. She expatiates on the use of afflictions to combat the seven deadly sins: suffering turns pride into humility, avarice into generosity, envy into charity, gluttony into abstinence, lust into chastity, ire into docility, and idleness into labor. Afflictions also cure the six roots of pride (lineage, well-proportioned body, youth and beauty, eloquence and intellect, worldly dignities and honors, abundance of riches). Teresa then offers an interpretation of Job as an exemplar of patience, and concludes by defining what manner of virtue Patience is: Patience's dwelling is built on the foundation of the four cardinal virtues – prudence, temperance, fortitude, justice – and its stairway leads to the three theological virtues – hope, faith, charity – which, in turn, guide the sufferer to God.

Wonder at the Works of God

Teresa begins her defense with an apology to Juana de Mendoza for her delay in writing: both her will and her understanding have been severely undermined by the illnesses and physical sufferings that continually assail her; more consuming, however, is the spiritual turmoil which besieges her anguished soul like an invading army. Nevertheless, she calls upon the Lord to give her strength and understanding to write in his praise and glory.

The reason given for writing her second treatise is that some people have marveled at her authorship of *Grove of the Infirm*; while Teresa acknowledges this as a personal insult to her, she alleges to write because, more importantly, such doubts offend God and call into question the nature and extent of His mercy. Teresa then discusses the conventionality of miracles: all of God's creation is equally full of wonder; if we marvel at some things more than others it is because these things are uncommon. One marvels that a woman writes a treatise because that is not customary for women, only for men. Men have written for so long that it seems natural for a man to write and unnatural for a woman; that is, custom has been (mis)taken for nature. Yet, Teresa argues, God made men and women different not to give one greater advantage or excellence but that they might complement and help each other and secure the preservation of the human race. Certainly it is within God's power to grant to women whatever pre-eminences He gives to men, if He so chooses. The biblical example of Judith and Holofernes is analyzed to illustrate her point.

There are two types of wonder: wonder mixed with devotion and faith that praises and venerates God because in marveling at his blessings we admire His omnipotence, wisdom, and goodness; and wonder mixed with incredulity that offends God because we give more importance to the phenomenon that inspires our wonder than to its divine source. Moreover, two kinds of blessings derive from God: blessings of nature or fortune (bravery, beauty, good understanding, riches), which we often mistakenly attribute to the person who possesses them rather than to God; and blessings of grace, which are great and extraordinary, surpassing those of nature and fortune and attributable only to the superabundance of God's grace and mercy (among the examples provided is that of women writing treatises). Teresa then admonishes her detractors that to doubt her authorship of *Grove of the Infirm* is to question God's capacity for grace and generosity. She affirms her first work as a product of *her* experience and *God's* teaching, not of plagiarized male sources:

> People marvel at what I wrote in the treatise, and I marvel at what, in fact, I kept quiet, but I do not marvel doubting nor do I insist on my wonder. For my experience makes me sure, and the God of Truth knows that I had no other master nor consulted with any other learned authority nor translated from other books, as some people with malicious wonder are wont to say. Rather, this alone is the truth: that God of all knowledge, Lord of all virtues, Father of mercy, God of every consolation, He who consoles us in all our tribulation, He alone consoled me, He alone taught me, He alone read (to) me (102–3).

In closing her defense, Teresa compares her spiritually blind understanding, still bound up in worldly cares, to the blind man in the Gospel of Luke on the road to the worldly city of Jericho, "by which it is understood that all my thoughts were placed on the road of this world and my desires were closer to human attachments than to spiritual ones" (103–4). Teresa's clouded understanding calls out to God to see the Light, and ultimately God illuminates her understanding. *Grove of the Infirm* is defended as a product of this enlightened understanding:

> And I wrote that treatise that deals with this intellectual light and the lesson that I learned, which is to praise God and to know God, and to know myself and to deny my will and conform it to His will; and to take in the hands of my inner understanding the cross of the suffering I endure, and to follow my Savior in the footsteps of spiritual affliction; and to exalt God through the confession of my tongue . . . (109).

Teresa then examines the three powers of the soul – understanding, memory, and will – and concludes by exhorting her fellow sufferers not to permit the powers of their souls to be distracted by their physical senses or by vain material things, but to apply understanding, memory, and will to seeking God, who will respond with grace and mercy.

The Ideology of Gender in the Middle Ages
and Medieval Literary Theory

In the Middle Ages, the scholastic synthesis of classical and biblical authorities provided a coherent and systematic statement of the pre- and postlapsarian inferiority of women. In articulating the subordinate onto-logical status of women, scholastic arguments – most notably in the works of Thomas Aquinas – combined the authoritative traditions of classical philosophical discourse – primarily that of Aristotelian metaphysics and natural science – with the patristic and predominantly Augustinian inheri-tance which had shaped theological speculation through the twelfth century.[27] Aristotle's biological theories asserted that the female child represented a defective human being, a "misbegotten male," the result of an accident to the male sperm which was thought to contain the complete human being *in potentia* and to reproduce the likeness of its origin, another male.[28] An accident of nature, woman's condition, then, is one of essential absence: in her passivity, she is deprived of the active character of man; since she partakes of the cold and damp humors, she is deprived of heat; and with this deprivation of heat, she inevitably experi-ences the deprivation of the virtues associated with heat – courage, moral strength, and honesty among them (Smith, *A Poetics of Women's Autobi-*

[27] On Aquinas and women, see Eleanor Commo McLaughlin, "Equality of Souls, Inequality of Sexes: Women in Medieval Theology," in *Religion and Sexism: Images of Woman in the Jewish and Christian Traditions*, ed. Rosemary Radford Ruether (New York: Simon and Schuster, 1974), 213–66, and Elizabeth Clark and Herbert Richardson, eds., *Women and Religion: A Feminist Sourcebook of Christian Thought* (New York: Harper & Row, 1977), 78–101. McLaughlin notes that in the new anthropology of Christianity, equality of men and women occurred only within the resurrected state; however, this equality was problematic since "an essentially androcentric Christology fundamentally weakens the theoretical equivalence of the order of salvation" (220–21), and theologians continued to debate the issue of the sex of the resurrected soul.

[28] See Maryanne Cline Horowitz, "Aristotle and Woman," *Journal of the History of Biology* 9 (Fall 1976): 183–213; and Giulia Sissa, "The Sexual Philosophies of Plato and Aristotle," in *A History of Women in the West, I: From Ancient Goddesses to Christian Saints*, ed. Pauline Schmitt Pantel (Cambridge: The Belknap Press of Harvard University, 1992), 46–81. On the enormous influence of Aristotle on medieval scientific, social, and political thought, see Prudence Allen, R.S.M., *The Concept of Woman: The Aristotelian Revolution, 750 B.C. to 1250 A.D.* (Montreal: Eden Press, 1985); Sidonie Smith, "Renaissance Humanism and the Misbegotten Man," in *A Poetics of Women's Autobiography: Marginality and the Fictions of Self-Representation* (Bloomington: Indiana University Press, 1987), 20–43; and Claude Thomasset, "The Nature of Woman," in *A History of Women in the West, II: Silences of the Middle Ages*, ed. Christiane Klapisch-Zuber (Cambridge: The Belknap Press of Harvard University, 1992), 43–69.

ography, 27). Thomas followed Aristotle in his view that the male was created for noble activity and intellectual knowledge, while the female, though possessing a rational soul, was created solely for her sexuality, her body, as an instrument of reproduction for the preservation of the divinely authored species.

For the scholastics, Aristotle's androcentric biological hierarchy neatly provided a "scientific" basis for the rich antifeminist tradition inherited from the church fathers that was ultimately grounded on their exegetical readings of the creation narrative in Genesis 2–3.[29] The subordination and inferiority of Eve, and therefore of all women, were established even before the Fall. Adam, first in time and founder of mankind, was created in God's image; Eve, subsequently formed out of the matter of Adam's side, was made only in the image of Adam. Eve's supervenience defines her ontological status before the Fall and also accounts for her subsequent betrayal of mankind.[30] Lacking Adam's intellectual fullness, Eve is easily persuaded by the serpent to eat of the forbidden fruit; afterward, her deceptive words lead Adam to betray God's commandment.

Eve's misuse of language is an ironic inversion of Adam's earlier use of language in naming the animals as a means of intellection.[31] By understanding only the literal level of God's mandate, Eve betrays her inadequacy for intellection (considered the essence of maleness): she does not comprehend the symbolic order with its figurative language. Responding only to the literal meaning of the serpent's speech, she believes that the thing – *apple* – will give knowledge, and she is duped because she allows herself to express her own desire. Because that misuse of language in service to desire is a source of disorder, Eve's entrance into the realm of public discourse eventuates in the catastrophic expulsion of man and woman from Eden and in the identification of her word with the

---

[29] On the church fathers, see Rosemary Radford Ruether, "Misogynism and Virginal Feminism in the Fathers of the Church," in *Religion and Sexism*, 150–83.

[30] While both sexes are marked by the *imago dei* and the possession of a rational soul, Thomas follows Augustine in his view that man possesses the image of God in a way different from and superior to the image found in the woman. Rational faculties are stronger in the male than in the female because, as Aristotle notes, the inferior quality and reproductive finality of the female body exercise a deleterious effect on a woman's soul. Her sexuality, identified with her essence as a woman, involves a weaker and more imperfect body and affects the intelligence upon which moral judgement is based; the inequality between man and woman thus extends to the moral as well as the physical and intellectual. Moreover, even in her specific generative function, woman is inferior to man, for the man is the active and fecund force, the woman a passive receptacle. On every level, woman is subordinate and auxiliary (McLaughlin, "Equality of Souls," 218).

[31] Smith (*A Poetics of Women's Autobiography*, 28–30) offers a detailed analysis of the biblical myth of origins and the role of woman's speech which I excerpt and paraphrase in this paragraph.

serpent's speech: like the serpent, woman is double-tongued, captious, evil-speaking.[32]

The punishment for the Fall differs according to the proper function of each sex. The male of the species must procure its material support by the sweat of his brow, while the punishment of Eve aggravates her natural state of subordination. After the Fall, she becomes subject to male domination even against her will. Moreover, her specific generative function becomes a painful burden, with the introduction of the fatigue of pregnancy and the pain of childbirth:

> As a result, the malediction of Eve culturally embeds the appropriateness of woman's eternal subordination to man: her post-lapsarian curse is to be subject to and therefore subject of her husband's authority. And so, intellectually and morally, she remains a misbegotten man, denied the possibility of achieving full intellectual, ethical, and moral stature. Additionally, she must bear her children in pain and sadness, a curse that suggests the degree to which her end signifies simultaneously her difference from yet continued identity with nature. The menstrual blood and afterbirth expelled from her body in fulfillment of her auxiliary function become pollutions within the community, as do the immoral proclivities that emanate from her sexual nature: a desire for fancy dress, ornamentation, and cosmetics . . . Only her silencing by means of confinement in the private, circumscribed realm of domesticity and her exclusion from the public realm curbs the potential pollution threatening the community on the one hand and, on the other, ensures that she fulfills her natural, divinely authored destiny (Smith, *A Poetics of Women's Autobiography*, 28).

As Smith notes, however, not only is Eve socially silenced, she is, as all women after her, literally silenced. The biblical tradition expounded in the Old Testament, the New Testament writings of Paul, the church

---

[32] Carolyn Dinshaw likewise notes: "[I]f Adam is the first namer, associated with a language that is unified, perfectly expressive of intent or spirit, Eve is associated with fallen language (in the *Ancrene Riwle* it is Eve's speech that is said to be the cause of the Fall), with the division, difference, fragmentation, and dispersal that characterize the condition of historical language. If the first Adam is associated with the spirit of an utterance, Eve is associated with its letter, divided from intent or spirit, fragmentary, limited, and unstable" (*Chaucer's Sexual Poetics* [Madison: University of Wisconsin Press, 1989], 6–7). R. Howard Bloch extends the homology of woman and fallen language and examines related figures – woman as riot, woman as excess, woman as rhetoric – in "Medieval Misogyny," in *Misogyny, Misandry, and Misanthropy*, ed. Bloch and Frances Ferguson (Berkeley: University of California Press, 1989), 1–24.

fathers, and scholastic theologians all insist repeatedly on the necessity of proscribing female speech.

A defining characteristic of the female, in both the classical and Christian exegetical traditions, is her corporeality, her association with matter and the physical body, as opposed to the male's association with form and soul. The assimilation of male/female dualism into a soul/body dualism in patristic theology conditions the basic definition of woman, both in terms of her subordination to the male in the order of nature and her "carnality" in the disorder of sin. The definition of femaleness as body decrees a natural subordination of female to male, as flesh must be subordinated to spirit in the right ordering of nature. It also makes woman the symbol of the Fall and of sin, since sin is defined as the disordering of the original justice wherein the bodily principle revolts against its ruling spirit and draws reason down to its lower dictates (Ruether, "Misogynism and Virginal Feminism," 156–57).

Now the meaning culture assigns to sexual difference – the ideology of gender – has always constituted *a*, if not *the*, fundamental ideological system for interpreting and understanding individual identity and social dynamics (Smith, *A Poetics of Women's Autobiography*, 48). Medieval gender ideologies invade and inform those prevailing discourses – theological, philosophical, scientific, socioeconomic, political, literary – which define and prescribe woman as well as her relationship to language in the late Middle Ages. Feminist approaches to medieval literature have examined how this ideology of gender has inflected medieval literary theory and practice.

Some critics have focused on the intersection between ideologies of gender and ideologies of selfhood in theorizing a poetics of women's autobiography.[33] How does the writer's identity as woman produce certain literary strategies regarding the structuring of content, the reading and writing of the self, the authority of the voice, and the situating of narrative perspective? These considerations will be important in the concluding interpretive essay which approaches Teresa's first work as an "oblique" spiritual autobiography and, while theorizing the text as

---

[33] See especially Smith, *A Poetics of Women's Autobiography*, 3–83; and also Shari Benstock, ed., *The Private Self: Theory and Practice of Women's Autobiographical Writings* (Chapel Hill: University of North Carolina Press, 1988); Bella Brodzki and Celeste Schenck, eds., *Life/Lines: Theorizing Women's Autobiography* (Ithaca: Cornell University Press, 1988); Estelle C. Jelinek, "Introduction: Women's Autobiography and the Male Tradition," in *Women's Autobiography: Essays in Criticism*, ed. Jelinek (Bloomington: Indiana University Press, 1980), 1–20; Domna C. Stanton, "Autogynography: Is the Subject Different?" in *The Female Autograph*, ed. Stanton (Chicago: University of Chicago Press, 1987), 3–20.

self-writing, examines the ways in which *Grove of the Infirm* is *not* a formal or conventional autobiography.

While the ideology of gender has a profound impact on how women read themselves and how they, in turn, were read by their culture (the antagonistic reception of Teresa's first text), another important intersection is with how medieval women read.[34] If "writing is an inscription within an existing literary code, either in the form of an appropriation or rejection,"[35] then autobiography becomes a manifestation of a prior act of reading on the part of the author who rereads literary and cultural conventions (Smith, *A Poetics of Women's Autobiography*, 6). Feminist reception theory and reader-response criticism – particularly Fetterley's theories concerning the "immasculation" of the woman reader (how women learn to read like a man, adopting the androcentric perspective that pervades the authoritative texts of her culture) – are especially applicable to Teresa, given her intensely personal identification with her male source texts. In part, the concluding essay will trace the transformation of Teresa from an immasculated reader/writer in *Grove of the Infirm* to a more self-conscious and critical reader/writer in *Wonder at the Works of God*, intent on problematizing and subverting existing gendered literary conventions and on exercising her right to read and write according to her own experiences and interests.

Correlative to woman's position as a reader are the heavily male-gendered medieval theories of *auctoritas*, of both authorship and authority.[36] What does it mean to be a woman writer in a culture whose

---

34 See, in particular, Judith Fetterley, *The Resisting Reader: A Feminist Approach to American Fiction* (Bloomington: Indiana University Press, 1978), and Susan Schibanoff, "Taking the Gold Out of Egypt: The Art of Reading as a Woman," in *Gender and Reading: Essays on Readers, Texts, and Contexts*, ed. Elizabeth A. Flynn and Patrocinio P. Schweickart (Baltimore: The Johns Hopkins University Press, 1986), 83–106; and, in general, Elizabeth A. Flynn, "Gender and Reading," in *Gender and Reading*, 267–88; Annette Kolodny, "A Map for Rereading: Or, Gender and the Interpretation of Literary Texts," *New Literary History* 11 (Spring 1980): 451–67; and Patrocinio P. Schweickart, "Reading Ourselves: Toward a Feminist Theory of Reading," in *Gender and Reading*, 31–62.

35 Nelly Furman, "Textual Feminism," in *Women and Language in Literature and Society*, ed. Sally McConnell-Ginet, Ruth Borker, and Nelly Furman (New York: Praeger, 1980), 49–50.

36 A.J. Minnis notes that for medieval grammarians, *auctor* derived its meaning from four main sources: "*auctor* was supposed to be related to the Latin verb *agere* (to act or perform), *augere* (to grow) and *auieo* (to tie) and to the Greek noun *autentim* (authority). An *auctor* 'performed' the act of writing. He brought something into being, caused it to 'grow.' In the more specialized sense related to *auieo*, poets like Virgil and Lucan were *auctores* in that they 'tied' together their verses with feet and metres. To the ideas of achievement and growth was easily assimilated the idea of authenticity or 'authoritativeness' " (*Medieval Theory of Authorship* [Philadelphia: University of Pennsylvania Press, 1988], 10). On the problem of *auctoritas* in medieval women's writing, see Maureen Quilligan, *The Allegory of Female Authority: Christine de Pizan's "Cité des Dames"* (Ithaca: Cornell University Press, 1991).

fundamental definitions of literary authority are exclusively patriarchal? How does Teresa as a woman writer revise or rewrite her precursor texts which are without exception male-authored? How does a medieval woman writer reproduce in her text a female authority, and how does this construct relate to the prevailing master discourse about femaleness? The interpretive essay will also define and explore the "anxiety of authorship" Teresa displays in *Grove of the Infirm,* her different literary strategies to negotiate this anxiety, and its resolution in her second apologetic text.

Finally, medieval hermeneutics is also intricately gendered: medieval literary practice associates acts of writing and related acts of signifying – allegorizing, interpreting, glossing, translating – with the masculine and identifies the surfaces on which these acts are performed – the page, the text, the literal sense, or even the hidden meaning – with the feminine.[37] In the literary culture of the late Middle Ages, whoever exerts control of signification, of language and the literary act, is associated with the masculine. While these gendered conventions are implicitly and necessarily violated once Teresa de Cartagena allegorizes, interprets, glosses, and translates in her first work, *Grove of the Infirm,* they are, as we shall see, explicitly thematized and intentionally subverted in her subsequent defense, *Wonder at the Works of God.*

---

[37] Dinshaw, *Chaucer's Sexual Poetics,* 9. Dinshaw examines the lively tradition of sexualized literary discourse in the Middle Ages and the sexual metaphorics that were commonplace and influential in late medieval literature: "The variety, range, and popularity in the Middle Ages of works which represent literary activity by means of gendered models argue for the fundamental nature of this correlation between the use and interpretation of language, on the one hand, and the social relations and organization of gendered bodies on the other hand" (14). She persuasively argues for the continuity of patriarchal thinking about signification from Augustine to Lévi-Strauss to Lacan. Dinshaw is concerned with the masculine and the feminine as socially constructed roles or positions that can be occupied or performed by either sex.

Grove of the Infirm (*Arboleda de los enfermos*)

This treatise is called *Grove of the Infirm*,[1] which Teresa de Cartagena composed, being afflicted with grave ailments and, in particular, having lost completely her sense of hearing. And she wrote this work in praise of God and for her own spiritual consolation and that of all those who suffer illness so that, forsaken of their physical health, they may place their desire in God who is true Health.

Long ago, virtuous lady,[2] the cloud of temporal and human sadness covered the borders of my life and with a thick whirlwind of anguished sufferings carried me off to an island called "Oprobrium hominum et abiecio plebis"[3] where I have lived for so many years – if life this can be called – without ever seeing anyone to direct my steps onto the road of peace or show me a path whereby I could arrive to any community of pleasures. Thus in this exile and shadowy banishment,[4] feeling myself more in a sepulcher than a dwelling, it pleased the mercy of the Most High to illuminate me with the light of His compassionate grace so that I might place my name in the register of those about whom it is written: "The people that walked in darkness, have seen a great light: to them that dwelt in the region of the shadow of death, light is risen" [Isaiah 9:2].

---

1   Alan Deyermond ("'El convento de dolençias': The Works of Teresa de Cartagena," *Journal of Hispanic Philology* 1 [1976]: 21) notes that the allegorical use of the *locus amoenus* in Teresa's title reflects common late medieval practice (*Bower of Consolation, Garden of Noble Maidens, Orchard of Princes*). Hutton (24–26) examines the allegorical use of landscape as a site for spiritual solace in the Franciscan mystical tradition, notably in the works of Ramon Llull.

2   The identity of Teresa's "virtuous lady" addressee is unknown; however, Teresa directs her second work to Doña Juana de Mendoça with the same epithet.

3   The island derives its name – "The Scorn of Mankind and Outcast of the People" – from Psalm 21:7: "But I am a worm, not a man: the scorn of mankind, and the outcast of the people" (my translation).

4   Pedro de Luna likewise opens his *Book of Consolations* with the commonplace of life as an exile ("considering the tribulations, anguish, and misery of this exile that we commonly call life," 563) and his forced abdication of the papacy as another kind of banishment ("thus, overthrown from our proper seat by rebels against the apostolic faith and impugners of justice and obedience to the Roman Church, enduring this manner of exile with more joy than justice, we thought to compose this work . . .," 563), *Libro de las consolaciones de la vida humana*, ed. Pascual de Gayangos, *Escritores en prosa anteriores al siglo XV*, Biblioteca de Autores Españoles, 51 (Madrid: Sucesores de Hernando, 1884), 561–602.

And with my understanding enlightened and the cloud of my heavy sadness dispelled by this true Light that illuminates everyone who comes into this world,[5] I saw that this island, indeed, was a good and healthful dwelling place for me. And although this island cannot be populated with residents – for you will find few people or none willing to dwell here since it is so sterile of temporal pleasures and dry of vainglories and the fount of human honors is far away indeed – it can be populated with groves of good counsel and spiritual consolation so that my painful isolation from worldly conversations is converted into the companionship and familiarity of good customs.[6]

And since my suffering is of such a treacherous nature that it prevents me from hearing good as well as bad counsel, it is necessary that my consoling counsels be able to bring me to the cloister of their gracious and holy wisdom without shouting into my deaf ears; for this, I must recur to my books which have wondrous graftings from healthful groves.[7] And since the lowliness and grossness of my womanly mind do not allow me to rise higher, aspiring to the nobility and sanctity of the very virtuous king and prophet David, I begin to look in his most devout songbook[8] called the Psalter for some good consolations. And I found more there than I sought, for I looked for consolation and found admonishment; I sought counsel and found without doubt so much good advice that were I to live by it, I would fill my solitude with a gracious grove under whose shade my body could rest and my spirit receive a healthful breeze.]

And since not all these counsels will fit on my small plate, I will omit some which are nevertheless profitable and more than good, and take some for the beginning of the meal and others for during the meal, and I will reserve some for after the meal;[9] and I intend to make use of only those counsels that aid most the purpose of my suffering and the growth

5   See John 1:9: "That was the true light, which enlighteneth every man that cometh into this world."

6   In his consolation for solitude, Pedro de Luna recommends seeking company in good thoughts, in good books, and in conversation with God: "Thus, the wise man is never alone; for he always has near him good thoughts. And he has books full of good examples . . . And if he has no one to speak with, he speaks with God, considering himself to live with his company" (*Libro de consolaciones*, 583).

7   Pedro de Luna also refers to the garden landscape of Holy Scriptures: "And St. Bernard says, 'Truly religion is a paradise with the green meadows of Holy Scripture and a delightful fountain of flowing water which love derives from the delights of Holy Scriptures' . . ." (*Libro de consolaciones*, 592).

8   Here Teresa uses the term *cancionero* to describe the Psalter; *cancioneros* are fifteenth-century collections of courtly verse.

9   Teresa presents the many examples of good counsel found in Psalms as dishes in a meal; because they are so numerous, they will be served at different intervals. The idea of God's words as spiritually nourishing food is also found in Pedro de Luna: "And if you find a sweet

of my devotion and spiritual consolation. And although my tongue is not eloquent and my sense is ill prepared, [I am writing this treatise] to avoid succumbing to these two dangers, solitude and idleness; and since I cannot rid myself of solitude, I want to drive idleness away so that it cannot join with solitude, for this would be a dangerous marriage. And if my hand could thus drive off solitude from my right side and idleness from my left, do not doubt that it would ever tire from this travail; for according to the nature of my suffering, if you look closely, you will see me more alone in the company of many than when I retreat to my cell all by myself.

This is the reason why: when I am alone, I am accompanied by myself and by this poor sense I have, but when I find myself in the company of others, I am completely forsaken, for I cannot profit from the joy of companionship nor from the speech of those around me nor from myself. My sense escapes me, for it is too busy feeling the inordinate pain that I feel when my reason abandons me with the reasonable torment it endures. My discretion is slight, but even if it were great, it would have more than enough to do to move human restlessness to patience. And where hearing fails, what good is speech? One is left dead and completely isolated. Thus, for these reasons, and because my experience lends them credence, you can well believe how very lonely I am; and since I cannot rid myself of this unsparing and lasting loneliness, I want to combat my idleness by busying myself with this little treatise, which one might well say is neither good nor even ordinary, but rather completely bad.

However, since it is written for a good purpose, a greater good consequently may ensue. And because of my good intention, may our sovereign Lord, who judges intentions rather than works,[10] find my writing,[11] which seems vexing and reprehensible to some people, pleasing and acceptable to His merciful eyes. And with this desire and directing my purpose only to Him, I have cared less to attend to the polish of my words than to declare the reality of my truth; and it does not please me so much to be diligent in investigating or searching for graceful eloquence as to be desirous of revealing to those who want to know what is revealed in me, so that as I know it, all may know it. And as I give thanks to the

---

fare, that is, some word of God, taste it and you will be refreshed by it. And drink from the wine cellar His wine of spiritual happiness . . ." (*Libro de consolaciones*, 586).

Ronald E. Surtz ("Image Patterns in Teresa de Cartagena's *Arboleda de los enfermos*," in *La Chispa '87: Selected Proceedings*, ed. Gilbert Paolini [New Orleans: Tulane University, 1987], 297–304) examines the network of food imagery in *Grove of the Infirm*.

10 See Proverbs 21:2: "Every way of a man seemeth right to himself: but the Lord weigheth the hearts"; and Luke 16:15: "And he said to them: 'You are they who justify yourselves before men, but God knoweth your hearts; for that which is high to men, is an abomination before God.' " See also 1 Kings 16:7.

11 Teresa refers here either to the act of writing or to the product of that act, her treatise.

sovereign Lord, let all give thanks and praise to Him to whom all praise should be given. And while I wish to please Him alone in all my acts, let whoever so desires judge if these are bad or good. For I, bereft of human praises and unworthy of them, here end this prologue and begin this slight and defective work, and I take the following words as its foundation: "In camo et freno maxillas eorum constrinje qui non approximant ad te" [Psalm 31:9].[12]

When I look at my suffering in temporal terms, it seems very painful and anguished, but when I turn my thought from these concerns, drawing it unto my breast, and I see the solitude that my suffering imposes, separating me from worldly transactions, I call it a kind solitude, a blessed solitude, a solitude that isolates me from dangerous sins and surrounds me with sure blessings, a solitude that removes me from things harmful and dangerous to both my body and soul.[13]

And it appears that what has happened to me is like what we see happen when many speak in a mad rush, and it seems they hear voices from far away. And they make a sign with their hand to be still and listen, and they fall silent in order to better distinguish the voices that seem to answer from far away. And there are some, foolishly unaware that it may be to their advantage to be silent and listen, who keep on gabbing. But if among them is a discreet man who knows that those voices are worthwhile to hear, he makes a sign with his finger to his lips, and thus lets them know that it behooves them to be quiet, and then their foolish persistence ceases completely. And although it is hard, they maintain silence, above all if he who makes these signs is someone whom they must fear and obey. From this it follows that they listen by force to what they did not want to hear willingly.

And thus enmeshed in the confusion of worldly chatter, with my understanding disordered and bound up in worldly cares, I could not hear the voices of holy doctrine that Scriptures teach us. But merciful God, who was with me in this din and with discreet observation saw my perdition and knew how important it was to my health to have the chatter cease so that I would better understand what was necessary for my salvation, signaled me with His hand to be quiet. And one may well say that this suffering is given to me by His hand. And even our customary way of speaking demonstrates that this is true, for when we see someone afflicted with great pain or suffering, we exhort him to have patience,

---

12   Psalm 31:9: "With bit and bridle bind fast their jaws, who come not near unto thee."
13   Compare the beginning of Pedro de Luna's consolation for deafness: "Likewise, do not be upset if perchance you are deaf, for thus you are spared the occasion of hearing vain words and evils harmful to you" (*Libro de consolaciones*, 600).

saying, "Have patience, since our Lord gave this suffering to you. And why must you be sad since this is from the hand of God? etc." Thus the hand of God signaled me to be quiet and cease worldly chatter. And I, silenced by force, did not willingly listen to what I should hear; rather, burdened with my foolishness, I struggled to further my own harm. And merciful God added a second sign with His finger to His lips, clearly indicating that it is not His will that I speak of things of this world but that I be completely silent.

And it seems clear enough that this sign was made to me by the divine hand when my suffering is increased to such a degree that, even though I want to speak, I cannot, and even though people may wish to speak to me, they cannot. I know well that one could say that my suffering prevents me from hearing but not from speaking, for my tongue is free from affliction. To this I respond, "What is the principal reason why we have been given language and speech?" I truly believe the principal reason to be the one that we exercise least, which is to praise and bless God. However, aside from this, who doubts that speech was and is given to us in order to ask questions and to be answered? And it even seems to me, if I understand it correctly, that the Prophet tells us so when he says, "Ask thy father, and he will declare to thee: thy elders and they will tell thee" [Deuteronomy 32:7]. And it is clear that speech and language are given to us, in addition to the principal reason, which, I have said, is to praise and bless God, in order to ask questions and to be answered, since there would be no usefulness or profit if each person were to converse only with himself; for such a thing would seem more the act of a madman than of a person with common sense. So with reason I am angered when people beg me and say, "Go to so-and-so; for they want to see you and even though you cannot hear them, they will hear you." And while I understand that this is said in good friendship and innocence without any malice, nevertheless it still annoys me, knowing as I do that speech is pointless without hearing, like faith without works. For just as faith without works is dead[14] and leads to greater pain than profit, so speech without hearing is worth nothing and only increases one's torment.

Thus language by itself is only valuable in two ways: one is to praise and bless God, the other to preach to the people; for these two things one can do without any reply. But in all other actions, to be able to speak without hearing is as pointless as hearing well and not being able to speak. For in these instances the purpose of hearing and speaking has been eliminated. For he who does not hear, how can he respond? And he who

---

14 Compare James 2:26: "For even as the body without the spirit is dead; so also faith without works is dead."

expects no response, how can he ask? Such a person, if he were discreet, would keep his silence. And since God has placed such cloisters on my hearing, it is clear that with equal seriousness he prohibits my speech; thus with His second sign of His finger to His lips our sovereign Lord commands me to keep silent, showing me clearly by increasing my suffering that it is His will that I avoid any worldly chatter and maintain complete silence in order to better understand what with the din of worldly distractions I would not be able to hear.

For without doubt man's understanding deserts him when he is too preoccupied with worldly things, and he is better able to withdraw into himself when he separates himself from these things. When someone is very engrossed in something, we say that he is lost in thought; however, to recover best one's scattered understanding and concentration, it is necessary to impose silence on everything else. Silence has already been imposed on me by the hand of God, who commands me to be quiet, and my foolish persistence has been checked with that finger that I now understand, showing me openly that it behooves me to be totally silent, to cut myself off completely from worldly chatter and desires; for it would be of little profit to separate myself from these worldly things if my desire and care were still involved with them. For any involvement would produce so much noise that I could not understand the voices; in order to hear them, I am commanded to maintain such an extreme silence.

Thus we see happen sometimes in conversations between people that although the speaker is very careful and diligent in what he says and those who are listening are silent, if the listener's thoughts and attention are preoccupied with things other than the conversation directed to him, no matter how much the speaker rants and raves, the listener will understand nothing of what he is told. Then the speaker says, "You, friend, are not here; come to your senses or rather return to yourself." Likewise, not only is it necessary for us to remove ourselves from worldly chatter and conversations, imposing total silence, we must also remove our desire and care; and it is imperative that we withdraw ourselves and our will completely if we want to listen without hindrance or noise to what is so fitting to our health.

Oh wondrous charity of my sovereign Lord! You show me such manifest signs so that I may listen to what is necessary to my health, for not only have you removed my hearing and speaking from worldly conversations but, with the merciful hand of His divine grace, you have removed completely my desire, which used to cause me so much trouble! Oh beneficial sign that confirms and sustains previous signs![15] My desire

---

[15] Carmen Marimón Llorca (*Prosistas castellanas medievales* [Alicante: Caja de Ahorros

now conforms with my suffering and my longing is thus reconciled to n , affliction, so that I no longer wish to hear nor can people speak to me nor do I want them to speak to me. What I used to call my crucifixion, I now call my resurrection. Now are my two enemies reconciled, my desire and my suffering. Oh merciful Lord, you have directed my desires along another path, smoother and straighter than I deserved! Oh, change imposed by the right hand of our Redeemer most high, you so manifestly display the grandeur of your mercy![16] For you not only cut me off from the dangerous mob of worldly distractions but you have removed from me my desire agonizing but undying, your mercy sparing me a lengthy battle between those two enemies, which are my wanting and my not being able. And I, who up until now desired but was not able to spend my time in worldly conversations, am no longer able nor inclined to have the power to fulfill such a harmful desire.

Certainly these words thanking God for having removed all my obstacles and hindrances should be a very helpful example for others. I am already cut off from human voices, for my ears cannot hear; my gossiping tongue is already silenced, since because of my deafness it cannot speak. My desire, thus withdrawn, is set less in temporal things than in my health, and what I cannot hear does not weigh upon me as much as what I have heard in offense to God. And I would have willingly endured this suffering from birth, so that no words that may have offended or disserved God could ever enter the cloisters of my ears. Oh Lord, I long to listen to and hear the sweetness of your voice! For without doubt I can say, "For thy voice is sweet, and thy face comely" [Canticle of Canticles 2:14d].[17]

And with the abovementioned silence, straining the ear of my understanding – since that of my body helps me not – I seem to hear spiritually these words resound:[18] "Listen, O daughter, and behold, and incline thy ear: forget thy people and the house of thy father" [Psalm 44:11; my

Provincial, 1990], 123) points out how Teresa often closes thematic subunits within her treatise with a series of exclamations or rhetorical questions; see also 32, 34, 40. Hutton notes the similarity between these rhetorical series – typical of oral language – and the rhetorical devices of popular medieval sermons (31).

[16] As Teresa subsequently notes (49, 79, 80), God's right hand is associated with mercy, justice, and salvation, and His left hand with sin, punishment, and damnation.

[17] Compare: "Do not be sad if you have lost or are cut off from the pleasing conversation of those whom you loved, and have come to a solitude where you must be silent; for if you want to be strong in your religion, your strength must be in hope and silence, because he who is distanced from the speech of men is close to God. . . . And often the man who loves silence converses with God . . ." (*Libro de consolaciones*, 587). Pedro de Luna then recommends the reading of holy books in silence with divine company.

[18] Pedro de Luna also speaks of spiritual hearing: "Likewise, by being deaf, you will hear better through the ears of your soul the words God speaks within you . . ." (*Libro de consolaciones*, 600)

translation]. And the initial words that warn me again and again to hear and to ponder and to listen intently lead me to understand that the subsequent words about forgetting my people and the house of my father have another meaning than what is literally represented. Since, however, in order to understand it literally, one admonishment would have been sufficient, the reiterated command to hear, to observe, and to listen intently indicates to me that I should examine with great care not only what these words say but also the meaning that they convey.

However, let us consider first what is said literally in order to know better its meaning, for it says, "Forget thy people and the house of thy father." And it does not directly command us to forget our father, but rather his house. Now clearly this does not refer to his material house, since that makes no sense, but rather to his family. And our everyday speech confirms this, for when we say, "So-and-so has a very great house," we do not refer to the buildings or the size of his dwelling, large or small, but to his family and the number of his people. Now if we are commanded to forget our father's house, then it follows that we are commanded to forget and even abhor our father, since whoever truly loves his father not only could not forget his house, that is, his household of servants and relatives, but would love them, I believe, out of respect for his father. Therefore, in order to be able to forget his house, it is necessary to first forget and even abhor our father.

Now it is clear that these words must have another more reasonable and healthful meaning, since for us to forget in this way our people and the house of our father seemingly contradicts God's commandment to honor our father; for we cannot honor someone we do not love. Conversely, when we do not honor someone, it is a sign that we do not love him, even though sometimes honor and reverence are given in this world without love, as when we say, "One kisses those hands he wishes to see cut off."[19] But such things have nothing to do with the divine commandment to honor our father, since we honor and revere our parents in one way and our lords in quite another; for we honor our parents with filial love and willing obedience and we honor our lords with worldly ceremony marked by acts of courtesy and correctness rather than by heartfelt love. And so the commandment that states "Honour thy father" [Exodus 20:12] does not say "Honour thy governors, counts, and dukes." This indicates that the honor and reverence that we rightfully give to our father surely must proceed from great love; and even his very name demon-

---

19 "Manos besa hombre que querría verlas cortadas" (Spanish proverb). See Gonzalo Correas, *Vocabulario de refranes y frases proverbiales* (Madrid: Revista de Archivos, Bibliotecas y Museos, 1924), 191.

strates this, for in saying "Father" it seems as if a deeply felt love revives and quickens in our will. So since we are commanded to honor, it is evident that we are commanded to love, for otherwise the honor or service we do to our father would be feigned and cunning. Now, how could we be commanded to forget someone whom we are commanded to honor and love? For he who loves well, never forgets.[20] Therefore, it seems clear enough, because of the repeated forewarning of the initial words which so diligently admonish me to hear and ponder and listen intently, as well as the reasons mentioned above, that this command and counsel to forget my people and the house of my father has another meaning.

And straining the ear of my understanding as much as my rude and gross judgement allows, I interpret "people" to mean a mob of temporal and human lusts. And just as in a town or multitude of people one finds diverse lineages and conditions, so there is great diversity in human desires: some covet honor and fame, others riches, others to work for the glory of this world, and others to repose in that glory. And if I had to describe all the types of temporal and vain desires, I do not doubt that their number would equal the twelve tribes of Israel.

But let us leave aside their diversity to speak of the war these lusts wage in the land where they dwell. I say that just as in the city a great noise is produced if some of the people rise up in revolt, and if all the people revolt, the city is in great danger and in mortal combat; so any temporal lust that rises up against our soul produces a great noise in the city of our conscience, and if all this accursed population of desires rises up against our soul, it is in great danger of perdition.[21] And we may well call human lusts "people," for just as the more people multiply, the more they populate and fill a city, so the more temporal lusts multiply in our will, the more full the city of our conscience is of harmful dwellers and so crammed that if a good neighbor wants to come dwell there, he will find no lodging, especially if he is someone who the evil people fear will overwhelm them.

Since the virtues are of such great estate and power that they can overwhelm and overpower the vices, these wicked people that have filled the city of our conscience do not allow them to cross over the threshold,

[20] "Bien ama quien nunca olvida" (Spanish proverb); see Correas, *Vocabulario*, 82.
[21] Hutton (35) traces the graphic image of a city in revolt to the anti-Jewish uprisings during the fifteenth century; Deyermond specifically points to the anti-converso rebellion in Toledo in 1449, shortly before the composition of *Grove*, when the Jewish problem became the converso problem. Here the traditional Christian image of the city as a secure place under God's rule (Augustine's *Civitas Dei*) is transformed into the dangerous and vulnerable "city of our conscience" (Deyermond, " 'El convento de dolencias,' " 26–27).

lest they take over the captive city. And we may well call captive a
conscience that is full of sins, for just as a captive is held in captivity
against his will, so our conscience has been taken captive by these
perverse people. Since we cannot commit sin nor even think of sin without
our conscience rebuking and accusing us, clearly it is not pleased by sin
and is thus forcibly inhabited by its populators or, rather, its desolators,
the vices. Who is there who does not consider the warning to forget and
abandon all these enemy people to be healthy advice?

I come now to the second part of my admonishment, that I forget the
house of my father. I interpret this house to mean human inclination,
which houses the father and desire and habit of sinning; for just as the
father is the beginning and the engenderer of his children, so bad desire
is the beginning and engenderer of sins. And we can apply the Prophet's
words "He hath conceived sorrow, [and hath brought forth iniquity]"
[Job 15:35] to this abominable father when he consents to sin with
deliberate intention and commits sin for the sake of evil. Thus it is healthy
advice and a valuable warning to me to forget my people, who are the
temporal lusts and the mob of vain cares in the house of my father, which
is human inclination, where the desire and habit of sinning dwell, because,
in my view, here sin has its home. For as great as the desire to sin may
be, if it does not take refuge in human inclination, it could not have such
a great house. And a very grand house, indeed, it has founded, and one
very costly to our spiritual commerce, for with its relatives and followers
it has a greater clan than a marquis and has become, because of our
iniquity, the father of our wicked life.

And who could hear with the ears of his soul such healthy advice if his
physical ears were filled with the noise of human voices?[22] Oh merciful
Lord, how immeasurable is your sovereign goodness! Oh how incomprehensible are your judgments, how inscrutable your ways![23] For you not
only receive those who approach you and save those who walk along the
path of salvation, but even those who withdraw from you and freely go
towards their own perdition, you constrain with merciful bonds and bring
them by force to their everlasting salvation! For indeed I can repeat, and
even take as my own, David's most gracious and truthful song, which I
cited as the beginning and foundation of this simple treatise: "With bit

22 Pedro de Luna makes a similar distinction between spiritual and physical hearing: "Of this
our Lord says: 'The deaf shall hear and the blind see,' which can be understood spiritually
to mean that those who are physically deaf shall hear with the ears of their soul" (*Libro de
consolaciones*, 600).
23 See Romans 11:33: "O the depth of the riches of the wisdom and of the knowledge of God!
How incomprehensible are his judgements, and how inscrutable his ways!" (my translation).

and bridle bind fast their jaws, who come not near unto thee and want to approach thee."[24]

To better appreciate how this biblical authority suits my purpose, we must consider that a bit and a bridle are designed for dumb animals who lack reason so that with these bindings they may be brought almost by force to a place that suits them and pleases their master; thus they are guided by their bit and constrained by their bridle. And just as, for the reasons stated above, this bit and bridle are placed in the mouth and on the neck of irrational animals, so for similar reasons another bit and bridle are provided for rational animals. The bit is our reason and the bridle our temperance and discretion. For reason guides us toward all that is good and fitting for our temporal good and our spiritual well-being in the service of our Lord, and temperance and discretion constrain us to curb the disordered appetites of our human weakness.

And while every rational animal has in its power and desire these two tools to control itself, we see in observing their actions that not all employ them equally, for we see some sin licentiously, and others live virtuously and honestly, and others halfway, neither very dissolute in some things nor very perfect in others. Although we see these differences in their deeds, certainly their humanity is the same; for both the most righteous person as well as the greatest sinner, and both the moderate person as well as the dissolute, human inclination invites them all equally to sin. The most virtuous and honest person we can find can be strongly tempted and assailed by any sin the greatest sinner can commit.

Now clearly the reason why some consent and others resist is because those who live virtuously avail themselves of the bridle of temperance and discretion and employ their reason, while the others do not. And we can call the house of the former well ordered, for he who should command commands and he who should serve obeys, for reason rules and commands its subject, which is sensuality, and the latter obeys and serves reason.[25] And it is not necessary to bridle these people since their own discretion restrains them and separates them from vice. From this it follows that the man who does not know nor wants to know how to use his bit and bridle is an irrational animal since he does not exercise reason, for the proper use of reason is to admonish and constrain us to desire good and avoid evil. Therefore, it seems that whoever abandons good and

---

[24] Teresa rewrites the biblical quote by appending "and want to approach thee"; compare 26.
[25] Pedro de Luna also discusses the well-ordered soul: "thus the kingdom of the soul is well ordered when well counseled: when reason counsels well, the will rightly obeys and our physical senses obey our will; and it is virtue in our soul that imposes this good ordering, for virtue enlightens our reason and raises up our will to the eternal kingdom from its servitude to sin" (*Libro de consolaciones*, 595).

follows evil has forsaken reason, or reason has forsaken him. Accordingly, it is more than right that, like a dumb animal, he be provided with another bridle.

Now you will see how the biblical authority cited above – "With bit and bridle [bind fast their jaws]" – applies directly to me; and so that you may see more clearly this correspondence between us, I will state, inasmuch as my simplicity allows, how these verses relate to my poor and simple treatise. I say and affirm that with bit and bridle my sovereign Lord constrained the jaws of my vanities to benefit my spiritual well-being. Now, let me explain for those who have never suffered affliction – since those who have, already know from their own experience – how ailments can be called bit and bridle.

A good and lasting ailment is a bridle to humble the proud neck and a bit to constrain desires dangerous and injurious to the soul. We see an example of this in everyday life when a sick man dares not to eat all foods and even with less harmful foods he does not eat as much as he wants. If an ailment thus resists and curbs physical acts, imagine how it affects spiritual acts; for if our discretion imposes rules on eating to preserve our temporal health, it is a greater discretion of more lasting benefit to impose rules on our deeds to safeguard our spiritual health. While it is true that it is fitting and healthy for everyone to adhere to a strict diet during a harmful meal of sins, there is no doubt that reason more openly influences the infirm than the healthy. For although it is good for everyone to avoid harmful foods, certainly the invalid is more strictly constrained to avoid them than a healthy person. Likewise, a sick person will abstain with more rigor and necessity from foods harmful to his soul – from sins – than a healthy person.

Oh, the meaning is quite clear! What excessive negligence it would be for the sick to ignore spiritual matters! First, because the ailing person is so imprisoned in his suffering, he cannot avail himself or others of temporal or corporal things.[26] Second, and more to the point, because the sick person already appears to have one foot in the grave, even though sometimes it happens that the healthy person more promptly departs this miserable life than the sick person, for we see some people with great ailments live many years, and others, flourishing in good health, we have seen depart in a flash. Here let those blessed with physical health beware, lest the dream of their invulnerability deceive them in such a way that an accelerated and unavoidable death catches them napping. But I should

---

[26] I have altered the order of sentences here to follow a more logical sequence; in the manuscript, "What excessive negligence . . ." is interpolated between the first and second reasons.

not have omitted myself in addressing only those blessed with good health, for although my withered health exempts me from their number, the slumber of my sins lulls me as asleep as anyone else. For this reason, I mean to say let them and us beware – the sick as well as the healthy – so that this departure called death not catch us sleeping; rather, may it please our sovereign Lord that He may find us vigilant in virtuous works, so that these divine words may apply to us: "Blessed are those servants, whom the Lord when he cometh, shall find watching" [Luke 12:37].

And leaving this aside, since it is far from my purpose and remote from my task, for those reasons stated above and for many more that I refrain from saying, these ailments and physical sufferings can and should be called bit and bridle. And how much more this applies to my own particular suffering that invests all its force in removing me from one thing and drawing me towards another, so that, in spite of myself, I have to want what my suffering wants, and my suffering always rejects what I want. For if I want to hear, my affliction does not allow it; and if I want to speak, it signals me with its hand and clearly indicates that its intention is to prohibit what I want and make me want what I do not want. What I do want is to involve myself in worldly activities, and what I do not want is solitude or isolation from them. Well, if I examine my suffering, its intention is better than mine, for it wants my salvation, and I want my perdition; it wants to withdraw me from dangers, and I want to cast myself into them.

My suffering's intention is much better than mine. I am coming to know its goodwill, for it labors not so much to torment me as to save me, nor so much to make me suffer as to make me worthy. And if it makes me experience great pain, it does so desiring my salvation. Therefore, I praise greatly its good desire and repudiate my own rebelliousness, worthy of total repudiation, for I have fought long and hard against its merciful persistence. It is now time that I let it achieve completely its virtuous end, full of spiritual benefit because the Lord gave this suffering to me. Oh bit and bridle of my healthful suffering! If so far you have been dragging me badly behind you, now I want to willingly follow you! And since you pursue me, I want to place my dwelling where you guide me. How beneficial it is to me to be bound by these sufferings that cause my indomitable persistence to be conquered by His divine mercy! So, because I did not want to draw near to God, the jaws of my vain desires have been constrained with a bit and bridle.

How can one call vain desires jaws? Consider that what the Prophet called jaws, we call face or countenance,[27] and even this same Prophet

27 The Latin *maxilla*, "jaws," becomes *mexilla*, "jaws or cheeks," in Old Spanish. Teresa's

says in another place, "Convert us, O God: and shew us thy face, and we shall be saved" [Psalms 79:4]. And just as the face is the first thing we see in a human being, so vain desires are the first sign we see in youth. And it seems to me that all worldly desires inclined to vanity have a face and an obverse. The face of these desires is from childhood through youth, and from then on, as one matures, they turn around. And certainly vain pleasures or the desire for vain pleasures face outward in one's adolescence and youth because they appear in their time and their season. In old age, to have vain desires is the obverse and even may be called a mortal reverse; if the face of these desires be found, a bridle would not be necessary to tighten and constrain them, since age itself is enough bridle. But when these desires face outward, that is to say, in adolescence or youth, then a remedy is necessary.

Well, see how timely my sovereign Lord came to my aid with my suffering, for it is now twenty years since this bridle first constrained the jaws of my vanities! Therefore, let whoever remembers my birth or knows my age count well, and he will see whether this suffering came to me at an opportune time, better, in fact, than that of Escalona.[28] In this regard, one can well call my vain desires jaws, since they were faced out, and thus the biblical authority concludes,[29] "With bit and bridle bind fast their jaws"; and it says further on, "who come not near unto thee in a timely manner."[30]

Without doubt we should esteem these bindings, for their only purpose is to draw us near to God. And if he so desired, the Prophet could have said "of those who sin against you, of those who do evil, of those who without fear offend you." However, because of his goodness and courtesy, he passes in silence over our bad works, and only says "[of those] who come not near unto thee" in order to more clearly indicate that with much love and mercy these afflictions and physical sufferings are given to us, not so much on account of our sins, which well deserve them, as to draw us near to God, who is our sovereign good.[31] Oh, what abundant charity accompanies my pains, so that in them I see shine the greatness

---

affirmation that "what the Prophet called jaws, we call face or countenance" is based on the change of meaning to "cheeks."

28 "The rescue of Escalona, when water arrived, the village was completely burned down" (Spanish proverb). On the village of Escalona (near Toledo) and the proverb, see Sebastián de Covarrubias, *Tesoro de la lengua castellana o española* (Barcelona: S.A. Horta, 1943), 532.

29 The phrase "aunque desnuda y groseramente" has been omitted in my translation.

30 Teresa interpolates "in a timely manner" in her translation.

31 Compare Pedro de Luna: "Nor should you complain of the harshness of your suffering, for it is a sign of your blessing and a sign that God has chosen you and loves you" (*Libro de consolaciones*, 567).

of His mercy! For my sufferings are given to me only to draw me closer to God. Oh, merciful Lord, when did I deserve such good fortune? One can say that I achieved grace without meriting it, and even grace beyond grace, for grace to me is the pain and beyond grace His mercy.

Indeed, if it is good to bear the penalty of a just judge, it is much better to receive punishment from a father; and just as a discreet father punishes the culpable child with love and mercy, so our heavenly Father tried to correct my faults with paternal charity.[32] And in order to prove this, let us see how any discreet father should castigate and help his child. The first condition, I believe, is that the punishment should begin at a tender age. The second is that the child's whipping should be neither dangerous nor fatal but corrective. Whipping should begin in our first age, in early childhood, and, if necessary, continue into our second age, into adolescence. And if after these two periods the lashing does not emend his ways, paternal affection should not forsake the child in his youth;[33] rather, now the whipping should be redoubled, both because of the rebelliousness that the child displays in not improving his customs and because as he gets older his culpability increases and his punishment becomes more deserved.

For according to this, my own lashing demonstrates well the paternal charity and sovereign discretion this discipline has had and continues to have with me. My whipping began in my early childhood and continued into adolescence, just when, as noted above, my vain desires faced outward; then my punishment was redoubled in my youth, for at this age my suffering increased as you have seen.[34] To explain it further would be

---

[32] Compare Proverbs 3:12: "For whom the Lord loveth, he chastiseth: and as a father in the son he pleaseth himself."

Pedro de Luna also discusses the value of loving punishment: "And even your present affliction is a divine gift as our Lord says, 'Those whom I love, I rebuke and chastise' [Apocalypse 3:19]. And in Ecclesiasticus we read: 'He that loveth his son, frequently whips him, that he may rejoice in his latter end' [Ecclesiasticus 30:1; my translation]. And thus our Supreme Father always has his most beloved children under the rod of his discipline and he applies it to them many times . . ." (*Libro de consolaciones*, 572).

The theme of loving punishment is a commonplace in contemporary consolatory treatises; see also: "parents, although they love their children, this love is mixed with discipline and is thus more true, for with a whip they strike their children so that they may be good and accomplish excellent deeds" (Fray Martín de Córdoba, *Compendio de Fortuna*; cited by Marimón Llorca, *Prosistas castellanas*, 120).

[33] Teresa applies standard terminology in her fourfold division of the ages of man: *puericia o moçedat, adolesçençia, juventut,* and *vejez.* See J.A. Burrow, *The Ages of Man: A Study in Medieval Writing and Thought* (Oxford: Clarendon Press, 1986) and Elizabeth Sears, *The Ages of Man: Medieval Interpretations of the Life Cycle* (Princeton: Princeton University Press, 1986) for conventional systems of four (*pueritia, adolescentia, iuventus, senectus*), five, six (*infantia, pueritia, adolescentia, iuventus, senectus, senium*), and seven ages.

[34] In the Middle Ages, the ages are conventionally grouped in hebdomads: in a four-age scheme,

excessive, but I will say what the perseverance of my punishment demands. For when whipping and discipline persevere for so long and even increase, this indicates that my life has not improved and my actions have gone from bad to worse. Tell me, what do you think of the great obstinacy of my rebelliousness when the rod has been applied to my shoulders for so long and my actions still remain uncorrected? For were my faults corrected, surely my suffering would cease. Thus St. Ambrose, referring to the restoration of Zacariah's speech, says, "God knows how to change your punishment if you know how to correct your sins."[35] It is clear, since my punishment is unchanged, that my fault has not changed nor been corrected.

I said the second condition is that the whipping must be neither dangerous nor fatal but rather corrective. In truth, my punishment is such that I can say with the Prophet, "The Lord chastising hath chastised me: but he hath not delivered me over to death" [Psalm 117:18]. And not only did He not deliver me over to death, but rather the objective of His punishment is to free me from death. Therefore, it is not necessary to exhort me to patience, nor is it of great merit for me to exercise patience, for the blessing I receive is greater than the pain I endure. For we need only to suffer our pain and travails with patience and let patience work its deeds. Yet my pain, imposed with justice and mercy, is accompanied by so many blessings that I am obliged, insofar as I understand, to confess my guilt and love my pain and praise His justice and magnify His mercy. And my understanding should be so busy praising the Lord's justice and thanking His mercy that I should not even mention the pain that I feel, especially since my guilt is so great that it makes any pain seem insignificant. However, it is best that we do not forget our pain, for it has great value. We should feel the pain of punishment, for otherwise patience would forfeit its office, and the rewards of His mercy would diminish, and the great foundation of His mercy would be built on shallow ground.

pueritia (childhood) ends after fourteen years, *adolescentia* (adolescence) after twenty-eight, *iuventus* (youth or prime) after forty-nine, and *senectus* up to seventy or eighty years; in a six-age system, *infantia* lasts for seven years, *pueritia* for another seven up to fourteen years, *adolescentia* from fourteen to twenty-eight years, *iuventus* up to forty-nine, *senectus* comprises three more hebdomads to seventy years, and *senium* (decrepitude) the period after that. If Teresa assigned the conventional numerical value to *juventud*, she may have succumbed to deafness much later – in her thirties or even forties – than has been previously assumed; since she writes *Arboleda* twenty years later, its date of composition may be as late as 1465–80, the latter date given by the copyist Pero López de Trigo.

35   "Nemo ergo diffidat, nemo veterum conscius delictorum praemia divina desperet. Novit Dominus mutare sententiam, si tu noveris emendare delictum." See St. Ambrose, "Expositio Evangelii Secundum Lucam, Liber secundus," in *Opera omnia, PL* 15:1564.

Therefore, it is good that we feel the pain of the Lord, lest we forget the greatness of His mercy.

Let us not overlook justice: every time that pain is applied to guilt, justice is present, for the proper act of justice is to punish the guilty. Let us note how praiseworthy His justice is when His punishment is of such a nature that wherever sin seeks to rest its head, it immediately finds the pillow of torment. From this it follows that either we will avoid sin or, if we start to sin, we will immediately suffer. This I call praiseworthy justice, and it should be made public to – and not hidden from – the people. What equity of justice matches this, for it does not allow guilt without pain nor inflicts pain without mercy? It is right that we praise this most just and merciful justice; and it seems to me that I see another reason why this should be praised, for while each and every vice is punished, all virtues are left intact. For I see justice exercised so reasonably and discreetly that only he who deserves pain suffers and only he who is worthy is free from suffering. Thus this justice only imposes obstacles and inflicts pain on sins and faults, never on virtues and good deserts. If I were ever to give myself over to virtue, He would show me his countenance so gently and graciously, just as now He reveals Himself harshly and severely to my vices. And this is the reason that in worldly things that lead me to sin, He causes my good suffering and inflicts pain; but in spiritual things that direct us to God, He never punishes me but rather invites me to them, and He even pulls at my mantle to lead me to a rich supper.

And to what supper does my suffering lead me? I believe without doubt that it is the same supper as where it is written, "Blessed are they that are called to the marriage supper of the Lamb" [Apocalypse 19:9]. Although divine generosity invites and beckons everyone to this blessed supper, affliction pulls at the mantle of the sick and forcibly makes them enter. And so states the parable that our Lord relates in the gospel about the man who prepared a grand supper and invited many, and when it was time to eat, he sent his servant to tell the guests to come, for everything was ready. And the guests excused themselves from attending for various and foolish reasons; indignant, the paterfamilias said to his servant, "Go out quickly into the streets and marketplaces of the city, and bring in hither the poor, and the feeble, and the blind, and the lame . . . and compel them to come in, that my house may be filled" [Luke 14:21b,23b; my translation]. And he did not say "Tell them to come" as to the first guests, but rather "Make them come in."

Therefore, it seems that the sick are brought forcibly to the magnificent supper of eternal health, for affliction pulls at their mantle and makes them enter through the door of virtuous deeds; for if we do not enter through this door, we cannot reach such great heights of honor as to be seated at the table of divine generosity. Oh blessed convent of the sick, of those, I say, who enter willingly where affliction bears them by force and do not choose to remain outside in the street! And how do they enter willingly if they are led there by force?

It seems to me this should be understood in this way: any invalid, no matter how good or virtuous, suffers illness against his will; even though he may be just and saintly, he will desire to be free of physical suffering and he takes no pleasure in its company. Of this we have an example in Tobias, when our Lord permitted him to be blinded and when the angel Raphael greeted him, saying, "Joy be to thee always," the saintly man replied, "What manner of joy shall be to me who sit in darkness, and see not the light of heaven?" [Tobias 5:11–12]. From this it appears that his suffering did not please him. And who does not desire to be healthy rather than sick? No human, I believe, is so perfect that he will deny what he naturally prefers, which is to desire health above all things. So it follows that when someone is deprived of this blessing, force is imposed on his wants and desires, and the suffering he endures against his will leads him forcibly to this supper. Yet he enters gladly if he recognizes that it is given for his own good, and with devout patience and gratitude he conforms his desire to God's will, taking pleasure spiritually – not naturally, for that cannot be – in everything pleasing to the Lord. And he abandons immediately the streets and marketplaces where temporal pleasures are bought and sold and approaches the door of the house where the table of spiritual platters and true riches is prepared. And if he finds the door shut, he does not marvel, for it is locked by the bolt of his sins; instead of returning to the public streets, let him knock with the doorknocker of humble and devout prayer.

The gospel itself declares that prayer is the appropriate doorknocker to call at the door of God's mercy: "And all things whatsoever you shall ask in prayer, believing, you shall receive" [Matthew 21:22]. And He says elsewhere, "Knock, and it shall be opened to you" [Luke 11:9]. For it is very reasonable and fitting that we call steadfastly at the door with the doorknocker of prayer, especially since the Lord who invites us to supper is the same one who invites us to pray. It is clear that prayer is the beginning of the spiritual refection that nourishes the soul. And who most requires such spiritual nourishment if not the sickly, whose physical strength is depleted by sufferings and afflictions? For whoever falters in human and temporal things because of the weakness of his body should exert himself in spiritual and divine things through the fervor of his spirit.

But what shall I say of us sick who with our suffering could partake of such a rich supper but choose instead because of our sins to remain in the street? And who are these sick who remain in the street? Certainly they have no physical health to enjoy nor human honors to hold nor abundance of riches to attend to, for of a thousand invalids, you will find none rich, and if one is, his suffering will impoverish him in no time. Thus stripped of all worldly goods and attired only in their sufferings, they keep their desire and care in worldly things, so that no matter how much their suffering invites them and tugs on their mantle, it cannot bring them to the abovementioned supper. And they neither take pleasure from temporal goods nor want to enter the house of spiritual treasures, and so they remain in the street.

And just as the sufferer in the middle of the street seems useless and idle, so his desire and attention directed toward the streets of this world are likewise useless and idle things and profit no one and harm him. And such an invalid as this has his understanding more paralyzed than his body, and his discretion weaker than his physical constitution. I say this for myself, for I accuse myself of this crime, and truth itself accuses me, and the long perseverance of my suffering indicates my guilt, and my delay without any progress – for I have lingered in the streets of this world so many years – bears witness to the paralysis of my understanding and the weakness and infirmity of my discretion.

However, it has pleased God's mercy to show this sign of new life in me: I now realize that my willfulness and obstinacy are as dangerous as they are enduring. I now recognize the great good in my misfortune and the mercy God has shown me in making me suffer for so long. To make amends I confess my guilt, I love my suffering, I praise His justice, and I am thankful for His mercy. I acknowledge that I suffer and am punished justly, wisely, mercifully. Justly, for I more than deserve sufferings and grave afflictions from God. Wisely, for since my condition is acutely wicked, no other bridle could have been given to me. Mercifully – oh how mercifully! – for certainly since I examine my great sins and my fortunate suffering, I recognize and see clearly that with very great mercy our Lord has punished me and revealed to me the evil of my sins that merits this affliction. Mercifully also, I add, since this suffering was given to me for such great good.

And passing over in silence many other innumerable blessings, I only wish to make mention for now of the most important and source of all others, and it is this: if I with my suffering continue to offend God so much and to be so inclined toward vices rather than virtues, what would I do if I were free of my suffering? Certainly now my sins are very great, but they would be even greater; and while now I offend God greatly, doubtlessly I would offend him much, much more. Thus, because of all this, I must acknowledge and hope that everyone recognizes the great mercy of the Lord manifested in me. For what greater mercy could there be than to bridle evil and encourage good? And what greater wickedness than for man to be able to sin as much as he wants? And what greater good than not be able to sin even if he so wishes?

It is true that not to desire would be a greater good than not to be able, for it is more meritorious and praiseworthy not to want to sin than not to be able to sin. However, it is a great mercy to take the power to sin from someone who has his will inclined to sin. Thus Boethius says that the worst evil that the wicked have is the power to do evil.[36] And if the power is taken from these people, this lone blessing is added to their misfortunes. Indeed, what mercy He has shown me by adding this blessing to my misfortunes! What charity! What justice! What a full complement of blessings is enclosed in my suffering!

Oh great blessings proceding from true Good! How can we thank you if we do not know you? What was that small part of this blessing that I recognized? How shall I be worthy, or how shall I repay the Lord for the many blessings that accompany my misfortune? What praises or glory can I offer to satisfy such beneficence since, as St. Jerome says, praise in the mouth of a sinner is not pleasing.[37] Accordingly, I should cease offering praises, since I am certain that I have sinned and that my sins have multiplied more than the sands of the sea, and I am not worthy to see the heights of heaven because of the multitude of my iniquities. Nevertheless, I do not want to cease glorifying the Lord; and when all else in me fails, I will receive the healthful chalice of my arduous suffering invoking the name of the Lord...[38] And I will gladly glory in my sickness so that the virtue of Christ may dwell in me: "Libenter gloriabor..." [2 Corinthians 12:9b].[39]

If by glorying in our sufferings we can bring to our soul such a good guest as the virtue of Christ, no invalid should be sad; for this reason alone, leaving aside other regards, we who have professed in the convent of afflictions should rejoice. But do not think that this joy should be in

---

[36] "Nam si miserum est uoluisse praua, potuisse miserius est, sine quo uoluntatis miserae longueret effectus." See Anicius Manlius Severinus Boethius, *Philosophiae Consolationis,* Loeb Classical Library (Cambridge: Harvard University Press, 1962), 322.

[37] "Secunda ad sanctus, qui ad Dei canticum provocantur. Non est enim pulchra laudatio in ore peccatoris." See St. Jerome, "Epistola CXLVII," in *Opera omnia, PL* 22:1198.

[38] The passage is incomplete and badly copied; I have omitted two lines that cannot be deciphered.

[39] 2 Corinthians 12:9b: "Gladly, therefore, will I glory [in my infirmities, that the virtue of Christ may dwell in me]" [my translation]. *Virtus Christi* is translated in the Douay-Rheims version as "the power of Christ"; Teresa's translation, "the virtue of Christ," is incorporated in my translation. Although *virtud* also means "power" or property in medieval Spanish, as in the *virtud* or power of certain precious stones, I translate it here as "virtue" because of Teresa's wordplay in the following paragraph with virtues.

temporal things, for while I do not say that temporal and human joy is bad, it is not good enough to be called a virtue. And since it is not a virtue, how can it prepare a place or dwelling for the sovereign virtue of Christ? For it is said, "That the virtue of Christ may dwell in me." And it seems that we should glorify or rejoice in our ailments for this purpose alone, so that the virtue of the Lord may dwell in our souls. Nevertheless, temporal happiness has nothing to do with this, even if it is good and honest, for it does not suffice that it be only good, but rather it is necessary that it be spiritual, virtuous, and pure. Therefore, we should glory in our sufferings and afflictions in such a way that the virtue and purity of our devout joy may prepare an agreeable dwelling for His sovereign virtue.

And to this spiritual happiness I invite the infirm and I wish to be invited, so that, just as we are equal in our suffering, we may be equal in our resurrection where, it seems to me, temporal and human happiness have no place. Likewise, there should be no place for excessive sadness, nor should excessive sadness, were it to appear, be resisted with human pleasures, for such a resistance as this is neither praiseworthy nor meritorious. What merit is it to rid one's conscience of one vice and substitute a dozen others instead? What victory can one expect from combatting one sin with another? Excessive sadness is a sin. And who would call human pleasures a virtue? Only someone who is not acquainted with them and does not know their ways; concerning these pleasures, I can say, "Let he who does not know them buy them."

It is not a good war to have relatives fighting relatives, and although excessive sadness seems to be the opposite of human pleasures, it is not so; rather, sadness has a great family tie with them, because bad and sinful sadness proceeds from the lack of worldly pleasures. So it clearly appears to have a great bond and family relationship with them, and even more frequently human pleasures themselves engender and give birth to sadness. Therefore, if someone with great ailments were burdened with the kind of sadness that brings sin with it, he should not alleviate his sadness with a multitude of pleasures; rather, he should shun them and fear to summon them to his aid, for according to the great bond that they have with sadness, they will only compound the very grief that his afflictions caused him.

Thus, some are diligent in searching and procuring pleasures and pastimes from morning to night, and what is worse is that they consider this well done and virtuous because it removes their sadness and annoyance. But I wanted to ask of such people, when those recreations have finished and they must return home, what good or profit did they derive from them? And if they tell me that they have lost their sadness, so help me God, I do not believe them, for they have not lost the cause of their sadness. For since the cause of their vexation and fatigue is their ailment, and since human pleasure cannot remove their affliction, how can it remove their sadness? Let them look again, and if they still have their affliction, believe me that they return home with their sadness and vexation redoubled.

What destructive and wicked litigation and war does sadness wage! If we think to vanquish sadness, we ourselves are conquered. This is not a good way to rid ourselves of sadness, for it is better to be sad for honest causes than happy for dishonorable pleasures. Therefore, it is not right for the sick to seek remedies that redound with dangers, and if we want to combat sadness, let us not take vices for arms but rather virtues, for these are the true adversaries that wage war on vices. This I say wherever sadness may be so excessive as to be called a vice.

But if sadness is experienced with moderation, so that the virtue of temperance is not abandoned, it does not seem to me that this type of sadness should be reprehended, for it is not a vice. And if it is not a vice, we should not avoid this sadness since we cannot prevent it, for human sentiment constrains us to feel sorrow and complain about our own sicknesses. We should not avoid this because such sadness, insofar as it is reasonable, is beneficial; reasonable because it is the first effect of the sickness, and as the first thing that affliction produces in the ill, sadness is beneficial since from such sadness as this, spiritual happiness can be born.

Indeed, to find sadness in temporal and worldly things is a step to climb to spiritual joys. Thus the first step is physical sadness; the second, spiritual happiness. For if the heart of those who suffer illnesses is not gladdened with this spiritual happiness, they cannot truly say, "Gladly, therefore, will I glory in my infirmities." And you should not wonder if I say that sadness experienced with temperance and moderation is good and beneficial, indeed, most fitting and healthful. For if all tribulation causes sadness and sadness is nothing but tribulation, it brings with it a great benefit, for it inclines us to prayer since anyone grieved or sad should immediately pray and call upon the Lord; for the necessity of one's own tribulation constrains one to prayer and even makes one devout and accepting.

Of this the Prophet says, "Then they cried to the Lord in their affliction: and he delivered them out of their distresses" [Psalms 106:13]. And it was not said, "Then they cried to the Lord in their prosperity and happiness," for in these things we first call on the world rather than God, but "in their affliction" because tribulation places man in such a bind that it makes him search with diligence and care for his true remedy. Whoever searches with an anguished and devout heart will find his cure, and, therefore, it says, "And he delivered them out of their distresses," giving us to understand that not only does tribulation make the afflicted call to God for help, but it even makes them worthy of response, as this same Prophet more openly declares when he says, "He shall cry to me, and I will hear him: I am with him in tribulation, I will deliver him, and I will glorify him" [Psalms 90:15].

Thus sadness and tribulation are two spurs that goad us toward devout prayer. At least you will not contend that temporal pleasures can lead us to this blessing; and well these pleasures may be called temporal because just as temporal things are subject to sudden change – so that if one day the weather is clear and serene, the next it is immediately cloudy and rainy – this same unpredictability I see in human joys, for one day they make us happy and fortunate, and the next day they bring us clouds of sadness and rain of tears.[40] While truly it is better that these pleasures make us cry rather than laugh, both effects are harmful, for crying or laughing for the wrong reasons amounts to the same thing.

It is, therefore, good for us to flee from such damaging joys, especially the sick with whom I have signed a pledge of sisterhood. I address and admonish only the sick, sad and sorrowful with their ailments and suffering, so that, indeed, we may all use our tribulation and human sadness to procure spiritual joy with devout and healthy intention, and we may say with the Apostle, "Gladly, therefore, will I glory in my infirmities." And if we do achieve this spiritual joy, we shall gladly scorn human joys as they scorn us, for if we examine it well, all pleasures of this world have happy beginnings and sad endings full of anguish. But the opposite happens with spiritual matters, for their beginnings are difficult and sad and their endings prosperous and happy.

Therefore, let us postpone our pleasure for another time, for the end of this brief journey, and let us sow with our tears our future exultation and joy;[41] may we deserve to harvest healthful fruit, and we shall glory generously and willingly in our sickness so that Christ's virtue may dwell in our souls. And yet my devotion will not allow me to forget these verses, but rather it reminds me of what is written in the epistle of this saintly Apostle, where it says, "For virtue is made perfect in infirmity" [2 Corinthians 12:9a, my translation].[42] According to this, we should under-

---

40 The play Teresa establishes here between temporal things, change, and the weather is based on the double meaning of *tiempo* as both "time" and "weather."

41 Compare Psalm 125:5–6: "They that sow in tears shall reap in joy. Going they went and wept, casting their seeds. But coming they shall come with joyfulness, carrying their sheaves."

42 Again the Douay-Rheims version translates *virtus* as "power"; I include Teresa's translation, "virtue."

stand that we must avoid all vices, for virtue cannot be called perfect in the company of vices. So, if the hardship of illness afflicts us, let us strive to rejoice in the blessing and honor that it promises; and I know no greater honor or dignity in this life than perfection and virtue refined and purified in our suffering.

Let us endure our torment because of its end; let us love our pain not for its own sake, for it does not deserve our love, but because of its virtue; let us love whoever loves us and despise whoever despises us. Our pains and afflictions love us – it is right that we love them; health and prosperity despise us – let us despise them for God's sake. Why should we infirm strive for what we cannot have, for the only fruit of our diligence is our effort? We strive to bring within our reach human joys and they refuse to come. All the blessings of this world are food reserved for the healthy; so let us leave what we cannot have and get accustomed to our own diet, and let us partake of those foods that suit our stomach and help us suffer our travail.

It seems to me that we who endure suffering should partake of these six dishes: grievous sadness, enduring patience, bitter contrition, frequent and heartfelt confession, devout prayer, perseverance in virtuous works. And we can ingest without fear these six foods and related provisions; and although they may seem quite bitter to our taste, this is necessarily so, for few infirm enjoy their diet, even though it is beneficial and fortifying. Therefore, let us love the bitter since the sweet does not love us, so that what is bitter to our palate (that is, to our human senses) may be converted into sweetness for our soul.

And I do not know why we infirm should want anything from this world, for as much as we may wander, we shall never find anything in it that loves us well. Worldly pleasures despise us, health forsakes us, friends forget us, relatives get angry, and even one's own mother gets annoyed with her sickly daughter, and one's father despises the son who with chronic afflictions dwells in his home.[43] And it is no wonder that this is so, since even the invalid loathes and is vexed with himself. Let us not suffer such great hunger for these temporal things but rather procure

---

43 Compare Job 19:13–17: "He hath put my brethren far from me, and my acquaintances like strangers have departed from me. My kinsmen have forsaken me, and they that knew me have forgotten me. They that dwell in my house and my maidservants have counted me as a stranger, and I have been like an alien in their eyes . . . My wife hath abhorred my breath, and I entreated the children of my womb."
   This theme of familial rejection is, as I argue in the interpretive essay, a deeply personal one. Teresa returns to the theme when discussing the six roots of pride (58–61) and later speaks of the emotional pain the infirm suffer (69) when subjected to the humiliation and contempt of family and friends.

what benefits us most, that is, what is spiritual and healthful to our soul. For even if we want temporal things, they do not want us, and if we were to try to satisfy our hunger in the land of the sick with worldly pleasures, these would elude us or the bridle of our suffering would prohibit us from tasting them.

Therefore, let us forsake what forsakes us, and let us want only the One who wants us and love only the One who gives us our afflictions, so that we may despise the world and love only Him who loves us. Without doubt, He is our true Father, He is a kind Father, He alone is not vexed by our sufferings. He is the one who cures our sicknesses;[44] He is the one who redeems our lives from failure and danger and will crown us with His compassion and great favors. He will fulfill our desires with blessings and, like an eagle, will renew our youth.[45] Therefore, let us who languish in hunger for physical health in this strange land seek Him with fervent desire, for in Him we shall find such repose that our temporal and human sadness will be converted into enduring spiritual happiness.[46]

However, in all these abovementioned matters Patience has sovereignty, for if Patience does not rule and order the convent of the suffering, all our afflictions and our travail would be fruitless. It does not seem to me, therefore, that Patience should remain with only the mention she has received in previous parts of this simple and brief treatise, for it is reasonable to make special record of what Patience is and what she comprises.[47] And while I may not know how to say all that Patience deserves, may my limited faculty suffice, for I acknowledge my poor mind and employ it in her service, and since I have such need of her, it is good to strive to keep her content.

And if I choose to leave Patience for last, I do this to honor her more, as we see is customary in solemn processions where those subjects of lesser estate begin at the front of the procession and the prelates and dignitaries proceed at the rear, as guardians and custodians of their

---

44 Compare: "And you should consider that God is your father and loves you well, much more than your natural father, and He only sends you medicines to help you . . ." (Fray López Fernández Minaya, *Libro de las tribulaciones*; cited by Marimón Llorca, *Prosistas castellanas*, 121).

45 Based on Psalm 102:2–5: "Bless the Lord, O my soul, and never forget all he hath done for thee. Who forgiveth all thy iniquities: who healeth all thy diseases. Who redeemeth thy life from destruction: who crowneth thee with mercy and compassion. Who satisfieth thy desire with good things: thy youth shall be renewed like the eagle's."

46 From this point on, Teresa's personal experience is no longer the central focus of her work but functions secondarily as an exemplum, point of reference, or proof in her discussion of patience.

47 I have capitalized Patience here and translate the gendered "it" as feminine since Teresa subsequently personifies Patience as an abbess and female prelate.

subjects. And in this regard I wanted to leave Patience for the end of this badly ordered procession of considerations, as their guardian and the prelate of my sufferings and anguish, for we the suffering and afflicted must profess at the hands of this good abbess to live in observance of the virtues that our spiritual advantage requires.

Therefore, I want to say what I understand of this honorable prelate called Patience. And beginning with her discreet name, I do not know who her godfather was but certainly whoever gave her this name wanted to indicate clearly the nature of Patience. For what is patience if not to suffer with prudence, as its very name – *paçiençia* – declares? These first letters that spell *paz* [peace] denote suffering [*pasión*] or endurance [*padesçer*] and the last seven letters that spell *çiençia* [wisdom] thus demonstrate to us that patience is nothing else but to suffer with prudence. We endure our hardships patiently if our prudence is such that we convert hardships that are bad and from a bad source into something good and beneficial for ourselves. And if the hardships are good and from a good source – like those that come from God's hand – it is much more fitting that the sufferer be prudent and wise, so that we do not forfeit our reward for those hardships.

And I want to clarify what I mean by hardships that are bad and from a bad source: they are those travails and afflictions that the world gives to its servitors, for the more we love the world, the greater our worldly reward. For this reason, when we see these hardships befall someone, we say that whoever serves the world receives his reward from the world with all its attendant dangers. And without doubt bad hardships from a bad source we can call those that people endure because of their disordered desires. We all know the great hardships these people suffer, so much that if the crown of martyrdom could be obtained simply by suffering hardships we would see nowadays as many martyrs as in the days of Diocletian Augustus.[48] Yet because of our sins, the opposite happens, and we see many sufferers and few martyrs; for, as St. Augustine says, his pain does not a martyr make but rather his cause,[49] and he who suffers for a bad cause is not worthy of the name and less of the true crown of martyrdom.

Nevertheless, these covetous people suffer more torment and affliction than martyrs, for martyrs suffered only in their bodies, and their souls were free from any anguish and full of spiritual joy; but those who suffer

---

[48] Diocletian ruled as emperor of Rome AD 284–305; in 303 he initiated a persecution of Christians that is often called the Great Persecution.

[49] "Illud ergo praecipue commonendi estis, quod assidue commoneri, et semper cogitare debetis, quod martyrem Dei non facit poena, sed causa." See "Sermo CCLXXXV," in *Opera omnia*, PL 38:1293.

according to the world have a double torment, for they suffer great anguish in their bodies and even greater harm in their souls and hearts. And with reference to them, the Prophet says, "They mount up to the heavens, and they descend into the abyss: their soul pined away with evils" [Psalm 106:26; my translation]. And one can well say, "They mount up to the heavens," when they climb the stairs of their disordered appetites and try to obtain more than they should; and they descend into the abyss when for the same reason they are struck down to the ground and fallen into great dangers. How much more so if, may God forbid, for this reason they descend to hell, for thus they clearly descend into the abyss since their souls are assailed with evils. And I call these hardships bad and from a bad source.

Yet even with these ills that proceed from bad causes, it is better that they exercise patience, considering the meaning of its proper name, which is to suffer with prudence. And since, whether they like it or not, they must endure suffering, it seems to me that they should exercise prudence as best they can, for true prudence when applied to these hardships deserves the name of patience. And the sufferers of these hardships should not focus so much on the harm and dangers that befall them as on the trunk and root from which these evils and anguish originate.[50] And if they will draw back the veil of covetousness from in front of their eyes, they will see their hardships and pain on their right side, which means that these have befallen them because of their just deserving, and the trunk and root, which is their bad desire, on their left side.[51]

And if they were to exercise prudence, they would cut off completely the bad root from their excessive desires that were leading them down the left road to great harm, and would embrace, instead, the hardships on the right, knowing that they justly endure them. And accepting these hardships in their will as the initial payment of a great sum of torments that are owed them, with this good recognition, they could improve their life through divine grace, and thus the hardships proceeding from a bad source will be converted into good and profitable amends. And such a person will be called patient, that is, a prudent and wise sufferer, for it is no mean wisdom to know how to turn bad to good, and change harm to profit and danger to security.

I leave this aside to describe what falls to my lot, that is, my hardships that come from a good source and for my own good, which are those that come from the hand of God: afflictions, poverty, the death of family, and other similar misfortunes. And to better understand the patience required

---

[50] The copyist here repeats lines from the preceding folio which I have omitted.
[51] See 29 n. 16.

for these hardships, it is necessary to consider the three purposes why our Lord permits these hardships, for He punishes the righteous to test them, He punishes the sinful to correct them, He punishes the wicked to condemn them.[52] With regard to testing the righteous, their suffering is so full of prudence that the more the fire of their anguish torments them, the more refined and pure their righteousness, goodness, and character seem; and with reference to them, the Prophet has said, "Thou hast tried me by fire: and iniquity hath not been found in me" [Psalm 16:3b]. And the Church sings in praise of the test that the Lord conducts for His chosen: "The Lord tests his chosen as gold is tested in the fire, and receives them as a holocaust or sacrifice."[53]

Since it is best to avoid extremes, especially with regard to these three groups, for the greater the excellence and sublimity of the righteous on the one hand, the greater the discord and the mortal fall of the wicked on the other. Let us, therefore, leave alone the testing of the just, for it is not our fare, and likewise let us not fear the damnation of the wicked, for God's mercy offers us safe-conduct. Rather, let us approach the most certain and likely group, those hardships and afflictions that are given to us for the sake of correcting and emending our lives.

And those of us who are punished in this regard, if we want to exercise patience, we should endure our hardship with prudence, so that the more our sufferings increase, the more our lives will be bettered. For if we sustain the hardship of our suffering and not improve our ways, our great torment would be stripped of our sovereign Lord's healthful and beneficial purpose in permitting our afflictions. And not only would the sufferer be divested of this good purpose but also of the reward and desert that such hardship was preparing for him. Therefore, although we think that some have much patience because we see them suffer their illnesses with moderation and temperance, unless there is more to this, this cannot be called great patience, according to the interpretation of its own name, which is to suffer with great prudence. For it does not seem to me very great prudence for a man to be able to win with one malady a dozen blessings and through negligence or lack of effort remain with only his affliction.

---

[52] Compare: "Tribus modis Deus in hac vita castigat homines. Scilicet ad damnationem percutit reprobos; ad purgationem corripit quos videt errare electos; castigat justos ad augendam gloriam meritorum." See St. Bernard, "Liber de modo bene vivendi, XLIII, De Infirmitate," in *Opera omnia, PL* 184:1264.

[53] "Et si coram hominibus tormenta passi sunt, Deus tentavit eos; tanquam aurum in fornace probavit eos, et quasi holocausata accepit eos." See "Common of Several Martyrs, the Communion of the First Mass," in *The Saint Andrew Daily Missal*, by Dom Gaspar Lefebvre (St. Paul: E.M. Lohman Co., 1956), 25.

With regard to this, one must consider that there are two degrees of patience, one that is good and reasonable and another even better and of greater perfection. The one that is reasonably good is when a man sustains his hardships with an eye to two considerations. The first is to take note of who gives or allows the illnesses and hardships, for it is our sovereign, powerful Lord and no one can flee His hand; He is great and abundant in the singular benefits that He bestows on us each day and He can bestow others even greater. The second is to note the quality and even the quantity of our hardships and our own impotence, for they are such and our power is so weak, that although we may want to butt heads with them, we would shatter our heads before we drive them away.

And whoever examines well these two considerations has patience in his dwelling. For with regard to the first, which is God, we should bow our shoulders as much as possible and humbly endure all that our Lord may allow. And with regard to the second, which is our own advantage, we should avoid grieving too much, realizing that excessive anguish or complaints will only increase our pain. And this is properly called patience, for to suffer with prudence and wisdom and to weigh well these considerations and to conduct oneself with moderation proceed from prudence.

And for this reason when people utter words of pride or clamor loudly in their suffering and afflictions or complain more than what is due, we say that they have little patience, and other times – even more frequently – we say that they have no prudence. And to have no prudence or to have little patience is one and the same, according to these expressions, for in saying "They have no prudence" we mean that they lack this virtue completely; and we do not say "They have no patience" but rather "They have little patience," which is very appropriately stated, because whenever something is described as "little" it is well understood that there is a part of this thing present and a part is lacking. The part that is present is what we call "little," for it is clear that there is something even though it is little. And the part that is lacking is what the same word denotes, for to say "little" is the same as saying a diminished thing, something that can and should increase.

And thus saying that they have little patience, we indicate that they have one part of patience and another part is lacking. The part that they have is the suffering and enduring. And it is clear that suffering is the first part of patience, for where there is no suffering, there can be no patience. For no matter how much prudence one may have, if one does not suffer some hardship, he will be called very prudent but not at all long-suffering, since suffering afflictions is the precondition for patience, and without suffering some hardship one could not have patience. Therefore, whoever has this abovementioned suffering has a part of patience but lacks the other part, which is better and more fitting, and this is prudence, which when joined to suffering makes patience whole, virtuous, and complete.

Of this the Apostle says, "And patience hath a perfect work" [James 1:4]. Now, how can something be perfect if it lacks virtue or is separate from virtue? And in order to better understand this, we must consider that prudence by itself is a complete and praiseworthy virtue, but the endurance of hardships alone is not a virtue, even though it may be a precondition for acquiring virtue. Therefore, it is necessary that a virtue be added, and since prudence is a virtue (for it admonishes and teaches us to endure our maladies so that we neither offend God nor increase our harm), prudence should be our companion in our sufferings. And therefore, when we endure human suffering with this virtue, which always brings good issue, we can say that our patience is a perfect deed; for it has in itself perfect virtue, not because our afflictions are a perfect or virtuous deed but because to tolerate our afflictions wisely and discreetly is a virtue without which we cannot arrive to a state of perfection. And this suffices to explain the first degree of patience, as far as my poor and womanly intellect can comprehend and sense. I call it the first degree of patience not because of any advantage it has over the second degree of patience, but because whoever exercises this well can then advance to the second, which is greater and of greater perfection.

The second degree of patience, of much greater excellence and merit, seems to me to be this: the sufferer is not only prudent in enduring his maladies and afflictions and in fulfilling the above prerequisites, but strives with all diligence and care to obtain spiritual benefits from his hardships, like the good and faithful servant in the parable who received five talents from his lord and through his own industry and hard work earned another five.[54] And to better understand this, let us analyze with care and count well and with deliberation how many talents we the afflicted and suffering receive on the field of our suffering, so that we may better know what we should earn with these coins and which course to follow.

And I find, according to my poor judgement and my own experience, which makes me know more in this regard than what I have learned from books, that we who are strengthened by our afflictions and physical suffering receive five talents of precious metal from our sovereign Lord. The first talent is singular love, the second our very afflictions, the third is the mortification that they deservedly impose, sapping the strength of

54 The parable of the talents is told in Matthew 25:14–30; see also Luke 19:12–27.

our bodies, the fourth talent is the humiliation and scorn they occasion, the fifth is the time they consume, preventing us from wasting time in vain and mundane things. And if our patience is so strong that it can be called great patience, that is, to suffer with great prudence, with these five talents that we who have our shoulders burdened with suffering and sorrow cannot deny having received, we can earn with divine grace another five talents as profits in our spiritual investment. And my simplicity tells me that the five additional talents should be these: the first is reverential love, the second filial fear, the third mortification of sins, the fourth willing humiliation, and the fifth repayment or act of gratitude.

And to be better informed in this spiritual transaction, we should know the quantity and quality of each of these talents, of those talents we receive and of those talents that reason obliges us to repay to the Lord. To this purpose it seems to be fitting enough to speak of each one separately, if the faculty of my poor judgement suffices; but to tell the truth, although with my diminished discretion I have been able to name them, I am badly equipped to discern and explain them in theory or in practice. However, guided more by my devotion than my knowledge and informed more by my suffering than my discretion, I shall say what God through His infinite mercy has wished to reveal to my simplicity.

I have said that the first talent we sufferers receive is singular love. And to better understand why this is first and why it has such a name, let us consider that in whatever we do, first comes the intention or purpose why it is done, for this is the beginning or basis of the work we wish to do. And thus the intention and purpose of our scourging must first be heeded, for this is important in the benefit we receive. And while the beginning or cause of our afflictions and travails can be attributed to our own sins and to the particular condition of our human weakness, it is necessary to go one step further; for if our illnesses occur only because of our sins or human weakness, the righteous would never be subjected to this rule nor would the wicked ever be exempt.[55]

Yet we know this is not so, for although we are all sinners and human, some of us are plagued with illness and sorrow, and others – in the majority – spend their lives free from this adversity. Therefore, certainly there is another, more principal cause that is the intention or healthful purpose why God gives us these sufferings, which we cannot deny is good and for our own good and manifest profit, and whoever desires our good clearly loves us. And whoever, in addition to desiring and wanting our

---

[55] A loose translation is given here because the passage is corrupt.

good, provides us with the means to recognize and achieve it, demonstrates to a greater degree the love that He has for us.

And what else are our afflictions and physical suffering, if we consider them well or, better yet, if we virtuously endure them, but a sure means to search and find the straight path to our salvation? For there is no other path to paradise except through the suffering of anguish and tribulations, and by means of this narrow path we shall find our spacious, everlasting resting place.[56] For it is written, "Strait is the path that leads man to eternal life,"[57] as if to say, "Grievous and very narrow is the road of travails we must travel if we wish to go on to eternal life."[58] And if the saints could not get to heaven without passing along this road, how can we sinners expect to follow it without enduring much suffering? Of this St. Gregory says, "No one can achieve great rewards without enduring great travails."[59]

Nevertheless, one can suffer hardships in one of two ways, either voluntarily or forcibly. Voluntary suffering is what the martyrs, confessors, and numerous other servants of God suffered, and nowadays some devout people guided by their own particular will endure abstinence, fasts, vigils, scourges, and many other travails, postponing the pleasures of this life for the benefits of heaven. Imposed suffering is when those people, against their will, are forced to suffer these same labors, those with no desire to go to heaven and even less inclination to travail or suffer any affliction; God, in His infinite compassion, heeds them and wounds them with His hand and makes them suffer in spite of themselves, giving them hardships which force them to step onto that narrow road which will lead them to eternal life.

And although the travails that God imposes are greatly diverse in manner and quality and designed by His incomprehensible wisdom to suit the individual sufferer, nevertheless, the primary excellence of all hardships is the suffering they bring, for in this suffering is manifest most clearly the true love and paternal nature of the Father of our salvation.

---

56 Compare Pedro de Luna: "And therefore be assured that the path of the chosen passes through harsh suffering so that they do not delight more in dwelling in this world than journeying to the other" (*Libro de consolaciones*, 567); "Of this St. Bernard . . . says, 'Our present suffering is the path to glory, the path to the city of paradise, and the path to the kingdom of God' " (*Libro de consolaciones*, 569).

57 Compare Matthew 7:14: "How narrow is the gate, and strait is the way that leadeth to life: and few there are that find it!"

58 Compare Pedro de Luna: "For the path of our present adversity is a narrow road that leads to everlasting life" (*Libro de consolaciones*, 565).

59 "Sed ad magna praemia perveniri non potest, nisi per magnos labores." See St. Gregory the Great, "Homiliarum in Evangelia, Liber II, Homilia XXXVII," in *Opera omnia, PL* 76:1275.

And while other hardships open our understanding and pierce our hearts so that we know the misery and mutability of this sad world and desire lasting blessings, our afflictions do more than this. For not only do they open our understanding and pierce our hearts and deaden the sufferer to worldly things, they goad us with their spurs, making us run along the narrow path mentioned above. For although it may seem that the afflicted stays still at home, he traverses more roads than we think and, even if bedridden, in the grip of a fever or some other painful affliction, he walks more, I believe, than a fifty-day journey. As God is my witness, to His honor and glory, I say that from the first day of my afflictions to the present, the painful spurs of my great suffering have forced me, to my dismay, to travel more day-journeys than from here to Rome. And if I, a sinner, with the heavy burden of my innumerable sins am forced to journey so many miles . . .[60] Therefore, I believe we can say what the Prophet says in the Psalm: "They shall go from virtue to virtue: the God of gods shall be seen in Sion" [Psalm 83:8b]. Therefore, among the other travails that God gives us to suffer against our will and for our benefit, our afflictions, as I have said, have the advantage and recognized excellence.

Now let us examine the difference between voluntary and forced suffering to ascertain if the first talent we infirm receive should take the name my simplicity invented and be called singular love. And it is certain that voluntary and willing suffering is very praiseworthy and, therefore, whoever suffers willingly should give God great thanks; and imposed and unwilling suffering is not at all praiseworthy in those who receive it but only in Him who gives it. Whence it follows that the difference between these two types of suffering should be distinguished in this manner: those who suffer gladly and willingly receive special grace from God, and those who suffer beyond or against their will receive from God singular love. And this is the reason why it seems clear that those who suffer willingly love themselves and truly desire their own salvation. However, with those who suffer against their will, it is apparent that He who makes them suffer loves them more than they do themselves, for given their negligence and carelessness, they would rather choose to go to hell at their leisure than get to heaven through their labors. And He who deprives them of their harmful leisure and gives them profitable labor shows them great love, and with much reason this should be given renown and be called singular love.

---

[60] Here the copyist has omitted some lines and conflated the beginning of this sentence with the end of another; the exact meaning is garbled but the sense is that the rigors of the journey incline the traveler to virtue.

And one can well say singular love for the abovementioned reasons and because this love is not shown to everyone; for although we, the idle and negligent along this road to heaven, are many, only a few, in my view, are afflicted with lasting suffering. And this diligence or special care that God shows to those He so scourges certainly proceeds from great and singular love. In proof of this, one can cite many examples, but as St. Gregory says in one of his sermons, "Whatever truth itself declares, human frailty does not presume to question."[61] And thus, leaving aside the streams and returning to the fountain, which is called the fount of living water,[62] what more proof do we want than what He Himself declares and proves where it is said, "Those whom I love, I rebuke and chastise" [Apocalypse 3:19].

Therefore, the first talent that we the suffering and afflicted receive is singular love, which we should repay with reverential love. And this repayment signifies loving God with much reverence and deeply felt devotion, not that our love can surpass or in any way equal His, for merely to think this would be presumption and manifest error. But this reverential love should be understood in this manner: we should multiply our love for Him beyond simply loving Him for Himself and for His innumerable blessings, so that in exchange for that talent of singular love that He gave us, He may find in us a corresponding special type of love by which we feel more obligated to love and serve Him above all others.

And when, because of our frailty or lukewarm devotion, this special love wanes or fails, may we recognize our baseness and hold ourselves guilty and unworthy of so many blessings, confessing with humility the fault of our ungratefulness. And if we were to do so, surely He who with great love wounded our humanity with grave afflictions with even greater charity would wound our hearts and souls with His divine love, showing us grace that we can repay with reverential love. And I say reverential because, although we well know the sovereign reverence that we as His creatures owe Him as our Creator and we as His redeemed sheep owe Him as our universal Redeemer, in consideration of the singular love He demonstrates in our suffering, we should have for Him exceptional reverence and fear that come from contemplating His blessing and special favor in disciplining us and in choosing us over others to be chastised by His hand for our own good and profit; this each one of us feels in his spirit

---

61   "Quam enim per semetipsam Veritas exposuit, hanc discutere humana fragilitas no praesumit." See St. Gregory the Great, "Homiliarum en Evangelia, Liber I, Homilia XV," in *Opera omnia, PL* 76:1131.

62   The imagery derives from Jeremias 2:13: "For my people have done two evils. They have forsaken me, the fountain of living water, and have digged to themselves cisterns, broken cisterns, that can hold no water."

better and more completely than I can say. And in this way we can and must repay the talent of reverential love in return for the first talent we received, which, as I said, was singular love.

The second talent we suffering receive, which is the very affliction and physical suffering we endure, is a coin of such metal that I know no one would want to receive. But this is because we do not recognize the virtue of this coin, nor the healthful practices it imposes wherever it finds the appropriate capacity and disposition; for if its workings were truly recognized, no one would repent of having received such a talent. And whoever wants to learn of the virtue and profit that accompany affliction should listen to St. Bernard when he says, "Suffering wounds the body and heals the soul."[63]

Blessed is the illness that is converted into our health! And what is our most important health if not the health of our soul? And since our soul is held in greater esteem than our body, we should appreciate the greater worth of any medicine that heals our injured soul. Yet such is our perversity in spiritual matters that experience tells us that we would rather have our soul burning with continuous fever than suffer a tiny pain in our toe. For although in order to heal a physical ailment we will suffer great torments, swallowing bitter draughts of medicine or submitting our bodies to burning instruments or the surgeon's blade or even consenting to amputation if required to save our lives which, despite all these measures, are always subject to death,[64] yet, in order to cure the continuous fever in our souls, to undergo any intervention seems bad to us.

Oh, invalid, do not be deceived by your physical pain or let human affliction cloud the light of your understanding! For this very suffering that you despise loves you well, that which you fear protects you, that which you try to push away draws you closer to true Good. And if you want a physician who will cure you, look only to your affliction, for if you allow it to work within you, it will purify you of bad humors more than you think.[65] And what are these bad humors if not the seven deadly

---

63 "Adversa carnis, remedia sunt animi: aegritudo carnem vulnerat, mentem curat: languor enim vitia excoquit, languor vires libidinis frangit" (St. Bernard, "Liber de modo bene vivendi, XLIII, De Infirmitate," in *Opera omnia, PL* 184:1264).

64 Pedro de Luna also discusses bitter remedies to avoid death: "Likewise, do not consider it bitter or shameful to confess your sins and ask forgiveness, as the sick person who joyfully takes bitter medicine to avoid a more bitter death; thus it behooves you much more to confess joyfully your bitter sins in this life so that you avoid bitter death in hell" (*Libro de consolaciones*, 574).

65 Medieval medical theory was based on Galen's theory of humors or body fluids. The ancient Greeks believed that the body was made up of four humors: blood, phlegm, yellow bile, and black bile. A person was supposed to be healthy when the body's four humors were in proper balance. Each humor was associated with one of the four fundamental elements (air, water,

sins? Without doubt these cause our souls to burn with continuous fever. Well, attend with discretion to the marvelous cure that physical suffering can effect in your soul and you will find truly that suffering shatters pride and fosters humility, it removes avarice and gives generosity, it curbs envy and encourages charity, it prohibits gluttony and imposes abstinence, it extinguishes fires and promotes chastity, it takes away anger and brings meekness, and it never allows idleness into its house.

Where can you find a physician so adept in medical arts that with one potion he cures his patient of all his ills? For no matter how much a doctor knows, if he cures your spleen, he injures your liver; if your stomach is healed, your head aches. But physical ailments are medicine confected and measured by that sovereign Physician whose sole word can heal all things.[66] And this elixir alone, if it is well received and held in the stomach, purges the soul of all seven bad humors mentioned above.

And just because I give these praises to my afflictions, do not think that I do so because of any special affection I have for them, although, given their perseverance and diligence in healing me of my spiritual fever, I do not deny that I hold them in good affection, for I love them as much as they do me, and everyone knows they afflict me as much as they could any human being. Yet, despite the spiritual well-being they give me, I would not offer praise that is untrue, nor, despite the continual hardship that they cause me, would I want to deny the perfect blessing that the Lord of all blessings wanted to inject into them, following in this case that ancient law that says, "You shall not deny glory to the good nor punishment to the bad."

And to better demonstrate the operations and marvelous cure that these afflictions produce in whomever they take in their hands, I want to briefly survey these seven fevers already mentioned that make our souls frantic in order to see how physical suffering can cure them. And first one must consider pride, captain and origin of all bad spiritual humors. And leafing through the book of its genealogy, my simplicity discerns that pride proceeds from six principal roots: the first is from illustrious lineage and great ancestors; the second is from being well proportioned and worthy; the third, from youth and what we commonly call beauty; the fourth, from gracious eloquence and an elevated mind; the fifth, from dignity and worldly honors; the sixth and least of all, from abundance and wealth and

earth, fire), the four seasons (spring, winter, autumn, summer), four temperaments (sanguine, phlegmatic, melancholic, choleric), and the four directions (east, north, west, south). Teresa presents the seven sins as bad humors expelled from the body by the medicine of suffering.

66 On Jesus as physician, see Luke 5:31–32: "Those who are healthy do not need a physician but the sick do, I have not come to call the righteous to repentance but sinners." See also Matthew 9:12–13 and Mark 2:17.

copious riches. Now let us see how affliction combats all these things with
armed resistance.

Suffering combats the first root of pride – the glorification of great
ancestors and family – in this manner: even if one is the son of a duke, an
admiral, or a marquis, if he is inflicted with great suffering or an embarrassing wound, not only will his friends and relatives hold him in contempt, but his own father and mother will dispatch him quickly from their
house and put him where he can cause them no detriment or disorder. And
even though he is the firstborn, he will be considered as lastborn, not only
among his own relatives or peers but among the lesser servants; he will
be despised by all and not held the equal of the least of them. Well, who
can take pride in what rejects him? It would be more to the point to
complain about the lack of compassion of his relatives than boast of their
nobility and more reasonable to humbly distance oneself from their
company than take pride in their power.

The second root of pride is the symmetry, proportion, and gallantry of
one's body. Affliction also overcomes this, for no matter how well
proportioned one is, if suffering comes to visit with a firm and solid
harness and continuously dwells within him, he will not have, I believe,
enough strength left to brag about nor will the proportions of his body
remain so symmetrical that some imperfection is not found.

The third root of pride is youth and beauty. Suffering robs this with
more daring than all other things, for there is no hardship in the world that
so quickly converts beauty into ugliness as suffering, which can turn white
to black and black to dark green. And suffering so impugns youth that it
makes a thirty-year-old seem more ancient than Simeon the Just,[67] not
only in visage but even in actions, for suffering burdens the young so that
they act like octogenarians.

The fourth root of pride is charming eloquence and elevated intellect
or wit. These things suffering never fears, for it converts witty sayings
into rude remarks – such as "Oh, my head! Oh, my stomach! Oh, blessed
Mary! Oh, St. Peter!" – so that the invalid wastes all his time in loud
complaints. And do not think that suffering overlooks a great mind, for
however learned or quick-witted one may be, suffering puts him in such
straits that neither his good sense nor that of his neighbors can help him.
How much worse is the affliction or suffering if one loses one's hearing
or one's speech, for no matter how subtle his intellect, he can only exercise
it for himself; and never fear that he may use his mind in vainglory, for
his very illness safeguards him from such an occasion.

---

[67] See Luke 2:25.

The fifth and very vigorous root of pride is worldly dignities and honors which, although they accrue to others, avoid the sick like the devil flees holy water. And it is no wonder that this is so, for suffering sustained by humble shoulders is holy water that cleanses and washes the conscience of the invalid; and worldly dignities and honors are like idols, coveted and pursued with such disordered fervor and struggle as if they in themselves offered salvation to those who possess them. For idols in ancient pagan times were held in place of the gods, and the devil entered the image or figure of stone or metal and deceived the people. In this same way human dignities and honors were constituted and are revered like God by those who receive them. And at times it happens that the prince of darkness enters the figures of prelates or pontiffs, leading them and their subjects to a bad end. But returning to our purpose, since his own dignity is lacking, the invalid cannot give or receive human dignities or honors.

The sixth and final root of pride is the abundance of many riches. This asset has made many arrogant, and sometimes raises them to such heights that they fall to the depths of spiritual poverty. But where suffering dwells there are no riches or, if there were, they could do no harm because suffering knows how to bring riches to its feet, and of this we need say no more.

However, since I have discussed briefly all the principal roots of pride and since the abundance of money and temporal goods is a very thick and green root from which the branches of pride grow and extend throughout the world, I wanted to include it in this account to more clearly show that wherever pride can prevail, there suffering impedes and countermands it. For it is likely that if suffering can combat a great force, it can completely overwhelm a lesser one. And there is no doubt that the blessings of nature are greater by far than the blessings of fortune. And since, as mentioned above, suffering combats and destroys the blessings of nature, it follows that with greater force and victory suffering will defeat those of fortune. And since temporal riches are gifts of fortune and totally subject to its jurisdiction, suffering can more easily combat and scatter them, and even they themselves show their fear of suffering, so much that only rarely will you see riches near the sick. Accordingly, as I said earlier in one section of this treatise, "For of a thousand invalids, you will find none rich, and if one is, his suffering will impoverish him in no time."[68] And even when riches abound so that there is enough to both spend and save, the invalid is still poor in that his wealth cannot alleviate his suffering; it is clear that

[68] See 40–41 above.

someone made poor by nature cannot be made rich by fortune. And in this way suffering knows how to cure the soul of the dangerous principal humor that is called pride.

Now let us see if avarice can be cured by suffering. Yes, indeed, for however avaricious someone may be, when he falls ill, he becomes liberal and generous, since the natural desire that man has for his own health is the key to immediately unlock the doors of avarice and exercise liberality. For not only is the sufferer compelled to spend abundantly in the cure of his own person and health, it behooves him even more to be generous with his physicians and to spend openly on all who serve him. For since nowadays charity is so cold and even completely frozen in the world, if generous incentives do not quickly warm their hearts, people will tire of serving. And not only is it fitting for the invalid to exercise generosity in the abovementioned matters, but like it or not, he must spend his money on pious works and devout sacrifices, giving alms and sponsoring masses so that God may grant him the health he desires.

Now the third and very harmful humor is envy, which clearly undermines and erodes our spiritual health; believe that suffering well knows how to greatly reduce envy. And since envy is to sorrow over someone else's good fortune and since the principal blessing of this life is our health, whoever is deprived of good health is so involved in his own misfortune that he cannot even remember the good fortune of anyone else, nor is it possible for an invalid to have envy of anything except physical health. And since physical health is a natural desire, to envy it is not a sin, as long as we do not wish harm to someone else's health, for that would more appropriately be called exquisite malice than natural envy.

And thus curing the soul of these three principal humors, suffering quickly dispatches the other four humors with sweet medications, for the fire and vigor of suffering immediately suffocate carnal desires. And see if an invalid can exercise gluttony, for where there is sickness, there you will find abstinence and fasting, so that even if the invalid does not want to, suffering makes him endure more than four quarantines of fasting.[69] Talking does not suit him, for his pain robs him of sleep, and he carries his scourges on his shoulders. What else does suffering do? It converts ire into meekness. It is no wonder that if God has given suffering the power to diminish our natural strength, He also gives it the virtue of meekness to diminish our occasional impetuousness.

And suffering never allows sloth. Whoever says that the invalid is idle does not know what affliction is, for were he to know it, his own

---

[69] A quarantine is a period of forty days, here derived from the forty days of Lenten abstinence.

experience would teach him how the invalid is always busy in worthy and secret labors, hidden without doubt from all human praise. There are some people who say in ignorance, "How well off are the suffering in their leisure!" I call this kind of ignorance malicious ignorance, full of spiritual envy. Their ignorance is not knowing or never taking the bitter medicine of afflictions. And their malice and spiritual envy consist in being so distanced from charity or pity of their neighbors that, seeing them subjected to extreme suffering, they not only have no compassion for them [. . . but, moreover, they accuse them of sloth . . .][70] so that even the afflicted notice their disdain. Based on my experience I can say that I believe the invalid confined to his bed labors more than a worker who keeps his hand to his hoe from morning to night.

And thus St. Bernard says a very great truth, that suffering wounds the body and cures the soul of these seven humors that assail it continuously.[71] And, furthermore, suffering readies our will for spiritual matters and removes the cloud of vain temporal blessings from the eyes of our understanding and makes shine the light of true knowledge. Thus we read about our glorious father St. Francis[72] that when he was committed to worldly affairs and ignored and disdained spiritual concerns, the hand of the Lord descended on him, according to the story of his life, and chastised him with a grave and tedious illness and enlightened him from within with the balm of the Holy Spirit, and from then on the light of his great perfection began to shine.

Therefore, let not those of us who suffer afflictions and physical pain be ungrateful nor deny the great good that comes to us through suffering, for without doubt we have received a talent of very healthful metal from God with which to earn many blessings. Our reason, however, especially admonishes us that we should earn and acquire filial fear, for the invalid will earn a great and beneficial talent, indeed, with the affliction that God gave him if he is instructed by his suffering to have fear of God. Of this the Psalmist says, "The fear of the Lord is holy, enduring for ever and ever" [Psalm 18:10], and in another passage, "The fear of the Lord is the beginning of wisdom" [Psalm 110:10].

And while our books are full of praises and admonishments about this saintly fear, there are actually two ways of fearing: one from servitude and the other filial. The servile fear is how the servant fears his master, and filial fear is how the son fears his father. And although both these

---

[70] My reconstruction; the copyist skipped lines and the rest of the sentence is garbled.

[71] See 57 above.

[72] Teresa's reference here to "our glorious father St. Francis" has led to the speculation that she belonged to a Franciscan convent.

types of fear are owed to God, Father of all creatures and Lord of all lords, there is a great difference between these two fears, and one is superior both in quality and merit, for a servant's fear proceeds from necessity while a son's fear proceeds from natural love.

Therefore, although we should fear God with servitude as our sovereign Lord, we also should fear Him with great love, for this type of filial fear is more pleasing to God and more praiseworthy in us, as we see if we examine their difference. For the servant fears his master because he has dominion and power over him and he can persecute him and throw him out of his house. All this refers back to the self-interest of the servant, as we see from experience; for a man when he lives with his master holds him in fear and reverence, but if the master throws him out of his house and takes away the livelihood he had with him, the servant immediately loses his fear of him.

However, the son does not fear in this same way, for he knows well that his father will neither persecute him nor throw him from his house; rather, he fears him only with natural love and filial reverence, mixed with his own desire not to anger him. And just as servile fear depends on the interest of the servant and on his own harm or benefit, filial fear is based totally on the honor and paternal reverence of the father. Therefore, this fear, insofar as it is more perfect and worthy, is the talent we should earn with the scourging of our suffering.

And it even seems to me that afflictions bring with them this fear and invite us to fear: for just as the first talent that we receive is singular love, with which we should earn reverential love, so with the second talent of our suffering – itself an act of God's singular love that binds us, for right after His love comes His punishment, chastising and correcting our faults like a sweet father – we should immediately add as spiritual gain the talent of filial fear; not only because we fear His incomprehensible and absolute power, which can cause us to lose body and soul in hell, and the great danger that can befall us, or because we fear losing worldly blessings or the greater and more perfect blessings of the future, but because we do not want to offend Him. This filial fear is of such strength and virtue that it can drive away servile fear; although I do not say it should, rather I admonish that just as God should be feared by all his creatures everywhere so we should fear Him always with great vigilance. Nevertheless, this filial love can give us faith and hope in our Lord to assure us that His sovereign and paternal charity will not permit our ultimate perdition.

The third talent that we receive is the mortification that our afflictions impose on our physical strength. This mortification is like the source or stamp of our suffering, for just as a seal placed over wax leaves its own impression, so afflictions with the stamp of mortification impress on the body and face of the sufferer the seal of its own coat of arms. Hence we recognize whether people are sick or healthy by the imprint of this abovementioned seal; for when we see the color of their pale face, their labored and feeble walk, the translucent bones of their hands, we immediately know that that man or woman has been or is ill. And if the person is an acquaintance, the imprint of this seal can be such that we may not recognize him. Thus the mortification that undermines and erodes the strength of our bodies is the seal with which our afflictions make the impression of their own coat of arms.

And with regard to strangers, this impression lets us recognize them as part of suffering's retinue, while with our acquaintances, the donning of suffering's livery renders them unrecognizable because of changes in their appearance. And afflictions can impress this seal of mortification with such force that not only is the invalid not recognized by those who know him and recognized by those who have never seen him before, but he is even unrecognizable to himself, for he has changed into another person. For if he was heavy, he finds himself now withered and thin, and if he had strength for great deeds, he finds himself now incapable of small ones; and if walking through the village used to cheer him, now he thinks only of reposing quietly at home.

Oh invalid, how powerful is this talent of physical mortification! Awaken your great discretion so that, aided by divine grace, you may discover how this talent is forged of the metal of insinuation.[73] For this coin of mortification advises and teaches you, admonishing you with a human voice how you can earn another coin to repay the Lord, who originally lent it to you. And so that we can better consider what it advises and teaches in spiritual matters, let me describe more openly and in depth how this talent of mortification operates in both human and spiritual affairs. For not only does it sap our external strengths and make us almost powerless in worldly exercises, it undermines in our mortified will even our hidden thoughts.

And in order to more clearly understand this, let us consider how human thought is as fleet as a dromedary, which I have heard say and even read walks more in one day than any other beast could walk in four. And likewise human thought travels far in a short space of time, for what we think in one hour we cannot hope to accomplish in one year, and our thoughts can so quicken their steps that in ten years we could not achieve what in one hour we understand. And suffering does not impede our

---

[73] The phrase "metal of insinuation" refers to how mortification impresses itself on the sufferer.

thought, for although suffering makes the invalid powerless in outward deeds, it makes him powerful in inward thought. It lets him scatter his thought wherever he wishes, so that although he may be feverish or crippled, his thought lets him imagine that he is hunting or wearing his armor or jousting or engaging in other worldly acts.

However, only physical mortification represses these vain thoughts and weakens and drains them to a great extent of their own vigor and force, for although thought can carry off our heart whenever and wherever it wishes and without any delay take it where our strength could not reach, as soon as physical mortification arrives at our door, all these vain thoughts are left cold. But when thought turns around because of our weakness and lack of strength, we realize that we are not prepared for the least enterprise our fantasy, oblivious to our state, imagined. And in this way, the mortification of our outward strength makes our inward thoughts faint and completely powerless. Well, this is not without reason: God thus arranges to advise and show us what we should earn with this talent of physical mortification, and that is the mortification of our vices.

This applies not only in deed but in thought, for it is not enough for the invalid not to sin in deed; rather, it is fitting that he not sin in thought, for intention is esteemed over works. And just as we are not compelled to do good works beyond our ability, it follows that when we cannot commit bad deeds because we are unable, we deserve neither punishment nor glory. Therefore, only what is within our power to do or not to do makes us worthy of merit, either good or bad as required by the quality of the act. And thus one should not commend the invalid for avoiding those sins which the healthy commit, since his afflictions make him powerless to commit these sins; but if he wants to improve on his own merit, he must separate his will from sin and mortify his desire to sin. For not to be able to commit sin in this case is a result of his suffering, but not to want to desire to sin is an act of his own virtue.

Therefore, let us leave the exercise of mortifying our vices to our afflictions, for their goodness charges them to do this more than we the infirm desire. And for this physical mortification, although it may be good and very praiseworthy and a cause of good health, thanks are due only to God.[74] But the mortification of our desires and thoughts is done in our will, which is within our control. This is what makes us worthy, this is how we should repay the Lord, if we do not want to go away emptyhanded from the spiritual attainment that this third abovementioned talent advises us to earn with it.

---

[74] Several lines repeated by the copyist here have been omitted in the translation.

Therefore, it is fitting that we follow these steps in this way: that just
as our physical strength grows faint and feeble, so may our temporal
desires, fears, and cupidity diminish little by little until they are level with
the impotence or weakness of our bodies, so that the sufferer too weak to
pray is also too weak to utter reproach, and he who is not empowered to
do good and meritorious works refuses to empower his will to desire
vicious and evil works. For whoever cannot serve God with material
deeds, let him not offend God with spiritual pride. For without doubt to
have one's desire inclined to evil is a great confusion and shame to
whoever has neither the strength nor the health to do good.

Consequently, it seems wrong not to have enough health to go to church
to adore Him who is our true health and yet spend four hours at the gaming
table or wandering around the village. Such a weakness damages more
than it benefits, for to have one's strength to do good works so dead and
one's desire to sin so alive are two very great torments which are full of
danger, empty of merit and spiritual benefit, and separate from the virtue
of prudence, which is the greater part of patience. For whoever seeks
remedy for his travails in this way, no matter how much his afflictions
stifle and harrass him, shall be called a sufferer but not long-suffering.
For a prudent and discreet sufferer does not multiply his misfortunes by
making one travail into four, or out of negligence or ignorance turn a
physical affliction into a spiritual danger.

Therefore, prudence, which is the second and better part of patience,
should here provide a remedy by aiding and exhorting the sufferer to leave
these vain remedies and turn instead to spiritual remedies, putting into
action that very lesson that his physical mortification advises and teaches,
which is to kill the bad thoughts and desires and human conflicts within
his will with the sword of mortification. As soon as his vain thoughts and
harmful meditations heed this mortification, they will lose their force, and
persisting a little against these thoughts, he will stifle them in their
dwelling within the secret walls of his heart. And of this mortification and
secret victory that the patient invalid should have over his enemy thoughts
that rob him of the great blessing and merit that his afflictions bring, St.
Jerome says in a letter, "He will be praised, he will be proclaimed blessed
who as soon as he begins to imagine stifles his thoughts and ties them to
a stone."[75] This stone is none other than that cornerstone rejected by the

---

[75] "Quia enim impossibile est in sensum hominis non irruere innatum medullarum calorem,
ille laudatur, ille praedicatur beatus, qui ut coeperit cogitare sordida, statim interficit
cogitatus, et allidit ad petram: petram autem Christus est" (St. Jerome, "Epistola XXII ad
Eustochiam, Paulae Filium," in *Opera Omnia, PL* 22:398).

builders,[76] for whoever heeds this firm stone or turns his thoughts to it, believe me, will find himself unbound and free of any evil fancy and diabolic conflicts. Of this the most saintly doctor Augustine says, "Whoever is bitten by Satan's cunning should contemplate Christ on the cross."[77]

But leaving aside this sovereign medicine and singular victory, I would say that this stone is the virtue of fortitude, which can be called not only stone but even precious stone; stone for the properties it has in itself, precious for its virtue. And to better understand how the virtue of fortitude itself has properties of stone one must consider that a material stone has, among other properties, two singular or principal features; one is immobility and the other resistance. For because of its immobility it receives great and strong blows without moving from its place, and because of its resistance it resists and surpasses powerfully the weak and little blows. Thus a stone, unaltered, wounds and breaks whatever is weaker.

These two properties also pertain to the virtue of fortitude, for it receives great and strong blows – the great hardships and afflictions of this life – without altering its own being and virtue; and it resists and powerfully withstands the weak and little blows – the secret subjugations and conflicts enclosed in our will – and does not change its own purpose and proper being and even wounds and breaks whatever has less strength than it has. And since our imaginations and temptations proceed from our human weakness and all weakness is incomparably less than fortitude, no vices and bad thoughts can remain in the presence of the virtue of fortitude; rather, even if they cause confusion, they are wounded, hurt, and in the short duration of this struggle die off completely. Therefore, he will be praised and proclaimed blessed who, as soon as he begins to imagine, stifles his thoughts and binds them to this precious stone called the virtue of fortitude, which is no less necessary than prudence if we want to exercise true patience, for the truly patient sufferer is strong. Thus the Prophet says of the Lord of patience and Lover of patient sufferers, "God was merciful, powerful, patient."[78]

For all virtues accrue to true patience, as I shall explain below, but for now suffice it to say this about the virtue of fortitude. For just as suffering

---

[76] "The stone which the builders rejected: the same is become the head of the corner" (Psalm 117:22). Compare also Matthew 21:42 and 1 Peter 2:7.

[77] Compare: "Crux illa vexillum nostrum est contra adversarium nostrum diabolum: pugnavit enim Rex noster pro nobis contra adversarium nostrum." See St. Augustine, "De Symbolo, Caput V," in *Opera omnia, PL* 40:664.

[78] Compare Psalm 85:10,15: "For thou art great and dost wonderful things: thou art God alone. . . . And thou, O Lord, art a God of compassion, and merciful, patient, and of much mercy, and true."

hardships and afflictions without the virtue of prudence is not complete and virtuous patience, so patience is greatly endangered if not immediately aided by the virtue of fortitude, which, with its own strength, wounds and shatters all vice and remains ever intact and whole. Therefore, let us take fortitude as an arm to resist and kill hidden vices, since public vices are resisted by our afflictions. What that glorious and saintly doctor instructed us in his abovementioned quote cannot, I believe, be passed over in silence; rather, it merits repetition: "As soon as he begins to imagine." Whence it appears that the mortification of inner thoughts and vices admits no delay but requires immediate remedy, because the longer wicked thoughts grow in our will, the more difficult and doubtful is our victory. Therefore, he says that "as soon as he begins to imagine," as if he were saying that at the very moment that a bad thought is conceived, we must immediately begin to oppose and resist it.

And thus this talent of mortification that we infirm suffer in our physical strength is a talent of very healthful metal, for it teaches us and shows us the way to earn mortification of our vices and inner and hidden thoughts, for if we ever achieve this victory so that our vices completely die in thought and intent as in deed, without doubt our virtues shall resurge. Truly it is not a bad exchange to abandon vices for virtues. We can rightly say that whoever suffers in this way has great patience, for he knows how to suffer with great prudence and wisdom and how to win with his travails, since he obtains from his hardships the best and most gracious and acceptable sacrifice that a human creature can offer to God, which is to be mortified in the flesh and unified in the spirit.

The fourth talent that we afflicted receive is the humiliation and contempt that our afflictions cause us. This talent is of such metal that experience can describe it better than tongue or pen, all the more so because enough was stated about this humiliation when I spoke earlier of the roots of pride, for what admits no exaltation necessarily breeds humiliation and contempt.[79] Therefore, since the quality of this talent is well known to those who have tasted its bitterness, let me state what we can earn with this coin, and that is voluntary humility. And to better understand what voluntary humility is and why with it we should repay the Lord from whom we receive so many blessings, let us consider that the humiliation and contempt that our afflictions cause us are not to our liking, but rather against our will; therefore, this counts as one of the talents we receive from the Lord. To give back to God what He gives us is bereft of merit, worthy of neither thanks nor praise.

---

[79] See 58–61 above.

Let us compare this kind of humiliation and contempt with the man who received a single talent and buried it in the ground. Of this St. Gregory says in his homily on this gospel, "To bury one's talent in the ground is to receive intelligence and to apply it to earthly acts, not seeking spiritual gain, never raising one's heart above lowly thoughts."[80] For whoever in his travails looks more to human concerns than to the spiritual never raises up his heart from lowly and earthly considerations. And whoever, having received from God such a healthful talent of humiliation and contempt, leaves it buried in the soil of human sentiment without earning with it voluntary humility, does not seek spiritual profit.

Therefore, it is very fitting that we add to the hardship of our travails and suffering in such a way that if our affliction bows one of our shoulders, our humility and devout patience will bow the other. And if extrinsic humiliation can bring upon us the scorn of other people, let us strive so that our natural and voluntary humility makes us scorn ourselves. For the foundation of true humility, I believe, is for man to despise himself more and esteem and value himself less than his detractors do. Beyond the worthy spiritual benefits this allows, two great temporal advantages can ensue: one is that the contempt that others show us does not offend us or provoke us to anger, and the other advantage is that our suffering – our inward spiritual suffering, not our physical suffering – will be alleviated to a great extent.

And to better understand spiritual suffering and how voluntary humility can alleviate it, let us consider how our afflictions and physical suffering not only scourge and wound our bodies, causing our heads, eyes, and arms to ache, but even more harshly cause our hearts to ache and afflict our spirit and inner feelings. It is not that our physical suffering alone completely causes these inner pains; rather, they are caused by this aforementioned talent of humiliation and contempt. For when the invalid sees himself so humiliated and despised by his neighbors, there is no doubt that his heart is stung with great affliction and feeling, so that, depending on the quality of the contempt and the person who receives it, someone can be more tormented by this type of anguish than by his many physical pains.

This inner suffering is what I say will be alleviated to a great extent by despising ourselves and striving to humiliate ourselves more than our travails and afflictions do, for the travails of this miserable life are not in our power to drive away; of this it is written, "Man is born to labour and

---

80 "Talentum in terra abscondere est acceptum ingenium in terrenis actibus implicare, lucrum spiritale non quarere, cor a terrenis cogitationibus numquam levare." See St. Gregory the Great, "Homiliarum in Evangelia, Liber I, Homilia IX," in *Opera omnia, PL* 76:1107. St. Gregory's ninth sermon is on Matthew 25:14–30.

the bird to fly" [Job 5:7]. We can, however, alleviate our travails somewhat by accepting them, for there is no hardship in this life that can hurt us too much if we convince our will that that hardship pleases us. Therefore, to have voluntary humility we must be pleased with the contempt that others show us, for this contentment in received scorn is the basis of true and voluntary humility. When the slights and humiliations that others inflict cause suffering and assail our hearts, this is a signal that we hold our persons in more esteem than we should according to our virtue; for humility is not only to conform to what our condition or worth requires; rather, we must lower ourselves further and humble ourselves more than our being or suffering does. Therefore, first of all, we must willingly receive the abjection and disdain that the affliction or wound that God gave us elicits from other people, and from this we can arrive at voluntary humiliation, which transcends mere satisfaction in what necessity imposes. Let us advance further so that this firm edifice of humility may be wrought with happy contentment, on the one hand, and devout exercise, on the other.

The fifth and last talent that we infirm receive is the time that our afflictions impede and detain us, preventing our involvement in vain or worldly things. This talent is of such great, precious, and valuable metal that my intellect fails to grasp or understand it. But it seems to me that in order to give it a name that conforms to its particular being, it should be called the talent of provision, for its very exercise is understood to be this: to provide and prevent – to provide remedies for present dangers and to prevent against future dangers.

Now, who can think or say how much this aforesaid talent is worth and how many more we should repay to the Lord? I do not know who could understand it better than someone who has seen it with his eyes and felt it with his hands. Therefore, if you, invalid, want to know the diversity and greatness of blessings contained in this fifth talent, begin to imagine and reflect on the multitude of sins you committed when your time was free of afflictions. And then you will be able to sense how many blessings we receive from God, who impedes and detains your time from dissolute living, and you will realize that these blessings are innumerable, for as many days, hours, and minutes as you are afflicted with grave suffering, that many days and hours are you provided with sweet blessings.

Of this the Prophet says, "For thou hast prevented him with blessings of sweetness" [Psalm 20:4]. Oh, how sweet are the blessings that separate us from the bitter curse of sin and lead us away from the horrible oppression of hell! For during the time we are engaged in our suffering not only are we diverted from worldly things that we cannot attend to, but we are, moreover, in a state of grace and true penitence. And certainly we are in a state of grace and true penitence that without deserving we should desire and strive to achieve, yet only by God's goodness do we receive such grace, for the deeds and desires that used to guide us toward the pains of hell are corrected with a merciful and fatherly whipping.

And if our attaining such a correction were not a special blessing proceeding from divine grace, the Church would not have begged for it, saying thus, "Correct me, O Lord, but with mercy and not in fury."[81] For without doubt, whoever is corrected with mercy and not with anger is provided with God's compassion at an opportune time so that amends may be achieved before that day of great ire and bitterness when amends can no longer be attained. And therefore, he who achieves this is in a state of grace, and very great grace, and of true penitence. For the true penitent is disciplined and punished by the hand of the great Prelate and sovereign Pontiff, Jesus Christ our Lord.[82]

For there is no truer penitence than that which proceeds from the fount of truth, even more so when beyond this special and even singular state of grace I have mentioned necessarily ensues a general and sacramental state that is confession and communion, which the sufferer should procure and frequent with total devotion. And in case some member of this family of afflictions be so worldly and emptyheaded that he does not know the one nor procure the other, even so, in spite of himself, during the time of his suffering it behooves him to be spiritual and devout. Thus, even if he does not want to do good, at least he cannot do bad things or sin so freely as he used to during the time of his health.

Therefore, this talent of prevention and detainment through afflictions and sufferings is so full of diverse and great blessings that we cannot repay with it any good or worthy deed that is not already in it. Thus I think that we should repay such a multitude of blessings with a multitude of thanks. And just as someone who has passed through a great dangerous and dark sea and finds himself free of its waves gives heartfelt thanks to whoever freed him from so much danger, with greater reason and more devout exercise the infirm should offer uncommon thanks to the merciful Lord, who in the secure ship of arduous suffering has freed him from the dark waves of this dangerous sea and provided his injuries with such healthful and sweet remedies.

Consider, invalid, that whoever prevents your danger and provides your remedy with such diligence, with equal diligence observes your heart

---

[81] Compare Jeremiah 10:24: "Correct me, O Lord, but yet with judgment: and not in thy fury, lest thou bring me to nothing."

[82] Compare Hebrews 4:14: "Having therefore a great high priest that hath passed into the heavens, Jesus the Son of God: let us hold fast our confession."

and feelings to see if you express your gratitude through good works or at least offer a repayment through thanks. For the affliction or suffering we endure should not fatigue us but rather glorify the manifest diligence that our Lord shows in wanting to detain us in conversation with Him so that we do not embark on the dangers of this world. And the more lasting and strong the affliction we endure, the longer the conversation our sovereign Lord beckons us to and invites us to share, communicating to us His marvelous secrets. For the pained and afflicted never cease to talk with God in prayer or in supplication or in confessing and praising his blessings.

And certainly I would say that the patient invalid always prays and blesses God; even though he may be quiet, his very pains pray for him and bless God and invoke His aid. Thus we read of St. Lazarus, for as many wounds as he had on his blessed body, as many mouths he had clamoring to heaven, and with all his mouths he praised and blessed God.[83] And if our physical pains and sufferings bless God and confess the magnitude of His saintly works, what should the intellect, heart, and spirit of the sufferer do, since these three things are more capable of knowing, sensing, thanking, and serving God's blessings? Therefore, let us praise God in our afflictions; let us praise God with confession of our word and thought; let us offer him thanks with our heart and soul continuously and unceasingly. For the sufferer who wastes his time without giving thanks to God for his afflictions and sufferings and for the manifest benefit they bring him is in great spiritual danger.

But, what shall I say if instead of giving thanks we give him offense, if instead of recognizing our blessings we ignore them, considering ourselves as badly served with this aforesaid coin we received from God and esteeming those who enjoy complete physical health as more blessed, more God's friends than we who are poor in health? Or if instead of worship the invalid curses himself and offends God with proud words? See what offense God receives from this. Certainly, this invalid is gravely ill, suffering as he may be, and even if his doctors say that his affliction is not life-threatening, I say he is in great mortal danger, wounded with such a pestiferous wound that not only should the healthy flee from his sight but the infirm should be separated with reason from his company. May it please God this be not so!

Yet wherever this happens there must be a great lack of prudence, for if prudence were present, it would examine at length all the blessings that

---

[83]   For the parable of the rich man and Lazarus the beggar, see Luke 16:19–31. Compare Pedro de Luna: "Thus Peter of Ravenna says that Lazarus the poor had as many clamoring mouths as wounds tormenting his body . . ." (*Libro de consolaciones*, 568).

in its absence seemed misfortunes and would speak of perfect and complete patience, revealing to the sufferer the five talents received from God and the quantity, value, and quality of each of the coins, and also how fitting it is to profit with them to repay the Lord. Thus from a sufferer he would be made patient, that is, a prudent and wise sufferer. Yet I believe that the lack of this virtue of prudence makes us have bouts of impatience, as we see happen in the fruits of the land, for when water fails, they dry up and are lost, and thorns and harmful weeds grow instead of grain. Of this we say that when bread becomes too costly, the common people suffer great hunger.

And thus, returning to my purpose, the fruit of the labors of our afflictions is patience, as mentioned above. But if patience lacks the water of the virtue of prudence, not only do our hardships dry up and become lost, but vices flourish in place of virtues, and the common people, by which we understand the community of the ailing and afflicted, suffer great hunger; for the sustaining bread, which is perfect patience, is so dear that I would sooner say that it rose to heaven because there is so little of it in this world, for I see the infirm as well as the healthy everywhere have great hunger of this virtue. Thus, if anyone has perfect patience, he is guided by heaven to his destination, directly to paradise.

But so that we do not remain completely starving for this bread of patience, let us work to have the royal coin that is called the virtue of prudence. And whoever has more need of the bread of patience should have his pocket more abundantly full of prudence. And who has more need of patience than the infirm and those wounded with suffering? And just as the infirm more continually suffer, so they should be continually full of patience, for there is nothing in the world more abominable or vexing than an invalid without patience who exaggerates his misfortunes and destroys his singular blessings with his indiscreet suffering and remains full of wounds and devoid of virtues because of his sin and manifest imprudence.

For who will love someone who abhors himself? Or who will suffer someone else's misfortunes when he himself refuses to suffer them? Who will exercise mercy with someone who is tyrannical and cruel with himself? Is there a greater cruelty in the world than for a man to multiply his misfortunes and not count his blessings? Surely the invalid without patience is more cruel than tyrants of the past, for while the latter martyred the bodies of others and preserved their own, the impatient invalid torments, crucifies, and kills himself. And if impatience during any hardship is an abuse, impatience in sufferers goes beyond abuse and becomes a mortal pestilence that kills the body and the soul. And who will visit an invalid who refuses to consider God's mercy? Who will visit mm? Someone who casts aside and refuses God's great gifts and benefits would never turn his face toward his neighbor nor welcome lesser human help.

Oh, invalid so infirm, because of your suffering you separate yourself completely from everlasting health! You complain of physical pains and you do not want to consider the great blessings they bring you; but first, if you want to recognize these blessings, you must meet the great doctor called Patience, medicine and conservator of the order of travails! Therefore, use your head, which is to say, your discretion; for if you exercise your discretion, patience is not far away; rather, it invites you and begs to be received in your company. Therefore, give yourself over completely to patience and it will be so friendly to you that you will suffer any hardship not to offend its gracious friendship. For, without doubt, whoever knows what patience is will know the blessings I speak of and many more I cannot recount, blessings that if known not only make us endure our ailments but even esteem them as precious jewels with which, through divine grace, we can reach the precious pearl that is the kingdom of heaven.[84]

And here ends the second and most perfect degree of patience according to the interpretation of its own letters, which denote suffering with prudence and wisdom: the first degree is tolerating one's misfortunes, and the second is recognizing one's blessings and obtaining from them spiritual profit, as stated above, or, in another better way, as it pleases the goodness of God to inspire in each devout soul.

Yet because my coarse womanly judgement gives my words little or no authority and because of my great desire that this virtue of patience be well known and honored by all, I am not content to know patience by name alone, nor does the interpretation of patience's name satisfy me. For I desire to have full information or more complete knowledge about what patience is and of what it consists, especially because some people are so deceived that they judge the natural feeling and pain one experiences from suffering as impatience, and they call dissembling and feigned happiness in hardships patience. This is as contrary to the truth as it is tiresome and annoying to the suffering, for instead of being consoled, they are reviled and accused of not having patience. This is because they are sad and weep over their afflictions and travails.

And so to contradict this and prove it wrong, I search for some well-lettered person so learned in this science that his doctrine deserves to have these two names: *façere e doçere* [to practice and to teach]. And

---

[84] See Matthew 13:45: "Again the kingdom of heaven is like to a merchant seeking good pearls."

because there are so few learned people of this type in our time, _ _
necessary to turn back to those of past and ancient times whose stories
the Scriptures recount for their praise and our example. These people
learned their laws not in Paris nor Salamanca but in the school of perfect
works, where they were and continue to be great teachers. Of these I shall
name one singular example who exercised complete *façere e doçere* in
the virtue of patience, for he practiced and taught perfect and true
patience. And to call him as I wish, let me recount how I remember a time,
before my ears closed their doors to human voices, when I had heard the
Master of Sentences referred to in sermons as a witness and authority for
what was said.[85] And in his stead, I wish to refer to the Master of Patiences,
not only as witness and authority of my simple sayings (for they do not
deserve so much) but to contradict those who give wrong judgements and
brand the sad and afflicted as impatient or imprudent sufferers.

Therefore, let us ask this famous example of patience, whose name is
Job, for through his deeds and words he will teach us and give us complete
knowledge of the virtue of patience. And although Scripture gives him
other very honorable names, for he is called a simple and just man,
God-fearing and remote from evil,[86] my devotion gives him the name
Master of Patiences. For the greatest and most exceptional hardships that
can occur in stages over the span of our lifetime befell Job all together in
the space of an hour and with all these hardships he exercised patience.
It follows that there were many kinds of patience in him, for whoever has
many diverse pains needs different kinds of patience, although these
become again one complete and perfect patience.

Therefore, he should be called the Master of Patiences; and in watching
and tracing the steps of his saintly history as much my rude intelligence
allows, I find that the first doctrine that he demonstrated through his deeds
was when, having heard the frightful mortal news of his very grave and
sorrowful misfortunes, he tore his clothes and fell to the ground. In this
he expressed the great anguish and natural feeling that he had from his
misfortunes, for in those days people were accustomed to tear their clothes
as a sign of great pain and sorrow. Hence we read that the patriarch Jacob,
with the great sorrow he had when shown the stained tunic of his most
beloved and saintly son Joseph, tore his garment, saying, "An evil wild
beast hath eaten him, a beast hath devoured Joseph" [Genesis 37:35].

---

85 Peter Lombard (1095?–1160) was called "Master of Sentences" because of his famous
   compilation, *The Four Books of Sentences* (1158), which served as a standard textbook in
   theological studies for three hundred years. See "Liber quatuor sententiarum," in *Opera
   omnia, PL* 192: 519–964.
86 See Job 1:8: "And the Lord said to him: 'Hast thou considered my servant Job, that there is
   none like him in the earth, a simple and upright man, and fearing God, and avoiding evil?' "

And likewise the prophet David, when he learned of the death of Saul and Jonathan, took his garment and tore it.[87] And we read of many others who as a sign of great mourning and sorrow tore their clothes.

This shows us that the first thing that life's hardships cause and should cause is a natural feeling of sorrow from our misfortunes, whence it seems clear enough that to be sorrowful or sad because of the hardships and sufferings we endure does not contradict the virtue of patience but rather precedes and makes way for it, just as when someone of great estate or dignity wants to come to see us, he sends ahead one of his men to announce him so that he will be better received and more at ease. And thus great anguish and emotion from our hardships are the proper harbingers of patience that advise us that patience is near and wants to enter our dwelling, so that we do not close the door. Therefore, the first doctrine that this saintly man, the Master of Patiences, teaches us through his works is that he tore his clothes. I well believe that it is true that his heart was not whole nor free from sorrow, but torn and wounded with unbearable pain and natural emotions that advised his discretion and prudence how the greatest and most perfect patience of patiences was coming to visit him in order to justify and make his saintliness more clear and refined and worthy of eternal memory, and thus to demonstrate to us that the great emotion, affliction, and sadness that happen to us in our misfortunes are natural and reasonable and not in the least discrepant with the virtue of patience.

For if we examine it well, bitter weeping favors patience more than dissolute laughter, for to walk around the street or cloisters laughing at our ills is neither patience nor discretion. It may be true that in some sorrows or some respects, discretion is to show happiness or not all the sorrow one has stored up, but this I call discreet pretense, not true patience. And perfect patience does not extend its purposes to these human concerns, but rather to please God, and this was exemplified by this very saintly and just man when three of his friends, having heard of the misfortunes which befell him, came to visit him and said in rebuke, "You have taught many and you have strengthened the weary hands, and now the scourge is come upon you and you have fainted. Where is your fear and your fortitude? Where is your patience and the perfection of your ways?"[88] To this the very conscientious Master of Patiences, among his

---

87 "Then David took hold of his garments and rent them, and likewise all the men that were with him" (2 Kings 1:11).

88 Compare Job 4:3–6: "Behold thou hast taught many, and thou hast strengthened the weary hands: Thy words have confirmed them that were staggering, and thou hast strengthened the trembling knees: But now the scourge is come upon thee, and thou faintest: it hath touched

many discreet words full of pain, responded as follows: "What is my end that I should keep patience?, etc."[89] Oh, most prudent sufferer of great pain, who in so few words showed us the straight road to true patience, saying, "What is my end that I should keep patience?" As if he were to say, "My patience is not directed to worldly arrogance for people to see and praise; it is a prudent sufferer in the hardships that have befallen me and a diligent observer of its sovereign purpose, which is God. Therefore, what is my purpose? It is not to satisfy human judgements but rather not to offend God."

And what is our purpose in patiently enduring our suffering and adversities if not God alone? For we should observe this end with devout diligence, prudently suffering his disciplines so that we do not offend him; rather, we should increase our fear of him and saintly service as the possibility of the hardship we endure requires. This the abovementioned Master of Patiences taught us openly when, having torn his garments (which signified his human affliction), he fell to the ground and worshipped. His falling to the ground teaches us prompt and willing humility; in all our hardships humility should come second after our natural emotion, and immediately without delay it should come, for one cannot have any kind of patience without humility. How much more so with great and perfect patience! This cannot be known or even glimpsed if there is any pride. By the act of adoring, Job teaches us heartfelt reverence and filial love, mixed with harshness and devout prayer.

And thus in all the other doctrines that this very reverend Master of Patiences teaches us, it is proven that true and perfect patience directs its purpose to God and takes solicitous care not to offend Him, but rather to serve Him and repay Him with an act of thanks, as this saintly man did. For whoever considers well Job's deeds will see them filled with knowledge of God and with repayment of thanks, and to recount them here would be too much; and for those who know less about Job's deed yet still more than I, what has been said is enough to prove that patience is not in whether or not one complains about one's pains, for this pertains to the discretion of the individual and even more to the quality and quantity of the pain that he experiences; rather, patience consists wholly in not offending God or uttering words of pride. And the conclusion of the praises of this very famous master and example of patience clarifies

---

thee, and thou art troubled. Where is thy fear, thy fortitude, thy patience, and the perfection of thy ways?"

[89] Compare Job 6:11–12: "For what is my strength, that I can hold out? or what is my end that I should keep patience? My strength is not the strength of stones, nor is my flesh of brass."

and confirms this where it says, "In all these things Job sinned not by his lips, nor spoke he any foolish thing against God" [Job 1:22]. It does not say that he did not weep but that he did not sin; nor does it say that he was not sad but that he did not speak vain or proud words against God.

And what do we need to know to recognize true patience? Surely true patience is to endure our hardships, ailments, and sufferings with fear and reverence of God and with great diligence not to offend God; not to say vain nor proud words against God nor judge as unjust the disciplines and corrections God sends us, since all that He does or permits proceeds from true justice and sovereign goodness; not to be ungrateful for the benefits we receive from God; not to be idle in our afflictions, but to strive to gain that spiritual patience that is contained in the five talents. So thus enduring our ailments and sufferings, may we deserve to savor the spiritual consolations that perfect Patience, prelate of the infirm and conservator of all the orders of the afflicted, will give us to know and enjoy if we use our suffering well and persevere in patience.

And whoever has this patience, whether sad or happy, tearful or smiling, has, I say, true patience dwelling in him, although it may be true that patience is more secure where there is crying than where there is laughter, because of that sentence where it says, "Laughter I counted error: and to mirth I said: 'Why art thou vainly deceived?' " [Ecclesiastes 2:2]. For if vain laughter is a sin and patience by its own nature flees from all vice, it follows that patience is more at home and secure with sad people than with happy people, and more certain where people are weeping than where they are boisterously laughing. But if some laughter or honest pleasure could be had, as long as it does not offend God, I well believe that Patience will allow her subjects to have it.

Know well, infirm, who Patience is and you will find that there is no other prelate in the world so discreet and prudent, nor so beloved by her subjects, for her office is none other than to prepare for them a straight road to heaven and steal them away from the world and take them to heaven. Therefore, observe with diligence your own works, for in them you will know if you are obeying this saintly and honorable prelate; and if you feel this, you will know yourself to be under her jurisdiction and you will consider yourself to be without doubt a most blessed invalid. And if you should see yourself far from Patience, you should sorrow more for her absence and your separation from this virtue than for the many wounds you have, for the invalid that first searches for a doctor rather than for patience neither knows the misfortune that he has nor where his good fortune lies.

Thus it seems that those infirm that beg God to give them health and do not pray that He give them patience do not know what they request.

And sometimes it happens through God's mercy that they receive the same response that was given to the mother of the sons of Zebedee: "You know not what you ask" [Matthew 20:22].[90] And if we do not receive this response in words, we receive it in deeds, when God through His infinite mercy not only denies us the health we request but even increases the ailment we suffer. And what He quite clearly leads us to understand is that we do not know what we request, for whoever asks for less instead of for more, for what is doubtful instead of what is certain, clearly asks in ignorance, for if we could know what is better and more certain, we doubtlessly would ask for that. Therefore, those of us who ask for health and not for patience do not know what we request, for we give up the best for the worse and the certain for the doubtful. For one day of perfect patience is worth ten years of physical health, which is the least certain thing that we have in this life, for quickly and through some slight mishap our health and our life may be destroyed and end.

Thus if we ask for health and forget patience, we do not know what we ask, just like that saintly woman who asked that her two sons be seated at the right hand of our Redeemer and at the left. In this her saintly ignorance and maternal affection made her err so that, while loving her sons with equal love and wishing them both true and complete good, she requested diverse and contrary judgements and petitions, for she asked as much blessing and glory for the one as she sought pain and damnation for the other. But He who loved them better and had them both already appointed to be seated upon the twelve thrones at His right hand replied to her, saying, "You know not what you ask."

And thus returning to our purpose, our own natural inclination that in this regard we can call mother, together with the desire that we have for our salvation (for however sinful we may be, certainly we desire our salvation, and even robbers and evildoers want to be saved rather than condemned), thus this desire for our salvation combined with our natural inclination for physical well-being makes us ask God these two petitions: health for our body, salvation for our soul. For there is no one, no matter how ardent his desire for health, who does not request it combined with his salvation. And however indevout he may be, he at least requests his health in this manner, saying, "Oh, Lord, heal me of this suffering or sickness for Your holy service!" And although he may not extend his reasoning, in these few words he makes both petitions, for in saying "Heal

---

90 See Matthew 20:20–22: "Then came to him the mother of the sons of Zebedee with her sons, adoring and asking something of him. Who said to her: 'What wilt thou?' She saith to him: 'Say that these my two sons may sit, the one on thy right hand, and the other on thy left, in thy kingdom.' And Jesus answering, said: 'You know not what you ask.' "

me, Oh Lord," he asks for his health and in saying "for Your holy service," he asks for his salvation, for in serving God is all our salvation. And who would not believe this to be a very good, just, and saintly petition? So that when we ask in this way, we believe we have spoken well, yet one petition contradicts the other, for whatever health and repose we request for our bodies procures pain and confusion for our souls. For there are no two enemies in the world as contrary as are the body and the spirit.

But the Lord, who knows better what suits us and loves us more truly than we love ourselves, denies us the one petition that is the health of our bodies, which is like the left hand of the Redeemer, for in his inestimable charity He has us appointed for His right hand, which is the salvation of our souls. Therefore, if health is denied us and our suffering increased, let us know clearly that our Lord is responding to us, saying, "You know not what you ask." And He does not say, "You do not know. What are you asking?" but "You do not know what you are asking." Whence it seems to me that not only does He reprimand and accuse us of ignorance in what we request, but He prepares our path and invites us to what we should request, and this is saintly and perfect patience. Therefore, let us ask for patience in our prayers, for if we request it with devout and pure intention, we shall not be accused of ignorance, since we know very well what we request, for in asking for patience we ask for all the virtues and, moreover, we strive to reach the Lord of virtues.

So that we may know better what we are requesting, and so that the greatness and abundance of this virtue may whet our desire to pray for it with more constancy and fervor, let us see which number of the virtues is patience. It is not among the cardinal virtues, for these already have their number assigned as four; nor is it of the theological virtues, which are three; and it is not right to place patience among the seven lesser virtues assigned against the seven principal sins since these seven lesser virtues all serve patience. Therefore, we should give it a more honored position, although no matter how high we want to place it, we can give it no more honored site that what it has earned for itself. For patience has founded its dwelling over the four firm pillars of the cardinal virtues and climbs its stairway leading directly to the theological virtues.

What honor can we render to patience that does not pertain to it already? My weak ability will attempt to honor patience by briefly and simply explaining how patience dwells in the abovementioned virtues and they in it, although this may not be proven and demonstrated as well as it should, due to my weak judgement; for my limited faculty and the few years that I was at the University of Salamanca, while they make me fully responsible for the simplicity of what I said above, grant me no wisdom in what I want to say now. However, in spiritual matters we should neither heed nor fear the abuse of people nor desire their praise but rather continue our devout works with good intention until we arrive as far as our strength allows. Thus following my devotion in this spiritual work (yet not arriving where I wanted with regard to patience and only partially satisfying my desire), I wish to say simply and briefly how I understand patience.

It has already been said and demonstrated that the endurance of human tribulations and sufferings is worth nothing by itself alone nor constitutes complete patience, but is rather the beginning of patience. Whence the saintly master Augustine the Bishop says, "Tribulations work patience."[91] Clearly tribulations themselves are not patience but build patience and prepare its way. And it is necessary to add the virtue of prudence, as I noted in the interpretation of the name of patience, which means to suffer with prudence. And thus it is clear that the first moral or cardinal virtue, that is, prudence, not only sustains the edifice of patience but is a principal part of it.

As for fortitude, the second virtue, where will you see its proper strength if not in patience? If to sustain a great weight without falling requires fortitude, even more is required when the weightiest is loaded onto the weakest. And there is nothing in the world more heavy or burdensome than the hardships and afflictions of this life, nor is there anything more weak than our humanity, and for this reason it is called in the Scripture fragility, which, in my view, means weakness. And so that the shoulders of our human weakness can sustain the powerful burden of suffering without offending God or lacking patience, there is no doubt that the virtue of fortitude is necessary and that without it patience collapses. And for this reason, those three friends of Job,[92] believing in their ignorance that the natural emotion they saw in him undermined his patience, said, "Where is thy fortitude, [thy patience, and the perfection of thy ways?]" [Job 4:6], leading us to understand that if the virtue of fortitude were there, he would not fail in his patience nor could he flee from its company; and they even mention first fortitude before patience, not because fortitude is greater in dignity or merit but, rather, because it

---

91 "Nihil enim mali patiuntur, qui jam possunt dicere quod ille vir spiritualis exsultat et praedicat Apostolus dicens: 'Gloriamus in tribulationibus; scientes quoniam tribulatio patientiam operatur . . .' " See St. Augustine, "De Agone Christiano, Liber unus, Caput VII," in *Opera omnia, PL* 40:295. Compare Romans 5:3: "But we glory also in tribulations, knowing that tribulation worketh patience."

92 See Job 2:11: "Now when Job's three friends heard all the evil that had befallen him, they came every one from his own place, Eliphaz the Themanite, and Baldad the Suhite, and Sophar the Naamathite. For they had made an appointment to come together and visit him, and comfort him."

is the second firm pillar after prudence upon which patience is built and sustained. The Master of Patiences taught us this more clearly when he replied to them, "My strength is not the strength of stones, [nor is my flesh of brass]" [Job 6:12]. In these words he shows us that he had the virtue of fortitude, but of this he spoke very discreetly, saying, "My strength is not the strength of stones," as if he were to say openly, "God forbid that my fortitude cease being a virtue and become a stone without feeling." Indeed, for a man not to feel his misfortunes is foolishness, not virtue. Yet to feel and sustain hardship and emotion without falling into the sea of impatience and offending God is the proper virtue of fortitude, which is the second pillar and foundation of patience, as I have said above.

The third cardinal virtue is called justice, which is to maintain equality in all things. What requires justice more than patience, which always has a scale and a balance in hand to measure with equal and exact weight the afflictions, anguish, and travails that God imposes on us in order to maintain a continuous balance and avoid undue hardship, giving God the exact tribute in our hardships and sufferings that we owe? And quite rightly He obligates us to repay Him and yet avoids burdening the patient more than reason requires and his thin shoulders can sustain without falling or stumbling. For to alleviate his burden completely would be neither justice nor patience, nor would natural emotion permit it; rather, natural sentiment should not overcome reason but be in equal balance to it. And since these duties necessarily pertain to perfect patience, it follows that patience has the virtue of justice in its own dwelling and it forms the third pillar of its foundation.

The fourth cardinal virtue is called temperance, which, like the other three, is subject to patience. To contemplate the vexations and emotions of the hardships that befall us with so much moderation that we neither offend God nor increase our harm pertains to the virtue of temperance. While prudence and justice direct patience, temperance sets it to work. And if true and perfect patience is founded upon these four virtues, where these four are absent, there can be no patience at all; and where patience is, all four virtues are as well. And it seems to me, if my simple thought does not deceive me, that the virtues come en masse just like the vices, for where do you see pride without envy or envy without avarice? Thus, wherever one of these vices is, the other six gather. And so it seems to happen with the virtues, for wherever the virtue of prudence is – if it is *true* prudence – the other virtues are also.

And why do I say true prudence? This implies that there are also deceitful and evil prudences. May God forbid that its name be thus impugned! For to know how to deceive and to do bad deeds is knowledge, but not prudence. Of such knowledge it is written, "They are wise to do evil, but to do good they have no knowledge" [Jeremias 4:22]. And if prudence were to extend itself to knowledge of evil as well as good, it would not be called a virtue, for it is not possible to be both a virtue and a vice, since two opposites cannot harmonize or endure together. But I say true prudence because there is a wisdom that in our observation is judged as prudence but before God and even in the presence of its owner's conscience it is a vice. To be a virtue prudence must know how to recognize vice, not in order to commit sins but to avoid them, for the true virtue of prudence includes knowing fully how to recognize good and evil, not just good alone. And I call this true prudence. And wherever this virtue of prudence is, there is the virtue of fortitude, and where fortitude justice, and where justice temperance.

Now you see that if all four cardinal virtues are enchased and united in patience, whoever has one virtue has all of them completely and whoever lacks one of them has none. Consequently, it seems reasonable that whoever has these four cardinal virtues and exercises them completely is not very far from the theological virtues. And since patience has inlaid in itself these four cardinal virtues and without them there cannot be true and perfect patience, it is clear that patience is not separate from the three theological virtues either and that someone who has no faith cannot exercise patience, for without faith it is impossible to please God.[93] And since patience directs its ends straight to God, to please Him exclusively and not offend Him, it follows that faith cannot be lacking in patience; rather, in patience more than any other good work the first theological virtue – faith – shines brightly.

And while faith is demonstrated in times of prosperity by the exercise of good works and caution not to offend God, faith is proven much more illustrious and great in the adversities and afflictions and travails endured and sustained with fear of God and solicitous care not to offend Him and with devout diligence to serve Him, which is the proper office of patience. To give thanks to God during times of material good fortune I do not reprove but rather praise, for doubtlessly this proceeds from faith. Yet this cannot equal that heightened faith that makes man conform his will with God's, for he directs to Him thanks for his great hardships and calamities as devoutly and sincerely as others do for their health intact and complete well-being.

And since faith pertains to true patience, clearly the virtue of faith is not separate from patience; rather, in and with patience faith proves itself

93 "But without faith it is impossible to please God. For he that cometh to God, must believe that he is, and is a rewarder to them that seek him" (Hebrews 11:6).

to be more certain and illustrious. For when someone is well equipped with physical health and rich with temporal blessings, if he gives thanks to God and fears and serves Him, this is a very great good. But who can judge whether this is his true faith or his concern either not to lose the blessings he has or to multiply his blessings? As we see happen sometimes when these blessings are in jeopardy, those who offer great petitions to God and involve themselves with much devotion in prayers or pious works fear losing their good fortune or hope to win it back. And when they have either lost or recovered the blessings and health they desire, their pious works disappear and devotion, spent, falls off so that it is lost with lost fortunes or forgotten with the recovered blessings.

Thus it appears that devotion and service to God, when exercised for temporal reasons, become attached to temporal fortunes and not to God, since such good works as these do not proceed from true faith; for true and holy faith believes in God, searches and desires God alone, and does its good works with respect only to God. Therefore, in afflictions and anguish, in ailments and calamities, the virtue of faith is refined and purified. He who has such hardships and serves God, loves and fears Him, and offers devout sacrifices of thanks, cannot be judged to have anything but great faith. And since this is due to perfect patience, without doubt patience has with it the first theological virtue. And if patience has faith, it is clear that it also has hope.

And let us leave aside the arguments and reasons why faith brings with it hope and charity and consider this: who is so perfect or holy in this life that without faith he could sustain the travails of this life in the manner mentioned above or another better way if he did not expect some reward for it? Of this the Prophet says, "I have inclined my heart to do thy justifications for ever, for the reward" [Psalm 118:112]. And he inclines or bows his heart before God's justice to suffer humbly and patiently the disciplines and afflictions that God gives him. And who could so incline his natural disposition to suffer in patience all his travails if he did not hope to receive some reward in exchange? Therefore, he who exercises true patience clearly has the virtue of hope; and thus with much reason we can conclude and believe that whoever continuously endures hardships and suffering with fear and reverence of God, continuously believes in God, and whoever continuously believes, continuously hopes, and whoever continuously hopes, without doubt continuously loves. And thus the three theological virtues – no less than the cardinal virtues – are required of necessity in the virtue of patience, because patience is an edifice as complex as it is praiseworthy.

It is certain and without doubt that all these seven virtues attend to patience's lofty and perfect work and that each one must place there its stone as a support: prudence to recognize in hardships which is the better part and to choose it; fortitude to sustain hardships truly without offending God; justice to exercise fairness; temperance to moderate our human emotions; faith to believe that God gives us these travails for our own good and to avail Himself of our patience; hope to aspire to the reward prepared for us by our hardships; charity to love above all else Him from whom and through whom we receive so many blessings and await even greater ones. Thus holy and perfect patience has its dwelling, as I said, founded upon the four cardinal virtues and climbs its stairway leading directly to the theological virtues that guide us straight to the Lord of virtues, who is the Lover of patience, true Health of the infirm, and glorious Repose of the afflicted, to whom be all honor and glory forever and ever. Amen.

Thanks be to God.

This treatise was copied by Pero López del Trigo.

Wonder at the Works of God (*Admiraçión operum Dey*)

Here begins a brief treatise which can be fittingly called *Wonder at the Works of God*.[1] Teresa de Cartagena, a nun of the order of . . . , composed it at the petition and request of Señora Juana de Mendoça, wife of Señor Gómez Manrique.[2]

I remember, virtuous lady, that I offered to write at your discretion. If I have delayed so long in committing this to paper, you should not marvel, for one's will is very inhibited when one's physical disposition not only does not co-operate but even impedes and contradicts it. If you consider, virtuous lady, the illnesses and physical sufferings that I have continually for companions, you will readily acknowledge that they are real obstacles to the intentions of my will and to my understanding, which, fatigued and disturbed at present with memories and emotions and constrained by its own need, draws unto itself the deliberations and inner desires of my will. And my understanding so detains and delays my will in the execution of its deeds that its own intellectual efforts are weakened by my physical hardships. Yet, even with all this, the debt I promised you would already be paid were my solitude content with only my physical suffering and not assail me with a secret and dangerous army full of inner conflicts and spiritual dangers, with a mob of vain and inconstant thoughts that, like a host of armed soldiers, besiege my anguished soul on every flank.[3]

And what can my weak womanly understanding do when it sees itself caught in so many dangerous snares? For it has enough work to defend itself from what is clearly evil, and its powers are too weak to recognize as bad what our adversary offers under the guise of good; so that unless sovereign Virtue strengthens and illuminates it, my understanding has no power or health at all. Thus, very discreet lady, may you perceive the diversity and intensity of these hidden spiritual scandals, along with others of equal quality and quantity that your prudence can well under-

---

1 *Admiraçión* means "wonder, awe" as well as "admiration, respect"; on the title as a purposeful composite of Spanish and Latin, see 131 n. 33.

2 Teresa's religious order was omitted – intentionally or accidentally – by the copyist. Gómez Manrique (1412–90) was a leading political figure and protector of conversos in Toledo, a major poet at the courts of Juan II and Enrique IV, and author of religious dramas. His wife, Doña Juana de Mendoza (d. 1498), was the daughter of Diego Hurtado de Mendoza and Teresa de Guzmán and lady-in-waiting to the *infanta* Isabel, princess of Portugal.

3 Compare *Grove* (31) for similar images of violence assailing one's soul; there, a rioting of the people against "the city of our conscience."

stand, which with their great strength have broken down the walls of my
weak judgement like a flood of water and have removed completely
everything that my understanding had prepared to write down.

And my memory tells me only the matter about which I thought to
write; and since the foundation was left unbuilt, the edifice itself is not as
good as should be presented to your discretion, but rather slight and weak
as one might expect from my poor faculty.[4] For since a bad tree, according
to a saying of the supreme Truth, cannot bring forth good fruit,[5] what
good words or devout works can you expect of a woman so infirm in her
body and so wounded in her spirit?[6] But I shall lift up my eyes to the
mountains, whence comes my help,[7] so that He who gives strength to the
weak and understanding to the lowly may open the ark of His divine
generosity, scattering His abundant grace over this dry and sterile land,[8]
so that a sinful woman removed from virtue may know how to form
her words in praise and glory of the most Holy and Lord of virtues.
And to return to the purpose and reason for my writing, its cause is as
follows.

Many times, virtuous lady, I have been informed that some prudent
men and also discreet women have marveled at a treatise that, with divine
grace directing my weak womanly understanding, was written by my
hand.[9] And since it is a brief work of little substance, I am amazed, for it
is hard to believe that prudent men would marvel so at such an insignificant thing. But if their wonder is certain, my offense is clear, since
apparently their awe does not result from the merits of my text but from
the defects of its author; as we see from experience when someone of
simple and crude understanding says something meaningful, we marvel
not because the saying itself is worthy of awe but because the person is
so reprobate and held in such low esteem that we do not expect anything
good from him. And for this reason when it happens through God's mercy

---

4   Compare Teresa's earlier reference to *Grove* as a "slight and defective work" (26).
5   Compare Matthew 7:17: "Even so every good tree bringeth forth good fruit, and the evil
    tree bringeth forth evil fruit."
6   Teresa here is apparently quoting the objections of her detractors.
7   See Psalm 120:1: "I have lifted up my eyes to the mountains, from whence help shall come
    to me."
8   The imagery recalls the opening of *Grove* where Teresa is exiled to the allegorical island,
    "sterile of temporal pleasures and dry of vainglories" (24). The intertextual network of
    images underscores the continuity between the two works; in effect, *Wonder* is a gloss as
    well as a defense of the earlier treatise. The image of the "ark of God's divine generosity"
    is repeated toward the end of her defense (see 111).
9   So begins Teresa's unwavering insistence that *Grove* is a product of her own writing
    enlightened by God's grace, a theme reiterated throughout her defense.

that such simple and crude people say or do certain things, although these may not be entirely good but even rather ordinary, we marvel a great deal for the reasons stated above.

And in this same way, I certainly believe, prudent men have marveled at the treatise I wrote, not because there was anything very good or worthy of wonder in it, but because of me and my justly deserved adversities and increased suffering; they cry out against me and call upon everyone to marvel, saying, "How can there be any good in a person afflicted with so many misfortunes?" And from this it follows that if a womanly text of little substance is worthy of reprehension among common men, with greater reason it would inspire consternation in exceptional and great men, for not without cause does the prudent man marvel when he sees that a fool can speak. And although it is said that their wonder is flattering, to me it seems offensive and clear that they offer me scathing insults and not empty praise; yet although insults cannot hurt me or vain praise benefit me, I do not want to usurp another's glory nor ignore my own offense.

However, there is something else I must not permit, for truth does not allow it: apparently not only do prudent men marvel at my treatise but some cannot believe that, indeed, I could do any good at all; and while my worthiness is even less than they presume,[10] greater blessings are found in God's mercy. And because they tell me, virtuous lady, that this abovementioned sheaf of rough draft papers has come to the attention of Señor Gómez Manrique and yourself,[11] I do not know if these same doubts surrounding my treatise have occurred to you. And since good works are known to sovereign Truth as true and certain, I have not objected very much when in the judgement of human beings my work is held as doubtful, although this can ruin the substance of my writing and undermines greatly the benefit and grace that God wrought for me. Therefore, to the honor and glory of our sovereign and generous Lord whose mercy fills the earth,[12] I, a small piece of dirt, dare to present to your great judgement these insignificant thoughts of mine.

---

10   Teresa's strategy here is an application of the concept of voluntary humility she discusses in *Grove*; that is, "for man to despise himself more and esteem and value himself less than his detractors do" (69). One of the spiritual advantages of voluntary humility, she notes, is that the contempt of others does not provoke one to anger.

11   It is not clear if this sheaf of papers refers to a copy of Teresa's *Grove*, "written by my hand," or if her detractors actually registered their objections in writing; if the "above-mentioned" sheaf refers to Teresa's own rough copy, then perhaps it was circulated to "virtuosa señora" before a formal copy could be made.

12   See Psalm 32:5: "He loveth mercy and judgment; the earth is full of the mercy of the Lord."

It is true, most discreet and beloved lady, that all things that God's omnipotence has made in the world are of great wonder to our human mind, so that the least thing that this sovereign and most powerful Creator has made is no less wonderful than the greatest. This is because the smallest thing in the world, like the greatest, could not be found unless God's omnipotence created it. And if all things, great and small, created by God's omnipotence are marvelous and worthy of great wonder and He can make on earth and in heaven whatever he pleases, why do we marvel at some things more than others?

And our glorious church father St. Augustine answers and satisfies my simple question in his homily on the gospel that recounts the miracle of the five loaves of bread. And he says this: "The greater miracle is the governing of the five thousand than the saturation of their hunger with five loaves."[13] Yet no one marvels at this, although it is no less a miracle that many spikes grow from few grains than that many people be fed and sated with a few loaves of bread.[14] And this saintly and learned man adds this sentence: "That is considered a miracle not because it is greater but because it happens few times or rarely."[15] And I think that he concludes that the cause of our wonder is not because some of God's works are less worthy of awe than others, but because those that we see every day we accept as the natural course of things, and those which rarely or never happen cause us wonder because they are not common or customary in this world. But if we lift up our understanding to contemplate or consider well God's works, we shall find that those we see occur daily in the natural course of things are no less marvelous or worthy of admiration than those that happen rarely or at great intervals of time.

Thus, returning to my purpose, I think, most virtuous lady, that the reason that men marvel that a woman has written a treatise is because this is not customary in the female condition but only in the male. For men have had the practice of writing books and learning and applying their

---

[13] Compare: "Miraculum grande factum est, dilectissimi, ut de quinque panibus et duobus piscibus saturarentur quinque hominum millia, et residua fragmentorum implerent duodecim cophinos. Grande miraculum: sed non multum mirabimur factum, si attendamus facientem." See St. Augustine, "Sermo CXXX," in *Opera omnia*, PL 38:725. On the feeding of the five thousand, see Matthew 14:13–21; compare Matthew 15:32–36, Mark 6:32–44, Luke 9:10–17, and John 6:16–21.

[14] Compare: "Ille multiplicavit in manibus frangentium quinque panes, qui in terra germinantia multiplicat semina, ut grana pauca mittantur et horrea repleantur." See St. Augustine, "Sermo CXXX," 725.

[15] Compare: "Sed quia illud omni anno facit, nemo miratur. Admirationem tollit non facti vilitas, sed assiduitas." See St. Augustine, "Sermo CXXX," 725.

learning since such ancient times that apparently this is assumed to be the natural course of things, and therefore no one wonders. But since women have not had this custom nor have acquired learning, and since their understanding is not as perfect as men's, it is considered a marvel. Yet it is no greater marvel nor less easy for God's omnipotence to do one more than the other, for He who could infuse the understanding of men with knowledge can thus infuse the understanding of women, even though our understanding may be imperfect or not as able or sufficient to receive and retain knowledge as that of males. For God's divine greatness can readily repair this imperfection and small insufficiency and even remove it completely and give perfection and ability to female understanding just as to male, for the sufficiency that men have they did not acquire on their own but because God gave it to them. Of this the Apostle says, "Not that we are sufficient to think anything of ourselves, as of ourselves: but our sufficiency is from God" [2 Corinthians 3:5]. For if the sufficiency of men comes from God and God gives to each one according to the measure of His gift, why should we women not receive the same when He judges it necessary and appropriate?

And you should consider, my great lady, that God created human nature, although He Himself was not human. Well, He who made such a great thing from nothing, can He not do anything in His creation? This most powerful Creator made the male sex first and the female second and adjunct to the male. And if He gave certain pre-eminences to the male more than to the female, I truly believe that He did not do this because He wanted to confer more grace on one condition than the other, but rather for a very secret purpose that He alone knows. Of this St. Jerome says in his sermon on the Assumption of our Lady, "Our Lord is such and so great and immense and good that He alone knows Himself or He alone understands";[16] as if to say openly that our Lord's omnipotence and magnificence are so great, and His divine and marvelous secrets so profound, and His holy works so abundant and beneficial, that He alone distinguishes their number and nature, He alone knows.

Nevertheless, leaving aside these hidden and divine secrets which surpass our human understanding, I ask what is the greatest pre-eminence that God gave to men more than to women, and my simplicity tells me that among all the pre-eminences that God gave the male sex rather than the female, this, in my view, is the principal one: that males are strong and valiant and of great spirit and daring and of more perfect and sound

---

[16] It has been impossible to identify this quote; Hutton notes (98), nevertheless, that there are many spurious sermons on the Assumption of the Virgin attributed to St. Jerome and possibly Teresa refers here to one of them.

understanding, and women, to the contrary, are weak and cowardly, faint hearted and fearful. For we see that a man awaits a brave bull with greater daring and strength than a woman would await a mouse that may pass by her skirts. And likewise, if we women see an unsheathed sword, although we know that it can do us no harm at all, we are naturally so fearful that in merely seeing it we are afraid. Yet men have no fear of using a sword and even of receiving on their bodies cruel and strong blows from its blade.

And God made these differences and oppositions in one and the same human nature for whatever unique purpose and marvelous secret that He alone knows. I, in my simplicity, daresay that our heavenly Father did this so that each would be the preservation and adjunct of the other, for everything that the Lord created and made over the face of the earth He furnished and equipped with marvelous preparations and provisions. And if you observe well the plants and trees, you will see how their outer bark or cortex is very robust and strong and resistant to the weather, to tempest and water and ice, and heat and cold. They are made in such a way that their firm and resilient bark protects the inner core or medulla enclosed within. And thus in this order the one works for the other, for the strength and hardness of the bark protects and preserves the medulla by resisting on the outside the inclemencies of the weather. The medulla, encased because it is weak and delicate, works inwardly and gives power and vigor to the bark; and thus the one preserves and helps the other and gives us each year the diversity and abundance of fruits that we see.[17]

And in this same way, I believe, our sovereign and powerful Lord wants these two opposites in human nature to operate: the masculine condition, strong and valiant, and the feminine, weak and delicate. For men with their strength and spirit and sufficiency of intellect preserve and protect things on the outside, thus procuring and dealing and winning fortune's goods, like ruling and governing and defending their country and lands from enemies, and all the other things required for the protection and benefit of the republic and consequently of its individual properties and persons; for this, it is fitting and necessary that males be robust and valiant, of great spirit and even of great and very elevated understanding. And women, weak and timid and not able to withstand the great labors and dangers that the procurement and government and defense of the abovementioned things require, encased or enclosed in their homes give

---

[17] Teresa applies allegorical conventions – inner versus outer, medulla versus cortex – to her discussion of gender, subtly and subversively privileging woman by associating her with the inner medulla. In allegory, the outer cortex is identified with the lower material and literal meaning while the inner medulla is associated with the higher spiritual and figurative truth.

strength and vigor and certainly no little support to the males with their industry and work and domestic labors. And thus human nature, made of such fragile stock, preserves and sustains itself, for without these complementary exercises and labors it could not survive.

Thus, neither these pre-eminences of men – to be brave and of great spirit and sufficient understanding – nor any other that God may have given them is to the detriment of women, nor likewise does the weakness and timidity of the female condition confer greater excellence to the male. Rather, these opposites are a marvelous arrangement ordered by God's great wisdom. Of this the Prophet says, "How great are thy works, O Lord! thou hast made all things in wisdom" [Psalm 103:24]. And thus, if it pleased God to make the male sex robust and valiant and the female weak and of little strength, one should not believe that He did this to confer more advantage or excellence to one condition than the other, but only, I believe, for the abovementioned purpose, so that with one helping the other, human nature might be preserved, and the marvelous works of His omnipotence and wisdom and goodness be noted.

We read in Genesis how woman is the helpmeet of man, for after God had formed man from the mud of the earth and had breathed in him the spirit of life, He said, "It is not good for man to be alone: let us make him a help like unto himself" [Genesis 2:18]. And one could well argue here whether the helped or the helper has the greater strength, and you clearly see what reason would respond. But these arguments and disputes make for worldly and vain arrogance and do not profit devotion and divert my intention from its purpose and end, which, may it please God, is not to offend the superior and honorable condition of prudent men nor to favor women but rather to praise the omnipotence and wisdom and greatness of God, who in women as well as men can inspire and effect works of great wonder and magnificence to the praise and glory of His holy name; for if He wanted brute animals to praise Him with speech, He could well achieve it.

Well, then, what excuse is there to doubt that a woman can understand some good and know how to write treatises or any other praiseworthy good work, even though this is not customary in the female condition? For our powerful sovereign Lord, who gave certain pre-eminences to men to have naturally and continually, can also grant them to women graciously and in due time, as His profound wisdom deems fitting, and He has done so in the past, although, even if He had not, surely He could.

And certainly I believe, most beloved lady, that there is nothing more difficult for a human being to do than to contradict his natural condition or do something against his own nature and vigor, for it is almost impossible for someone naturally weak and fearful to conquer the valiant or for someone simple and foolish to teach the prudent; surely you see that this is difficult and almost impossible, beyond our human efforts. Well, since a woman is considered to be naturally weak and timid and faint hearted, whoever would see her exercise the sword or defend her country against enemies or do other deeds of great audacity and vigor would marvel greatly! Yet this marvel He did once and He can do again now or whenever He wants, for He alone can work miracles.

Tell me, virtuous lady, what man could be found in past times or present of such strong and valiant character or fearless heart that he would dare to bear arms against such a great and strong general as Holofernes,[18] whose army covered the surface and extent of the land, and yet a woman had no fear of doing this? And I know well that men will respond that this was a special grace and skill that God conferred on the prudent Judith, and I agree. Yet according to this, it is apparent that supreme skill and grace transcend natural male forces, since what a great army of armed men could not accomplish was achieved by the ingenuity and grace of a lone woman.

As for industry and grace, who would consider them slight attributes except someone who does not know what they are? Certainly whoever God endows with these two singular qualities – whether male or female – will understand marvelous things and work wonders with them if he exercises his abilities and is not idle or negligent. Well, if God did not deny the female condition the grace and skill to do very difficult things beyond the power of their natural state, how will He deny us His grace to know and be able to do something more readily accessible to the female sex? For clearly it is more within the reach of a woman to be eloquent than strong, and more modest for her to be skilled than daring, and easier for her to use the pen than the sword. Thus prudent men should note that He who gave the skill and grace to Judith to accomplish such a marvelous and famous act can well give ingenuity or understanding and grace to any woman to do what other women and perchance some of the male condition might not know how to do.

And someone may well say that this case is not the same, insofar as prudent Judith was a virtuous and holy woman and a great observer of God's law, and because of her excellent merits God conferred this singular blessing upon her, and that, therefore, one should not deduce from this that other women may receive such exceptional skill and grace. To this I respond that this is true: although Judith was a holy woman and very

---

[18] Holofernes, commander-in chief of the armies of King Nebuchadnezzar, led an overwhelming Assyrian force against Israel and lay siege to the town of Bethulia; he was beheaded by Judith while he slept, as recounted in the Book of Judith.

solicitous in keeping God's law and very given to prayers and fasts and all spiritual exercises, we know that God does not confer blessings or grace according to our individual merit but only according to His own inestimable goodness; for, indeed, were our heavenly Father to dispense and distribute His blessings according to the sanctity and justice and merits of human beings, I believe that all the blessings we have here on earth would return to heaven.

Nor should we believe that God has the same manner and custom as kings and princes of the land, who grant benefits and privileges to those who are in their favor or serve their will, and to those who do not do their will or are held in disfavor, they confer no benefits at all. The King of kings and Lord of lords is not like this, for to both sinners and righteous men, to the bad and the good alike, to those who offend Him and to those who serve Him well, He gives blessings and privileges to us all; this He does only according to His own great goodness and mercy. Of this the Apostle says, "God has no favorites" [Romans 2:11; my translation].[19] For this kind of favoritism and special affection does not pertain to God who is the Father of all creation, for just as He is Father of all, so is He generous and merciful to all. And it even seems to me that the Church sings this in the first Introit for Lent when it says, "All-Merciful, have mercy on us all, O God, for nothing have you abhorred that you made in this world."[20] And thus God is a great lover of human beings, and as evil and sinful as we may be, He does not abhor us or deny us the benefits of His divine generosity and great compassion.

Therefore, while it may be true that this good lady and chaste widow Judith was indeed a holy woman, the blessings and privileges and marvels that God grants proceed from such a high fount that no one – no matter how holy he may be – could deserve them if God's goodness did not make him worthy. And despite the worthier and better preparation that the just and good have to receive these blessings of grace than the sinners, nevertheless, the more unworthy and wicked the sinner who receives these blessings, the more profound and great and marvelous the goodness and mercy and magnificence of God is shown to be.

And perhaps someone will say that although God has always granted great blessings and privileges to sinners and righteous men alike, such exceptional and notable blessings occur rarely and never to women. And

---

19　See also Acts 10:34–35: "And Peter opening his mouth, said: 'In truth I perceive that God has no favorites. But in every nation, he that feareth him, and worketh justice, is acceptable to him'" (my translation).

20　"Misereris omnium, Domine, et nihil odisti eorum quae fecisti . . . " See "The Introit for Ash Wednesday," in *The Saint Andrew Daily Missal*, by Dom Gaspar Lefebvre (St. Paul: E.M. Lohman Co., 1956), 110.

while this is certainly so, the more infrequently God does these things, the more marvelous they are, and the more marvelous they are, the greater wonder they inspire in our understanding. And the greater the wonder they inspire in us, the more thoroughly they teach us to know and venerate and praise the magnificence and omnipotence and wisdom and goodness of God. Thus, very fortunate lady, I think the only reason prudent men marvel is that mentioned at the beginning of this brief treatise: the act of composing books and treatises is not customary in the female condition, and all new and unaccustomed things always inspire wonder.

However, those that marvel should note that there is a kind of wonder that praises and venerates the Maker or Inspiration of the work that excites our wonder, and there is another wonder that neither praises nor serves our sovereign Maker but rather insults and offends Him. Therefore, it is fitting that we examine well when and how and why we marvel, so that our wonder may honor and glorify His wondrous name throughout the land. And the wonder that lauds and venerates and even serves, I believe, our sovereign Lord is when our wonder at His holy works and marvelous inspiration is mixed with devotion and faith, and we believe that His omnipotence and wisdom can do anything. For just as His omnipotence and wisdom know how to do anything, in His unique supreme goodness He has done everything to our profit and advantage. And although through His omnipotence, wisdom, and goodness so many divine blessings descend on the exiled children of Eve in this vale of tears, and we receive abundant blessings and exceptional grace from His great mercy and perfect charity, certainly no human intellect can understand this, nor human tongue speak of this, nor human hand write about this.

And to marvel at God's wondrous works with devotion and sound spirit, we should first elevate our wonder to the omnipotence, wisdom, and goodness of our most excellent Father, and then lower our understanding to marvel at the blessings and benefits, mercy and grace that He grants to human creatures. And first we should marvel at our general blessings: blessings of nature and blessings of fortune, which are very great and marvelous. And without doubt we will find in them enough to sustain our wonder for a long time; and after this we will marvel even more at the exceptional or special blessings that are called blessings of grace. And whence comes grace if not from God? For although all things in this world are His, there is nothing in this world that so singularly pertains to God as this alone, namely, grace.

For although we know that all the blessings of nature and of fortune and everything in heaven and on earth God made and created and rules and governs through His lofty and marvelous providence, and that He alone is the principal and natural Lord of all creation, still we always attribute blessings of nature and fortune to people here on earth and attribute only grace directly to God. Thus, we attribute bravery and high spirit, beauty and good understanding to the person himself rather than to God, although nature provided and equipped him with such blessings; likewise, we attribute riches and estates, villages and rents to the people who possess them rather than to God.

And we customarily say that fortune gave them these blessings, although this is neither well said nor in itself true; nevertheless, we attribute only grace as pertaining to God, proper to Him and reserved and guarded in His holy breast so that no one else can dispense the blessings of grace except God alone. Likewise, we see that the Holy Father, just as he is in God's place and acts as His vicar, very clearly has this same manner, for he gives power to the prelates of the Church to grant and provide benefits and privileges to all the clerical estate and to the religious orders as well, but he always reserves for himself certain cases and dignities as special and singular so that no one else can dispense them except His Holiness alone.

And thus our most Holy Father of fathers gives power and vigor to nature to give us natural blessings. And once He created temporal blessings, He immediately subjected them to the governance of man. Of this the Prophet says, "Thou hast subjected all things under [man's] feet" [Psalm 8:8]. And He gives ingenuity and art to man to win and possess the blessings of fortune, which can more appropriately be called good luck. However, the greater and more exceptional blessings of grace He reserved for Himself, for these blessings we attain neither through the effort of nature, nor the good luck of fortune, nor through any human art or ingenuity, but only through the goodness and mercy and grace of God; therefore, in truth, they have their proper name and cognate as blessings of grace.

And it seems to me that by this we mean blessings influenced or inspired by God's special grace or blessings that God gives graciously to whomever He pleases, for with blessings of grace it is not fitting to scrutinize or judge the condition of the person – male or female – nor the disposition and ability of his intellect, whether very capable or totally insufficient, nor the merit of his deeds, whether he is righteous or a very great sinner. For divine grace surpasses and exceeds all this and more and abundantly fills the blank spaces of our defects. And the Apostle says, "And where sin abounded, grace did more superabound" [Romans 5:20b; my translation]. And if God's grace superabounds where sin, a defect of our soul, is abundant, why cannot grace superabound where other defects and physical sufferings are abundant, since these are not sins? And certainly we can say that where our defects abound, there grace superabounds, for if we note well we will find that whatever nature and fortune withhold or distribute sparsely, the abundant grace of the Lord liberally restores and repairs; thus it is clear that these blessings of grace are greater and more exceptional than those of nature and fortune.

This is so for three reasons: first, because blessings of grace surpass the power of human nature, for divine grace can do marvelous things for and against human nature; second, because they are more excellent and enduring blessings and of greater benefit and repose to the soul than those of fortune; third, because they descend from the highest source, namely, from the grace of God. And for these reasons and for others better and more sufficient than my narrow capacity and womanly understanding can comprehend or sense, I believe certainly that the blessings of grace are greater and more exceptional than those of nature and fortune.

And the man or woman provided with these blessings or with one of them should hold them in great esteem and appreciation and should solicitously and diligently keep and employ these blessings in the service and honor of God, whence they come. And not only those who receive and have these blessings but even we, when we see shine in another person blessings of grace, should marvel devoutly, directing and guiding our wonder not with regard to the recipient of these blessings – whether male or female, learned or simple – but only with regard to our merciful Father who gives the blessings. And if we raise or direct our awe toward the inestimable sublimity and oneness of our sovereign Lord, we shall not marvel doubting what we see, but rather we shall marvel believing that not only the wonders we see, but even those we cannot see nor imagine, God can inspire and work in his creatures. And thus our wonder will ascend to contemplate the omnipotence and wisdom and goodness of God and all His other excellences, and then our awe will travel a straight path, for we shall venerate and honor the things He created and their sovereign Maker, and the good works that we see that His creatures do for the Inspiration and Giver of all blessings.

And I certainly believe that this is the truth that the Prophet teaches us in the psalm where he says, "O Lord our Lord, how admirable is thy name in the whole earth!" [Psalm 8:2]. For here with few words he praises God's magnificence: that is, His divine excellence and the blessings of nature He has given and gives to man, and how He made man superior to all other things on earth with what we call blessings of fortune, and how He continuously visits upon him special consolations and gifts, that is, the blessings of grace; and then, in conclusion to all this, he repeats his wonder again, saying, "O Lord our Lord, how admirable is thy name in all the earth!" [Psalm 8:10]. In this he clearly indicates to us that all the things that God does in the world are done to the honor and glory and magnificence of His holy name, and thus it seems right that in all these blessings – of nature and fortune as well as of grace, in our own particular blessings as well as in those God gives to our neighbor – we should raise our admiration and wonder and devotion to the supreme Fount whence all blessings descend.

And thus it follows[21] that when we see that God has made something from nothing, we shall praise His omnipotence; and when we see that He has made great things from little things, we shall praise His magnificence; and when we see that God makes simple and crude intellects learned guardians of His law, we shall praise His eternal wisdom; and when we see that God leads the sinful to understand and do good works, we shall praise His inestimable goodness; and when we see that the good and just receive from God recompense and rewards, we shall praise His justice; and when we see that God confers blessings and mercy on sinners, we shall praise his great mercy; and if we see that women write treatises, we shall praise the gifts of His holy grace and divine generosity. And thus in all things that God has done and does and arranges for human creatures, those that we see occur daily as well as those that happen rarely or at great intervals of time, we should direct our admiration and wonder to the glory and honor of God's name. And this admiration and wonder is the veneration and reverence and sacrifice of praise that human understanding offers to His Divine Highness. Of this the Prophet in the presence of the Lord of prophets says, "I will sacrifice to thee the sacrifice of praise, [and I will call upon the name of the Lord]" [Psalm 115:17].

There is another wonder or mode of marveling which neither praises nor serves the Lord who works these wonders but rather offends Him, and this is when we marvel so much and so excessively at some grace or blessing that God grants to our neighbors that it seems that we do not believe it. And this doubting wonder proceeds from having more regard for the thing itself than for the fount whence it comes, for we consider only the faculty or condition of the human being and not the greatness of divine power. When our understanding is completely engrossed in this regard, it becomes so heavy and ponderous and dull that only with great difficulty can it recognize the delicacy and subtlety of those blessings infused with divine grace.

Thus heavily burdened with human concerns some people marvel – or have marveled – and even consider it doubtful or impossible that a woman can write treatises or compose a meaningful work that may be good. Yet no one marvels if men write books or compendious treatises, for this is

---

21   Here Teresa begins a catalogue of seven blessings of grace in litany fashion – a style recalling sermon rhetoric – culminating with the blessing of grace that approximates her own.

attributed to the very brain and sufficiency of understanding of the male author and to the great and "natural" learning that he knows; and nothing is said about the glory of God, nor do I think they remember whence came this "natural" knowledge that men acquire in their studies, and even those who know these subjects do not remember from where they got their knowledge nor who taught them. Yet if they were to consider it well, they would find that those who now are masters in another time were disciples, and those whose disciples they were were taught by yet another master. And thus by men teaching each other and learning, acquired knowledge came into the hands of its present male practitioners; but were we to inquire further, we would find that knowledge as well as the ingenuity and grace to teach and learn all descended and descend from one Fount, for God alone is the Lord of all knowledge.

And it even seems to me that I have read this, near the beginning of August, in a history that we have, in the book called *On Wisdom*,[22] where it says, "All wisdom is from the Lord God, [and hath been always with him, and is before all time]" [Ecclesiasticus 1:1]. And it goes on to say, "He created Wisdom in the Holy Ghost, [and saw her, and numbered her, and measured her]" [Ecclesiasticus 1:9, my translation]. For He divides and measures and disseminates wisdom throughout His works and over all flesh, according to His gift, and He gives to His lovers or to those who love Him, etc.[23]

And if someone were to dedicate himself to this very healthful and holy study, namely, to love God, and were to implant in his soul the root of wisdom, that is, the fear of the Lord, God's grace would not be denied him; nor does our merciful Father disdain to sit in the seat of the understanding of the simple and to read to them marvelous lessons. Thus any man or woman who wants to exercise this study will be wiser than Solomon. For not only does He instruct and teach marvelous counsels and saintly inspirations to those who love and fear Him, but even to those of us who continually offend Him by not serving Him and are unworthy to receive blessings from such a holy and great Father; and therefore, if my own wickedness and human frailty could contain His teachings, the works my sovereign Master would teach me to do would be better than the words He instructed me to write.

Well, what an impious wonder it is to marvel so much at something

---

22 The reference is to the Book of Sirach or Ecclesiasticus; its earliest title was "Wisdom of the Son of Sirach."

23 Compare Ecclesiasticus 1:9–10: "He created her [i.e., Wisdom] in the Holy Ghost, and saw her, and numbered her, and measured her. And he poured her out upon all his works, and upon all flesh according to his gift, and hath given her to them that love him."

for being good that one considers it impossible or doubtful that God alone may have inspired it or taught the person who did it! And without doubt, we give God more offense than reverence when we think that one human being can teach another any branch of knowledge and yet doubt that the Lord of all knowledge can teach whomever He wants. And someone might argue here, saying that everyone believes this: that God is so omnipotent that He can make of a simple man, who never learned his letters nor took a course of studies, the most learned man in the world, but that, just as His omnipotence can do anything, so His eternal wisdom and marvelous providence provide all things with an order and manner and time for each one of them and thus He made the natural sciences,[24] for it pleased Him to give the order and means for them to be learned and taught, etc.

All this I accept, and I do not contend that someone because he loved and served God must be suddenly made a master of theology or a doctor of laws or a bachelor of canon law; neither does he need hope to be infused with the liberal arts. However, what I do say and mean is this: the quality of the science and wisdom that God teaches to any man or woman who may come to His school with love and reverence and humility is determined by His incomprehensible and perfect knowledge that knows what is fitting to the constitution of each one of us, for God is perfect Love. And just as His perfect charity loves us truly, His great mercy and goodness instruct us and instill in our minds and souls the wisdom we need to recognize and love and earn true blessings. For these other natural sciences are good, since God created them and implants them in the understanding of men, but we know that many of those who learned these sciences were condemned, while many others who did not were saved. For the only true science is that which teaches us and directs us and draws us to know and love and desire true Good, and God will not deny this knowledge to whoever desires it and searches for it with deeply felt care.

And if you want to know the school where one learns and praises this true science, I say it is the continuous remembrance of God's blessings. Oh, to be so diligent to continue to enroll in and attend this school, namely, to commit to memory and continuously reflect in our minds on the blessings we receive from God! Certainly we would then consider ourselves so obligated and bound to love and serve God that in return for the

---

[24] Teresa generally uses *çiençia* to denote acquired knowledge or learning and here the term *naturales çiençias* to refer to areas of knowledge or fields of study – including theology and philosophy – which she distinguishes from "devout and healthful wisdom" (101); I have translated the latter term literally as "natural sciences" although it encompasses more than the modern designation.

least blessing we receive in this world a thousand years would be spent in His service. And if the blessings that we receive in this world should incline us to love and serve our sovereign Lord, imagine what the blessings and rewards that await us in the next would do and how much, much more our Lord, supreme and perfect Good and abundant Fount of all blessings.

Therefore, let each one of us prepare a secret cell within his soul and thought where he can contemplate his blessings from God, and since, because of them, he will feel obliged to love Him, soon afterwards he will be inclined to desire Him, to serve and praise Him and recount to the people the magnitude and greatness of His blessings and abundant mercy. And since this good wisdom is very healthful and advantageous, God denies it to no one who needs it. And the prudent men who have read the treatise that I wrote[25] already know that it does not treat philosophy or theology or any other natural science but only this devout and healthful wisdom mentioned above, which is to know and commit to memory the blessings of God and to acknowledge and scrutinize and discover in my public misfortunes the hidden mercy of the Lord. Of this the Prophet says, "O how great is the multitude of thy sweetness, O Lord, which thou hast hidden for them that fear thee!" [Psalm 30:20]. And he seems to indicate with these words that unless we receive the disciplines and travails that God sends us in this world with fear and reverence and love, we cannot know or experience the sweetness of God's mercy nor feel the gentleness of His spiritual blessings which are enclosed and hidden in the trials we endure.

And if I was not and am not worthy of knowing such goodness – and God's blessings should be known and recounted and praised by all creatures – whatever was obscure and difficult for my womanly intellect, He who is the true Light and Sun of justice was able to make clear and easy. And certainly He is properly called Sun of justice because He infuses and spreads the rays of His clarity where He recognizes and knows that they are needed most. And where is light more necessary than where darkness abounds? And where is knowledge more necessary than where there is dangerous ignorance? And where is grace more necessary than where there is a multitude of sins? Where is consolation more necessary than where there is great affliction of spirit and body? And who will be the helpmeet of the poor and lowly? And I understand by poor and lowly a poverty of virtues and a lowliness and coarseness of intellect, for the rich can help those poor in temporal goods, and the mighty can favor those

---

[25] Here, almost without transition, Teresa's writing now becomes the concrete focus of her defense.

of lowly estate, but he who is poor and destitute of virtues and good merits, who can succor him or remedy his lack? Likewise he who is simple and foolish, who can make him prudent and learned? No human being, no matter how virtuous, can make another virtuous, nor can a learned person teach or make wise another of little or rude understanding.

Well, now you see that only God's omnipotence can do this and only His eternal wisdom can know this, for He alone knows who is poor in virtues and He alone recognizes the crudeness and lowliness and insufficiency of our understanding. And what only His unique wisdom can know, only His inestimable goodness and charity and mercy can repair. For just as a rich man is not obligated to give alms to a poor man if his own charity and good will do not compel him to do so, so God does not have to do what His omnipotence can do and His eternal wisdom knows that we need, unless His goodness and perfect charity and fatherly mercy intercede; for these three divine excellences – goodness, charity, and mercy – are great intercessors and mediators that help us achieve and attain those blessings and remedies and consolations that God's omnipotence alone can grant us, and His wisdom alone knows what the quality and quantity of our travails require.

And in truth I believe justice accords with this and does not turn its left face toward us.[26] For when God scourges us and gives us tribulations, He is moved by justice, and the very rod with which we are wounded is justice; and since through God's grace we sinners are converted and made penitent, who doubts that justice is our advocate? So it is indeed. And since God's eternal wisdom knew the extreme poverty and destitution of virtues in my soul and likewise knew the lowliness and insufficiency of my rude understanding and its scant capacity to recognize and know and praise and give thanks for the blessings given to me, through the intervention of His inestimable goodness and great mercy and perfect charity, His omnipotence that alone could remedy my grave ills provided this sinner with such remedies and healthful consolations that without doubt I can say with the Prophet, "According to the multitude of my sorrows in my heart, thy comforts have given joy to my soul" [Psalm 93:19]. You alone considered my travail and my pain and to You alone I revealed my cause, Defender of my life, my Lord, my God.

People marvel at what I wrote in the treatise and I marvel at what, in fact, I kept quiet, but I do not marvel doubting nor do I insist on my

---

[26] The justice of God's punishment is a continuous theme in *Grove*; compare, for example: "Let us not overlook justice: every time that pain is applied to guilt, justice is present, for the proper act of justice is to punish the guilty" (39). Regarding the moral and eschatological properties of left and right, see 29 n. 16.

wonder. For my experience makes me sure, and God of truth knows I had no other master nor consulted with any other learned authority nor translated from other books, as some people with malicious wonder are wont to say. Rather, this alone is the truth: that God of all knowledge, Lord of all virtues, Father of mercy, God of every consolation, He who consoles us in all our tribulation, He alone consoled me, He alone taught me, He alone read (to) me. He inclined His ear to me when I, besieged with great anguish and adrift in a deep sea of misfortunes,[27] called upon Him with the Prophet, saying, "Save me, O God: for the waters are come in even unto my soul" [Psalm 68:2].

And truly a very dangerous water was entering my soul, for I did not recognize in my misfortunes any blessings from God nor did I have any patience or even know what patience was. And certainly I believe that my understanding at that moment was like the blind man on the road near Jericho when our Redeemer passed by.[28] And just as that blind man, without seeing any light at all, felt that He who made light was passing near by him and that He could free him from his darkness,[29] so my understanding, blind and full of the darkness of my sins, felt the footsteps of my Savior, which are the good inspirations He sends to our souls before His coming so that once He has arrived we recognize Him and know to ask what we should rightfully request. And when, because of these signs, my blind understanding felt my Savior coming, it immediately began to shout with secret voices, saying, "Jesus, son of David, have mercy on me" [Luke 18:38]. And those who were coming and going chided this blind understanding of mine to be silent. And I can say without doubt that many disordered thoughts and a great mob of temporal human concerns were coming and going, rebuking and compelling my understanding to be quiet; for since I was on the road near Jericho – by which it is

---

[27] Compare *Grove*: "And just as someone who has passed through a great dangerous and dark sea and finds himself free of its waves gives heartfelt thanks to whoever freed him from so much danger, with greater reason and more devout exercise the infirm should offer uncommon thanks to the merciful Lord who in the secure ship of arduous suffering has freed him from the dark waves of this dangerous sea and provided his injuries with such healthful and sweet remedies" (71).

[28] The healing of the blind beggar is recounted in Luke 18:35–43, and in Mark 10:46–52; see also Matthew 20:29–34.

Here Teresa rewrites the initial landscape of *Grove* with New Testament analogues; the image of exile to a lonely island is replaced with the road near the worldly city of Jericho.

[29] A continuation of the imagery of light and darkness that pervades *Grove*; compare: "Thus in this exile and shadowy banishment, feeling myself more in a sepulcher than a dwelling, it pleased the mercy of the Most High to illuminate me with the light of His compassionate grace so that I might place my name in the register of those about whom it is written, 'The people that walked in darkness, have seen a great light: to them that dwelt in the region of the shadow of death, light is risen' [Isaiah 9:2]" (23).

understood that all my thoughts were placed on the road of this world and my desires were closer to human attachments than to spiritual ones – it was no wonder if the thoughts that came and went and passed through my understanding were residents of Jericho, namely, more related to the world than to the religion whose name I usurped at that time.[30]

Thus these thoughts and human commotions chided my blind understanding to be quiet; yet with its great desire for light, my understanding multiplied its secret voices more and more, saying, "Son of David, have mercy on me" [Luke 18:39b]. And it pleased the Lord to observe the difficult and devout struggle that my blind understanding waged against its obstructors on its own behalf. And through His great charity He stopped and waited until this blind man arrived to the true Light; and since it was guided by His divine grace, my understanding – constrained by its own great need, for it had no protection or help except from Him who made heaven and earth – was taken before the presence of my Savior where, for these reasons, it was fulfilled and brought to prayer, for we are properly in the presence of God when we pray devoutly and attentively.[31]

And, consequently, through His great mercy the same question was put to my understanding that our Redeemer asked of the blind man who shouted to Him on the road to Jericho, namely, "What wilt Thou that I do to thee?" [Luke 18:41]. And while my natural human desires invited and inclined me to request things contrary to my spiritual health, I realized that the Lord that asked me that question was my Savior and that if I were to ask for something contrary to my salvation, He would not give it to me. And then my understanding remembered what St. Augustine says about this verse in the gospel: "Quidquid p[e]cieritis Patrem yn nomine meo, etc."[32] Of this he says that whoever asks for something contrary to his

---

[30] The "many disordered thoughts and a great mob of temporal human concerns" recalls the "mob of temporal and human lusts" assaulting "the city of our conscience" (31). Jericho as the worldly city is opposed to the heavenly city of Jerusalem (108); the city of conflict is the soul, the site of violence assailed by the mob of worldly desires.

   The road near Jericho also recalls the street outside the supper of the Lamb where Teresa lingers with other reticent sufferers: "Thus stripped of all worldly goods and attired only in their sufferings, they keep their desire and care in worldly things, so that no matter how much their suffering invites them and tugs on their mantle, it cannot bring them to the abovementioned supper. They neither take pleasure from temporal goods nor want to enter the house of spiritual treasures, and so they remain in the street" (41).

[31] Recall that in *Grove* the doorknocker to be admitted to the Lord's supper is humble and devout prayer (40).

[32] "Whatever you ask the Father in my name, [he will give to you]" (John 16:23; my translation). See St. Augustine ("In Joannis Evangelium, Caput XV, Tractatus LXXXVI," in *Opera omnia, PL* 35:1852): "Proinde in omnibus misericordia ejus praevenit nos. Et fructus, inquit, vester maneat: quodcumque petieritis Patrem in nomine meo, det vobis."

spiritual health should not ask for it in the name of the Savior.[33] And, therefore, my understanding, stung with these fears, stopped asking for what my natural inclination demanded and only asked for what it felt would please the Savior.

Oh, how it pleases our Savior when we love what He loves so much, which is the health of our souls, and when we desire what He so desired; for, having offered Himself in sacrifice to the Father on the altar of the cross, He thirsted for the health of our souls! Indeed, what more just and gracious and acceptable petition can we ask of our Savior than the health of our souls or those things that pertain to this health? And as if my understanding with all its blindness heard my Savior asking, "What wilt thou that I do to thee?", it responded, "Domine, Domine, ut uideam lumen."[34] Lord, may I see the light to know that You are the true Light and Sun of justice; may I see the light to recognize in my public misfortunes the hidden blessings of Your great mercy; may I see the light to seek You with great fervor in my chastising suffering and desire You who are the true Healer of souls; may I see the light to have continuous remembrance of You, glory and good fortune of the saints, in this my affliction, confusion, and torment; may I see the light to illuminate my dark and womanly ignorance with the rays of Your supreme prudence. Come, send, my Lord, the wisdom at the seat of Your marvelous greatness so that it may be with me and mold me, and I may know always what is acceptable before You.

And thus my blind understanding persevered in these and other similar petitions, and it pleased the mercy of the Savior to say to it, "Respiçe" [Luke 18:42: "Behold"; my translation].[35] And that one word had such vigor and virtue that immediately the veil of darkness that blinded the eyes of my understanding was rent, and it saw and followed its Savior, extolling God. Therefore, let those who wonder, doubting the treatise I composed, leave their doubt, and let them wonder believing that the Lord is, indeed, the refuge of the poor, our helpmeet in both opportunities and tribulations.

Perchance someone will want to know the explanation of this word, namely, how my understanding saw and followed my Savior, exalting God. And to better understand this, let me first speak of the nature of the

---

[33] Compare: "Quod autem accipere salvandis non expedit nobis, non existimemus nos petere in nomine Salvatoris: sed hoc petimus in nomine Salvatoris, quod pertinet ad rationem salutis." See St. Augustine, "In Joannis Evangelium," 1852.

[34] "Lord, Lord, that I may see the light"; compare Luke 18:41, where the beggar replies, "Lord, that I may see."

[35] In the Vulgate and in Teresa's text, Jesus replies, "Respiçe" ("Have sight," "Look," "Behold"). See Luke 18:42: "Receive thy sight: thy faith hath made thee whole."

affliction, what blindness of understanding is, and from what humors intellectual darkness proceeds. For this, it is fitting to consider the powers of the soul, which are understanding, memory, and will.

Understanding is the first power of the soul, and it seems to me that it should be given precedence, for we cannot remember what we do not know, nor can we love what we do not know and understand. And so it follows of necessity that understanding precedes and exercises its office first, understanding and knowing and recognizing; and then memory and will exercise their habits and natural offices, remembering and loving what understanding intends and recognizes and knows. And these three powers of the soul are, therefore, naturally imparted and given to man through God's omnipotence and wisdom, and they cannot be idle for one moment; for it is necessary that our understanding intends something and that consequently our memory remembers what understanding perceives, and our will is inclined to love or abhor what our understanding and memory present, according to its quality.

And because we all, men and women alike, are generally called rational creatures, reason compels and inclines us to love naturally and be pleased with our own good and to abhor and regret misfortune when it happens to us. And since this natural inclination is so attached and familiar to every rational animal, it is very fitting and necessary that our understanding be healthy and have correct and clear vision to understand and recognize and discern what is good and what is evil, for clearly what our understanding presents to our memory is thus received by our will.

And I remember that I heard medical doctors say that the human body is governed by four humors, and when one of these changes and agitates too much, our body gravely suffers.[36] And this apparently happens to our understanding and the humors that govern it. And these humors, I certainly believe, are our five senses, for when our senses are well ordered and ruled, our understanding will be healthy. But when our five physical senses are uncontrolled and exert themselves too much in worldly things, our understanding suffers, and once rendered sick it cannot attend to its duty to be the first and principal power of the soul.

And the dissolution of our intellectual humors can even be so excessive that it causes our understanding to lose its vision. And certainly our understanding can become ill because of our senses, for who can prevent his understanding from knowing what his eye sees and his ear hears? Well, if what we see and hear is harmful and immorally perceived, the health of our understanding is hurt and our inner vision obscured. And when our

---

[36] On medieval medical theories regarding the four humors, see 57–58 n. 65.

understanding is sick, I truly believe that our memory and will cannot be healthy. And if the powers of our soul weaken, what will fortify our spirit? How can we know God if the understanding given to us in order to know God has lost its vision? How can we remember His many blessings if our memory is sick and absorbed in worldly remembrances? How can we love Him whom we should love when our will is damaged and engaged through the eyes of our understanding in affections contrary to the love of God?

And the eyes of our understanding are blinded in this manner because of our senses, for if we see the accidental light of day and do not see or heed the darkness of the night of our sinful living, which separates us from the true Light and carries us off in measured steps to eternal darkness, our understanding is truly blind. And whoever sees the darkness and confusion of his sins and recognizes the misery in which he lives and knows the goodness of God that awaits him in penitence has very clear vision indeed. And certainly a great light shines in the understanding of whoever knows himself and knows God. And this light was seen by blind Tobias when he taught his son such clear doctrine and admonished him, saying, "Fear not, my son: we lead indeed a poor life, but we shall have many good things if we fear God, [and depart from all sin, and do that which is good]" [Tobias 4:23].[37] And by poor life we should understand spiritual poverty, for whoever lives full of vices and empty of virtues leads a poor life, since virtues are the true riches of the soul. Of this St. Gregory says, "If you wish to be truly rich, love true riches."[38] Nevertheless, even those of us who lead a poor life with these true riches will receive many blessings if we fear God.

To fear God is to separate yourself from evil and do good works; thus the Prophet demonstrates that fear of God consists of these two things, saying, "Come, children, hearken to me: I will teach you the fear of the Lord" [Psalm 33:12]. And before he teaches about fear, he asks this question: "Who is the man that desireth life: [who loveth to see good days?]" [Psalm 33:13]. To love life is to abhor death, which is sin, and to love virtue, which is the life of the soul. For just as the body lives through the spirit, the spirit lives through virtue and through the exercise of virtuous works. Therefore, he immediately adds, "Who loveth to see good days." And what are the good days if not those that this same Prophet mentions when he says, "For better is one day in thy courts

---

[37] Pedro de Luna also cites Tobias's words to his son in discussing God's love for the poor (*Libro de consolaciones*, 580).

[38] "Si ergo, fratres charissimi, divites esse cupitis, veras divitias amate" (St. Gregory the Great, "Homiliarum in Evangelia, Homilia XV," in *Opera omnia, PL* 76:1132).

[above thousands]" [Psalm 83:11]. And since we cannot climb to this celestial dwelling and residence except up the stairway of virtuous works and good merit,[39] certainly with great maturity and prudence the Prophet teaches the discipline of fearing God; but before teaching us fear of God, he poses these questions as a preparation or provision. And immediately afterward, he teaches his doctrine, saying, "Turn away from evil and do good" [Psalm 33:15]. And how can someone separate himself from evil if he does not yet know the true Good which is seen not with our physical eyes but with the intellectual eyes of our soul? And if these eyes are obscured by our sins and blinded with the dust of earthly covetousness, we are in darkness and cannot see the road to our country and city of Jerusalem unless He who is the true Light enlightens our understanding.

Oh, eternal Light and Sun of justice, Key of David[40] and Scepter of the house of Israel,[41] come and free my grieving soul from this darkness and shadow of death! And, recognizing the quality of my spiritual ailment, what did the true Physician do in order to cure me? He closed the doors of my ears through which death was entering my soul and opened the eyes of my understanding, and I saw and followed my Savior. And I saw my hands empty of all vain human pleasures, and I saw my works burdened with anguished suffering, I saw the justice of the just Judge who wounded me with His powerful hand, and I saw the mercy of the most clement Father who awaited me in penitence, and I followed my Savior. And following my Savior can be understood in many ways, but the most appropriate and true is what He Himself says in the gospel: "If any man will come after me, let him deny himself, and take up his cross, and follow me" [Matthew 16:24].

And since to deny oneself is to contradict and impugn and negate completely one's own will and follow instead the will of God, in what should I spend my time if not in this agony and arduous conflict, namely, contradicting and denying my will and following His will, for His great mercy made me worthy of being scourged by His hand? So, at times through the grace of God's supreme goodness, at times through the force of His rigorous justice, I continually abstain from my own will and deny myself with difficulty and struggle to take my cross – the torment of my everyday pain – in the hands of my inner contentment. And bearing it

---

39 The image recalls the dwelling of patience sustained over the pillars of the four cardinal virtues whose stairway leads to the three theological virtues; see 80–85.

40 The Old Testament reference to the key of the house of David appears in Isaiah 22:22; on Christ as the Key of David, see Revelations 3:7; on the reinterpretation of the keys as the keys to the kingdom of heaven, see Matthew 16:19.

41 The scepter of Israel is mentioned in Genesis 49:10 and Numbers 24:17; the scepter is also referred to in Revelations 2:28.

painfully on the shoulders of my fragile humanity, I follow my Savior not with physical footsteps, but with the affections of my soul, pursuing the scent of His ointments that anoint His precious wounds, with which He, in His great charity, wishes to anoint those whom He chooses for Himself. And thus my blind understanding saw and followed and continues to follow my Savior, exalting my God.

And I praised God and I observed with devout diligence the greatness of His blessings and mercy and grace and made these manifest to everyone, to the glory and exaltation of His holy name, albeit with little devotion and even less prudence, according to my limited womanly capacity. And I wrote that treatise that deals with this intellectual light and the lesson that I learned, which is to praise God and to know God, and to know myself and to deny my will and conform it to His will; and to take in the hands of my inner understanding the cross of the suffering I endure, and to follow my Savior in the footsteps of spiritual affliction; and to exalt God through the confession of my tongue, giving laud and praise to His holy name, recounting to the people the fairness of His justice, the greatness of His mercy, and His magnificence and glory. Of the glory of His kingdom the Prophet says, "They shall speak of the magnificence of the glory of thy holiness: [and shall tell thy wondrous works]" [Psalm 144:5]; and "The heavens shew forth the glory of God, [and the firmament declareth the work of his hands]" [Psalm 18:2]; and let the earth, which is His human creation, recount His magnificence and glory, saying: "Sing ye to the Lord, for he hath done great things: shew this forth in all the earth" [Isaiah 12:5].

Thus the three powers of the soul that previously through the excessive dissolution of their physical senses had become confused and idle, now with the extreme abstinence of their senses can diligently and carefully attend to their proper duties. And it seems to happen to understanding, memory, and will what happens to some common women who frequently leave their houses and go wandering through the houses of other people; because of this bad custom, they become negligent and lazy in womanly duties and domestic and household chores, and they do not benefit from this habit; rather, their household and home suffer. And this appears to happen to our understanding when it frequently abandons and leaves its own home, which is the inward study of private meditation within the walls of our heart; for just as women enclosed within the doors of their home exercise their proper and honest duties, so understanding, withdrawn from outside things and confined within the doors of its secret meditation, exercises with more vigor its proper duty.

But that understanding that goes wandering outside its dwelling or inner study and involves itself very frequently in worldly transactions does not benefit from this action; rather, its household – its soul – suffers.

And like the gadding woman,[42] compelled to return home by the coming of night, who arrives so restless and unaccustomed to work that the little time she has left she cannot employ to her benefit or to the advantage of her house, so our understanding, as our senses withdraw from their labors at nightfall and worldly dealings and outside contact are silenced, is compelled by necessity to retire to its proper home, which is the secret meditation and soliloquy of its inward thought. But it returns so altered, so restless from the idleness of the day, that it cannot take advantage of the quiet of the night and attend to anything to benefit itself or its badly run house and estate, which is our spiritual health. In order for understanding to attend to its own well-being in repose and wisdom and to the advantage of its household, which is the health of its spirit, it is necessary that it be calm and remain in its dwelling. And as soon as it returns to its senses, it will attend more carefully and profitably to its proper duty, which is to know God and recognize His blessings and know the defects and faults of the soul and how it is prostrate and fallen in the cave of its sins because of its great neglect.

Oh what sublime wisdom it is to know God and what true prudence to know and recognize His blessings! And what a healthful and beneficial science it is for us to know ourselves and our own defects and faults! For perfect charity is engendered in the soul from the true knowledge of God, and heartfelt gratitude is engendered in the soul from the recognition of God's blessings, and comprehension and humility are engendered in the soul from the acknowledgement of one's own defects and faults. And this is the proper role of the three powers of our soul, especially of our understanding, for when it dedicates itself completely to work inside its house in this holy exercise and proper occupation, immediately memory and will join it, and all three powers of the soul will work together and strive to recover their proper title, namely, to be true powers of the soul in deed as they are in name; for they are called powers of the soul so that with these three powers – understanding, memory, and will – our soul is raised on high and strives against human weakness to reach and obtain the true Good for which it was created.

---

42 Pedro de Luna compares carnality to a gadding woman: "[Flesh] is that talkative, roaming, restless woman, adorned to deceive our souls, that Solomon spied from his window" (*Libro de consolaciones,* 599). Compare Proverbs 7:10–12: "Not bearing to be quiet, not able to abide still at home, Now abroad, now in the streets, now lying in wait near the corner." In line with Teresa's avoidance of sexual overtones (see 130 n. 32), she suppresses reference to the overt sexuality of the biblical figure: "And behold a woman meeteth him in harlot's attire prepared to deceive souls; talkative and wandering" (Proverbs 7:10). For background, see Carla Casagrande's discussion of women wanderers in "The Protected Woman," in *A History of Women in the West, II: Silences of the Middle Ages,* ed. Christiane Klapisch-Zuber (Cambridge, Mass.: The Belknap Press of Harvard University Press, 1992), 84–86.

But when understanding, memory, and will abandon their cell and dissipate themselves in material and vain things, they may be called weaknesses, not powers, of the soul, for they become stupefied and gross, and our soul grows weak because of their absence and neglect. And thus when they withdraw from worldly occupations, they become more solicitous and diligent in their proper spiritual duties. When understanding, memory, and will unite and dedicate themselves to this good and worthy enterprise, our sovereign Lord does not deny us His holy grace; rather, He observes with eyes of paternal love and true charity the wants of His children exiled in this vale of misery and tears. And when He sees the insufficiency and limited capacity of our human understanding that cannot ascend to where our soul aspires, without delay He opens the door of His sacred ark and from the sovereign fount of His great mercy sprinkles marvelous dewdrops over the earth ready to receive it, by which I refer to the disposition of all human creatures to receive spiritual blessings.[43]

For when the Prophet and saintly King David says, "God is wonderful in his saints" [Psalm 67:36], it is clear that he was and is one of the saints, and having himself felt divine magnificence, he wonders at how marvelous God is to His saints. Nevertheless, if we sinners want to speak according to what we ourselves feel about the magnificence of God's blessings, we can well say, "God is wonderful in his sinners"; for even though we are sinners, we are His, and if because of our sinfulness we are to be cast away from Him, the sovereign Truth would not have said, "I say to you, that even so there shall be joy in heaven upon one sinner that doth penance, [more than upon ninety-nine just who need not penance]" [Luke 15:7]. And if we want to know how wonderful God is with His sinners, let us consider with what patience He sustains us, with what solicitude He keeps us, with what long-suffering He awaits us, with what charity He corrects us, with what mercy He consoles us, with what graciousness He visits us, with what generosity He provides for us, with what intimacy He teaches us. How wonderful God is to His saints, for He gives them virtue and fortitude; and how wonderful God is to His sinners, for He shows us mercy and grace.

And God shows mercy and grace to us sinners when He scourges and corrects us in this present life, for this is a time of mercy and grace, and that which awaits us is a time of judgement and justice. For He who exercises justice during a time of mercy indicates that at the time of justice He will exercise mercy, and thus God's mercy and grace show sinners

---

[43] See 87 n. 8.

how to escape future ire, namely, the rigor of the Last Judgement. And let us acknowledge His mercy in deeming us worthy of forewarning and correcting in this present life, and His grace in illuminating our understanding so that we may know and recognize His blessing, and let us turn to God, for He is gracious and merciful.[44] And the trials, afflictions, and calamities that God inflicts on sinners, although these may seem from the outside to be the rigors of justice, inwardly they shout words of mercy and charity and admonish us as with a human tongue, saying, "Be converted to the Lord with all your heart."[45] And thus God is wonderful with His saints, for He gives them virtue and fortitude, and He is wonderful with His sinners, for He gives us mercy and grace to sustain and endure and our misfortunes to recognize His great blessings. And in order to know and praise and recount this to the people, whoever has a devout desire and a pressing thirst to learn and acquire healthful learning, let him come to God's school of patience and he will receive the Lord, Bread of life and of understanding, and He will give him to drink the water of healthful knowledge, and he will joyfully get water from the wells of our Savior.[46] And they will say on that day, "Confess to the Lord and invoke His holy name, quod est beneditum in saecula saeculorum. Amen."[47]

Thanks be to God forever and ever.

---

44 Compare Joel 2:13: "And turn to the Lord your God: for he is gracious and merciful, patient and rich in mercy, and ready to repent of the evil."

45 Compare Joel 2:12: "Now therefore saith the Lord: 'Be converted to me with all your heart, in fasting, and in weeping, and in mourning.' "

46 Teresa's final image celebrates the sufferer's admission to the supper of the Lamb to partake of the bread of life and understanding and the water of healthful knowledge.

47 "[His name] that is blessed forever and ever"; compare Psalm 144:21: "My mouth shall speak the praise of the Lord: and let all flesh bless his holy name for ever; yea, for ever and ever."

Interpretive Essay

From Anxiety of Authorship to *Admiración*: Autobiography, Authorship, and Authorization in the Works of Teresa de Cartagena[1]

The term "anxiety of authorship" was coined by Sandra Gilbert and Susan Gubar and applied to nineteenth-century women writers in their by now classic feminist study, *The Madwoman in the Attic*.[2] Like most women in patriarchal society – in the fifteenth as well as the nineteenth century – the woman writer experiences her gender as a painful obstacle or debilitating inadequacy. Indeed, the situation of those nineteenth-century women writers Gilbert and Gubar examine offers many direct parallels with Teresa's and is crucial to understanding her position as author and subject of her text:

> Thus the loneliness of the female artist, her feelings of alienation from male predecessors coupled with her need for sisterly precursors and successors, her urgent sense of her need for a female audience together with her fear of the antagonism of male readers, her culturally conditioned timidity about self-dramatization, her dread of patriarchal authority of art, her anxiety about the impropriety of female invention – all these phenomena of "inferiorization" mark the woman writer's struggle for artistic self-definition and differentiate her efforts at self-creation from those of her male counterpart (50).

Applying this paradigm to Teresa: the loneliness of being a female artist would only be exacerbated by her deafness; with regard to attendant alienation from male predecessors and need for sisterly precursors and successors, Teresa's deafness cut her off from the oral female subculture (women's songs, proverbs, convent chatter) and thrust her into the dominant culture of male letters. Her urgent need for a female audience (Teresa directs both her texts to an inscribed reader, "virtuosa señora," presumably Juana de Mendoza) together with her fear of the antagonism of male

---

[1] I have retained *admiración* in the title here because of its ambiguity: *admiración* means "wonder, awe, incredulity, surprise" but also "admiration, respect."

[2] *The Madwoman in the Attic: The Woman Writer and the Nineteenth-Century Literary Imagination* (New Haven: Yale University Press, 1979).

readers (implicit in certain literary strategies in *Grove* and subsequently realized in its antagonistic reception), her culturally conditioned timidity about self-dramatization (Teresa obliquely dramatizes herself through her literary authorities), her dread of the patriarchal authority of art (the "prudentes varones" as she refers to her detractors in *Wonder*), her anxiety about the impropriety of female invention (the formulaic repetition of disclaimers like "the lowliness and grossness of my womanly mind," "my poor womanly intellect," "my coarse womanly judgement") – all these phenomena of inferiorization – mark Teresa's struggle for artistic self-definition in *Grove of the Infirm*. Women writers have traditionally participated in a very different literary subculture from that of male authors; a fundamental difference is revealed when women's struggles for literary self-creation are examined in the psychosexual context of Harold Bloom's Freudian theories of patrilineal literary inheritance. Instead of the "anxiety of influence" Bloom traces in male writers, the woman writer experiences a debilitating "anxiety of authorship," built from "complex and often only barely conscious fears of that authority which seems to be by definition inappropriate to her sex" (*The Madwoman in the Attic*, 51).

Teresa, as anxiety-ridden as her nineteenth-century sisters, applies several strategies to obliquely *authorize* her own text. She directs both *Grove of the Infirm* and *Wonder at the Works of God* to the "virtuous lady" who has presumably requested their composition, and this fulfills two rhetorical functions: it takes responsibility from Teresa, since she is ceding to a request to write rather than initiating the act of writing of her own accord, and the inscribing of an accessible and receptive female reader facilitates communication to a more general audience. Another strategy is the use of gendered humility formulas as a means of *captatio benevolentiae*;[3] Teresa acknowledges her own inherent lack of authority as a woman by the inferiorizing self-references already cited and then appropriates the voice of a male authority to authorize her words:

> And since the lowliness and grossness of my womanly mind do not allow me to rise higher, aspiring to the nobility and sanctity of the very virtuous king and prophet David, I begin to look in his most devout songbook called the Psalter for some good consolations (24).

---

[3]   These are not, of course, original to Teresa; protestations of ignorance are a frequent strategy in women's writing, used even by such learned women as Hildegard of Bingen and Teresa of Avila.

Yet because my coarse womanly judgement gives my words little
or no authority . . . (74; a transition to cite Peter Lombard and
Job).

I wish to refer to the Master of Patiences, not only as witness and
authority of my simple sayings (for they do not deserve so much)
. . . (75).

The following is a more extensive example of how Teresa appropriates discourses of male authority; here she adapts the first-person
voice of the moralist in Pedro de Luna's *Libro de las consolaciones de
la vida humana* (*Book of Consolations for Human Life*), one of her
primary sources:[4]

Pedro de Luna, *Book of Consolations for Human Life*	Teresa de Cartagena, *Grove of the Infirm*
Likewise, you should not grieve if perchance you are deaf, for you are spared the occasion of hearing vain words and evils harmful to you (600).	When I look to my suffering in temporal terms, it seems very painful and anguished, but when I turn my thought from these concerns, drawing it unto my breast, and I see the solitude that my suffering imposes, separating me from worldly trans-actions, I call it a kind solitude, a blessed solitude, a solitude that isolates me from dangerous sins and surrounds me with sure blessings, a solitude that removes me from things harmful and dangerous to both my body and soul (26).
Whence our Lord said: "The deaf shall hear and the blind see," which we can understand spiritually, for those whose bodies are deaf shall hear with the ears of their soul (600).	And who could hear with the ears of his soul such healthy advice if his physical ears were filled with the noise of human voices? (32).
Likewise, by being deaf, you will hear better with the ears of your soul those words that God speaks within you . . . (600)	And with the abovementioned silence, straining the ear of my understanding – since that of my body helps me not – I seem to hear spiritually these words re-sound . . . (29).

---

4 Pedro de Luna, *Libro de las consolaciones de la vida humana*, ed. Pascual de Gayangos,
   Escritores en prosa anteriores al siglo XV, Biblioteca de Autores Españoles, 51 (Madrid:
   Sucesores de Hernando, 1884), 561–602. The parallels between Teresa's texts and Pedro de
   Luna's *Book of Consolations* were first established by Hutton (17–23).

Likewise, you should not be upset nor sad if you find your self alone, especially in the company of worldly men, for frequently they can obstruct the sanctity of holy men. Of this Origen says: "When man is accompanied by worldly men and carnal pleasures he cannot think of God, nor can he be saintly unless he isolates himself from the world." ... And moreover the company of men can obstruct and bar the road to God. For on this road he who walks alone without the company of men deserves the company of holy thoughts that is more worthy and secure and of greater salvation (583).

And thus enmeshed in the confusion of worldly chatter, with my understanding disordered and bound up in worldly cares, I could not hear the voices of holy doctrine that Scriptures teach us. But merciful God, who was with me in this din and with discreet observation saw my perdition and knew how important it was to my health to have the chatter cease so that I would better understand what was necessary for my salvation, signaled me with His hand to be quiet (26).

There are, nevertheless, important differences in the first-person voice of Pedro de Luna and that of Teresa de Cartagena. Pedro de Luna addresses his book to *tú* (the second-person familiar in Spanish), and the first-person narrator assumes the moralizing voice of a doctrinal work. Luna's voice is directed outwardly towards a younger male reader, the "beloved son" he purports to instruct. In a natural and traditional way, a hierarchy of authority is established in which a moralizing authoritative "I" instructs his inscribed reader. Teresa directs her text to the "virtuous lady" of her prologue, whom she addresses as *vos* (the second-person formal in Old Spanish); her inscribed reader is much more complex than Luna's disciple: "virtuous lady" is an accessible authority figure, a combination confessor/confidante, and ultimately, in *Wonder at the Works of God*, a ploy to indirectly engage the male detractors of Teresa's first work. Teresa's first-person narrator assumes the more intimate voice of a confessional work, which is directed inwardly, exploring her own personal experience as an example. The hierarchy of authority that structures Luna's *Book of Consolations* is missing in Teresa's text as she strives to establish a community with her fellow infirm, the "convent of afflictions." In contrast to Luna's text, in Teresa's, the first person is distinctly autobiographical, that is, it is both subject and object in the text.

In these collated examples, Teresa appropriates and personalizes the voice of the male moralist; in other instances, she cites other male voices to authorize her own statements. Teresa incorporates a multiplicity of male voices in her text, for she writes in the tradition of consolatory treatises modeled after Boethius, of Franciscan writers like Ramon Llull, of the sermons of popular and learned preachers, of the church fathers (particularly Jerome, Ambrose, Augustine, Gregory the Great), of *cancionero* poets, and, most importantly, of Scriptures. Ostensibly, *Grove of the Infirm* is a didactic treatise – a male-dominated genre in the Middle Ages – glossing Teresa's base text, Psalm 31:9: "With bit and bridle bind fast their jaws, who come not near unto thee." Among the instances of amplification are etymologies, the parable of the five talents, the seven deadly sins, the six roots of pride, and the cardinal and theological virtues. Yet underneath this self-consciously conventional didactic text dominated by borrowed male voices is a deeply personal female subtext, a subterranean voice that is Teresa's own, that oblique personal voice that informs her spiritual autobiography.

"This Slight and Defective Work": The Poetics of Teresa's Autobiography

Grove of the Infirm has been read as both a work of auto-consolation and an attempt through the act of writing to overcome the isolation imposed by Teresa's deafness. While critics invariably emphasize the autobiographical focus of Teresa's devotional treatise as distinctive to her work, *Grove of the Infirm* has not been critically examined as a piece of women's self-writing. Although Teresa's extended gloss of Psalm 31 may seem to randomly unfold through the association of ideas and imagery, its interlace pattern is firmly woven together by the autobiographical thread of Teresa's personal record. I do not mean to suggest that Teresa set out consciously to write a conventional autobiography proceeding from childhood to conversion to religious maturity;[5] instead, she intricately weaves together her life and her texts and represents her self obliquely rather than explicitly.

That *Grove of the Infirm* does not conform to canonic definitions of autobiography is not untypical in women's self-writing:

> When writing locates itself at the margins of genre or outside the
> limits of defined genre, or if the author is also marginalized . . .,
> it serves as a kind of "limit case." Writing that works the borders
> of definitional boundaries bears witness both to repressive in-
> scription under the law of genre and to the freedom and dispos-
> session of existence outside the law. Such cases – and women's

---

5 St. Augustine's *Confessions* was, of course, the prime model in the Middle Ages for what we now call autobiography, although it is clear that autobiography at the time was never defined or identified as a genre or tradition. For this reason, I do not mean to suggest that Teresa's hidden agenda was to write an autobiography, as this concept was not even available to her as a literary model. When I refer later to Teresa's transgressive autobiographical project in *Grove of the Infirm*, her transgression lies in the textualizing of her experience and the investing of her self as the subject of her writing rather than any overt intention, for, as she notes in her introductory remarks to *Wonder at the Works of God*, both the act of writing and her subject (her self, her experience) were rejected by her male detractors as inappropriate.

autobiographical writings are exemplary in this – are difficult to define in terms of "theory." As a result, the problems they pose are often avoided altogether . . .[6]

Teresa's devotional treatise crosses *into* the definitional boundaries of autobiography in a number of determinative ways. Her text takes the speaking "I" as the subject of the narrative, rendering the "I" both subject and object. Her "autobiography" is both the process and the product of interpreting her life, investing her past and the self she constructs with coherence and meaning. The complex set of intentions and expectations binding Teresa and her reader – the "virtuous lady" and her more general audience – acts as an autobiographical contract; that is, the fictions of the autobiographer are mediated by a historical identity with the intention of interpreting the meaning of her lived experience, and the reader suppresses the recognition of inevitable unreliability in an effort to expect "truth" of some kind. Contrary to this expectation, the self constructed in Teresa's autobiographical project is a cultural and linguistic fiction that is constituted by historical ideologies and figures of selfhood.[7]

Moreover, in its aberrance from standards of conventional autobiography, Teresa's text coincides with contemporary theories of women's self-representation: in her focus on the private rather than the public self

6   Shari Benstock, "Introduction," in *The Private Self: Theory and Practice of Women's Autobiographical Writing*, ed. Benstock (Chapel Hill: University of North Carolina Press, 1988), 2. Recent theories of women's autobiography have challenged androcentric paradigms of self-representation, their underlying assumptions about writing and sexual (in)difference, and their essentialist conflation of male subjectivity and human identity. Sidonie Smith offers an overview in "Autobiographical Criticism and the Problematics of Gender," in *A Poetics of Women's Autobiography*, 3–19. See also Benstock, "Authorizing the Autobiographical," in *The Private Self*, 10–33; Estelle C. Jelinek, "Introduction: Women's Autobiography and the Male Tradition," in *Women's Autobiography: Essays in Criticism*, ed. Jelinek (Bloomington: Indiana University Press, 1980), 1–20; and Domna C. Stanton, "Autogynography: Is the Subject Different?" in *The Female Autograph*, ed. Stanton (Chicago: University of Chicago Press, 1987), 3–20.

7   "As she examines her unique life and then attempts to constitute herself discursively as female subject, the autobiographer brings to the recollection of her past and to the reflection on her identity interpretative figures (tropes, myths, metaphors, to suggest alternative phrasings). Those figures are always cast in language and are always motivated by cultural expectations, habits, and systems of interpretation pressing on her at the scene of writing. Cultural scripts of signification . . . reflect privileged stories and character types that the prevailing culture, through its discourse, names as 'real'. . . . Precisely because 'every subject, every author, every self is the articulation of an intersubjectivity structured within and around the discourses available to it at any moment in time,' self-interpretation emerges rhetorically from the autobiographer's engagement with the fictive stories of selfhood" (Smith, *The Poetics of Women's Autobiography*, 47; the internal quote is from Michael Sprinker, "Fictions of the Self: The End of Autobiography," in *Autobiography: Essays Theoretical and Critical*, ed. James Olney [Princeton: Princeton University Press, 1980], 325).

(the *res gestae* of male self-representation); her fragmentary and discontinuous autobiographical narrative (versus the pretensions of linearity and totalization of male writing); her self-representation through her relationship to a significant "Other," in Teresa's case to the dominant and authoritative figure of God (versus the autonomous individuality and separateness of the traditional male subject). Ultimately, Teresa's representation of her experience (*bios*), sense of identity or selfhood *(autē)*, textuality (*graphia*), and reading or interpretive strategies all proceed from her marginalized position as a woman, as a deaf person, and as a *conversa*.

There are several specific examples of what I have called Teresa's "oblique autobiography" in *Grove of the Infirm*; the first is the initial inscription of her self in her text:

> Long ago, virtuous lady, the cloud of temporal and human sadness covered the borders of my life and with a thick whirlwind of anguished sufferings carried me off to an island called "Oprobrium hominum et abiecio plebis" ["The Scorn of Mankind and Outcast of the People"] where I have lived for so many years – if life this can be called – without ever seeing anyone to direct my steps onto the road of peace or show me a path whereby I could arrive to any community of pleasures. Thus in this exile and shadowy banishment, feeling myself more in a sepulcher than a dwelling, it pleased the mercy of the Most High to illuminate me with the light of His compassionate grace so that I might place my name in the register of those about whom it is written, "The people that walked in darkness, have seen a great light: to them that dwelt in the region of the shadow of death, light is risen" [Isaiah 9:2].
>
> And with my understanding enlightened and the cloud of my heavy sadness dispelled by this true Light that illuminates everyone who comes into this world, I saw that this island, indeed, was a good and healthful place for me (23–24).

Here Teresa represents her past history of illness and suffering in terms of an allegorical landscape; she is metaphorically swept away to an island called "The Scorn of Mankind and Outcast of the People." By means of an allegorical construct, Teresa can elaborate figuratively the initial loneliness, despair, and suffering she had experienced when she became deaf, without focusing on her concrete personal circumstance.[8]

8 This play between the literal and the figurative is distinctive to Teresa's writing: "Teresa's life was bounded by both her reclusion in a convent and her deafness, meaningful biographical elements that her treatise develops on both a literal and a figurative level. Although her

A somewhat different obliqueness in Teresa's self-representation occurs in her exhortation to her fellow sufferers to virtuously endure in their afflictions:

> All the blessings of this world are food reserved for the healthy; so let us leave what we cannot have and get accustomed to our own diet, and let us partake of those foods that suit our stomach and help us suffer our travail.
>
> It seems to me that we who endure suffering should partake of these six dishes: grievous sadness, enduring patience, bitter contrition, frequent and heartfelt confession, devout prayer, perseverance in virtuous works. And we can ingest without fear these six foods and related provisions; and although they may seem quite bitter to our taste, this is necessarily so, for few infirm enjoy their diet, even though it is beneficial and fortifying. Therefore, let us love the bitter since the sweet does not love us, so that what is bitter to our palate (that is, to our human senses) may be converted into sweetness for our soul.
>
> *And I do not know why we infirm should want anything from this world, for as much as we may wander, we shall never find anything in it that loves us well. Worldly pleasures despise us, health forsakes us, friends forget us, relatives get angry, and even one's own mother gets annoyed with her sickly daughter, and one's father despises the son who with chronic afflictions dwells in his home* (46, emphasis mine)

Teresa observes that worldly pleasures are reserved for the healthy; the infirm are seated at a different table and presented with a different menu. She encourages her fellow sufferers to eat of their bitter fare, for what is physically disagreeable is spiritually beneficial. Then, seemingly disheartened, she complains of the fare she has been served in life: "And I do not know why we infirm should want anything from this world . . ." Embedded in Teresa's allegorical supper of the infirm is a deeply personal – and obliquely autobiographical – revelation of painful familial rejection: "relatives get angry, and even one's own mother gets annoyed with her sickly daughter and one's father despises the son who with chronic afflictions dwells in his home."[9]

---

imagery is often biblically inspired, it is assimilated and personalized in such a way that it also functions on a vital level. Such interrelated image patterns mirror the interplay between received doctrine and personal experience that sets her treatise apart from other such devotional works" (Ronald E. Surtz, "Image Patterns in Teresa de Cartagena's *Arboleda de los enfermos*," in *La Chispa '87: Selected Proceedings*, ed. Gilbert Paolini [New Orleans: Tulane University Press, 1987], 303).

9   The theme of family rejection is reiterated more indirectly in discussing the six roots of pride:

The passage exemplifies the double-voiced narrative of women's autobiography: "Manifest in women's autobiography, therefore, is a kind of double helix of the imagination that leads to a double-voiced structuring of content and rhetoric. The voices of man and woman, of Adam and Eve, vie with one another, displace one another, subvert one another in the constant play of uneasy appropriation or reconciliation and daring rejection" (Smith, *A Poetics of Women's Autobiography*, 51). The opening remarks ("All the blessings of this world . . .") are voiced by the kind of authoritative first person we find in Pedro de Luna's consolatory treatise; the affective interruption and the rebelliousness of the female subject ("And I do not know why . . .") – Eve's disruptive language of desire – subvert the totalizing morality of the male voice.[10]

The obliqueness and pervasiveness of her self-references[11] suggest that while Teresa does not constitute her self as the focal subject of her

---

"even if one is the son of a duke, an admiral, or a marquis, if he is inflicted with great suffering or an embarrassing wound, not only will his friends and relatives hold him in contempt, but his own father and mother will dispatch him quickly from their house and put him where he can cause them no detriment or disorder" (59).

Teresa also sensitively analyzes the emotional pain of rejection and contempt when she discusses the talent of humiliation: "For when the invalid sees himself so humiliated and despised by his neighbors, there is no doubt that his heart is stung with great affliction and feeling, so that, depending on the quality of the contempt and the person who receives it, someone can be more tormented by this type of anguish than by his many physical pains" (69).

10 Smith ("Woman's Story and the Engendering of Self–Representation," in *A Poetics of Women's Autobiography*, 44–62) examines the complex negotiation of paternal and maternal narratives that characterizes women's self-writing; pages 52–54 are excerpted and paraphrased here. As the woman writer appropriates the story and speaking posture of the representative man (those male voices reaffirming the ideology of female subordination to male authority that haunt Teresa's text), she silences that part of herself that identifies her as daughter of her mother. Rejecting the realm of the mother for the realm of the father and his word (Teresa's entry into the family writing tradition of the Cartagena men), she colludes in her inscription "in the law of the same: same sexuality, same discourse, same economy, same representation, same origin" (Josette Féral, "Antigone or the Irony of the Tribe," *Diacritics* 8 [Fall 1978]: 6–7) and allows for her own recuperation in the symbolic order of patriarchy. Accepting tacitly the fictions of woman, including the story of her cultural inferiority (Teresa's gendered humility formulas), accepting the fiction of man as the more valued ideal toward which to strive, she takes her place on stage, not as Eve, but as Adam (hence her exclusively male literary analogues in *Grove*). Yet, as Smith warns, hers is always a complex, ultimately precarious capitulation, open to subversive elements both without and within the text. Although her story re-enacts the figures and supports the hierarchy of values that constitute patriarchal culture, it remains nonetheless the story of a woman (despite, as we shall see, Teresa's strategy to un-gender her story, her detractors will dismiss it as the story of a woman). Potentially more damaging, however, is the threat from within. The effaced voice of her repressed sexuality and her uneasy denial of the maternal inheritance can disrupt the figure of male-identified selfhood, betraying an alternative and private story that qualifies and sometimes even subverts the authorized and public version of herself (as in the supper of the infirm passage examined above).

11 "Teresa's works are full of herself; they are engendered from the depths of her reflection on herself and from there extend to other themes – women writers, the infirm – without losing

devotional treatise in the mode of a traditional autobiography, neither does she constitute her text(s) as separate from her self, that is, for Teresa the act of reading (as well as the act of writing) is profoundly autobiographical. While *Grove of the Infirm* is ostensibly a gloss of several biblical verses (Psalm 31:9: "With bit and bridle bind fast their jaws, who come not near unto thee"; Psalm 44:10: "Listen, O daughter, and behold, and incline thy ear: forget thy people and the house of thy father"; 2 Corinthians 12:9: "Gladly therefore will I glory in my infirmities, that the virtue of Christ may dwell in me"), in fact, these verses also serve to gloss and inform Teresa's spiritual autobiography, marking the divine infliction of her deafness, her separation from her family, and her final celebration of the spiritual benefits of her affliction.

In *Grove of the Infirm,* Teresa writes her self through her texts rather than through concrete referential details. Here we must remember that so much of what we know about Teresa actually comes from the initial rubrics to her texts:

> This treatise is called *Grove of the Infirm,* which Teresa de Cartagena composed, being afflicted with grave ailments and, in particular, having lost completely her sense of hearing. And she wrote this work in praise of God and for her own spiritual consolation and that of all those who suffer illness so that, forsaken of their physical health, they may place their desire in God who is true Health (23).

> Here begins a brief treatise which can fittingly be called *Wonder at the Works of God.* Teresa de Cartagena, a nun of the order of [. . .], composed it at the petition and request of Señora Juana de Mendoça, wife of Señor Gómez Manrique (86).

Ironically, when we first read *Grove of the Infirm* we have a surplus of circumstantial information – probably provided by the copyist – that Teresa did not intend for us to have. In contrast, Teresa's own text is marked by an erasure of the circumstantial:[12] she never names herself,

sight of the intimate personal experience that made these works possible . . . Twenty years of deafness – the loss of direct contact with the outside world – must have deprived Teresa of worldly experience but provided a great abundance of intimate life experiences that found an ideal outlet in the act of writing" (Carmen Marimón Llorca, *Prosistas castellanas medievales* [Alicante: Caja de Ahorros Provincial, 1990], 118).

12 The only exception to this is her reference to her studies in Salamanca ("although this may not be proven and demonstrated as well as it should, due to my weak judgement; for my limited faculty and the few years that I was at the University of Salamanca . . ." [80]), an ironic version of the humility formulas elsewhere in the text, since to study in Salamanca, even for a few years, would be a recommendation for, rather than a disclaimer of, knowledge.

never gives us her age, never explicitly reveals her profession as a nun, never divulges her family, never identifies her space, and any self-references are either represented obliquely or figuratively.[13] This literal anonymity permits Teresa greater freedom to elaborate the autobiography of her spiritual life and also magnifies her exemplarity, for the suppression of concrete personal details circumvents her limited symbolic value as an afflicted *woman* and casts her instead as a more universal exemplar of suffering humanity.[14] Thus she constructs her self largely through literary analogues, generally through male biblical figures and male biblical voices (David, Job, the blind man on the road to Jericho, Lazarus, and, ultimately, Christ): the self of a faithful sinner so beloved and chosen by God that He inflicts suffering to draw the subject closer to Him, to protect her from the dangers of this world, and thus to prepare for her salvation. This is a "culturally valued" fiction of male selfhood, a biblical myth rehearsed over and over again in the stories of the Old Testament and particularly in the Book of Job; Teresa's innovation is that the subject is female, and one of her strategies is to minimize the gendering of her own story by emphasizing the figurative spiritual dimension – that space where male and female are theoretically equivalent – over its literal details. This total permeation of self and text – unusual in the Middle Ages – explains in part the vehemence of Teresa's defense in the *Wonder at the Works of God*: while Teresa is offended that the "prudent men" wonder at a woman's right to write, what really galls her is that her detractors have called into question her authorship of her own text and thus rejected her fictive construction of her self.[15]

---

[13] In this regard, it is instructive to reread Teresa's text without the benefit of the prefatory material and to see how fully her story hovers in the figurative. When I distributed excerpts from Teresa's writing prior to giving a lecture at Emory University, one graduate student who had skipped over the initial rubrics offered a coherent and plausible figurative reading of Teresa's account.

[14] Teresa's exemplarity is based on the patristic principle that despite subordination on the level of creation, male and female souls are theoretically equivalent in the order of salvation; see Eleanor Commo McLaughlin, "Equality of Souls, Inequality of Sexes: Women in Medieval Theology," in *Religion and Sexism: Images of Woman in the Jewish and Christian Traditions*, ed. Rosemary Radford Ruether (New York: Simon and Schuster, 1974), 233–51. The failure of her strategy is recorded in the prologue to *Wonder* where Teresa's detractors re-gender and, therefore, reject her story.

[15] It would be interesting to examine the psychoanalytical implications of Teresa's constructed self. Stung by familial rejection, she is commanded to leave her people and forget the house of her earthly father, and she enters a convent. Castigated by a stern but loving Heavenly Father, she receives the first talent of singular love (53–57), which she repays with reverential love, and is ultimately enlightened and received by the Lord (108–9). It must have been profoundly painful for Teresa to experience the subsequent rejection of the fiction she constructed in *Grove*, cavalierly dismissed by her incredulous detractors as an impossibility.
    The prominence of the patriarchal father in her writing has been attributed by some (Hutton,

"The Cloisters of My Ears": Deafness, Gender, and Writing

Teresa's deafness is an important pivot of her self-presentation as an author. Deafness – and its correlate illness/affliction – provides the central metaphor of the treatise and functions both literally (Teresa's physical deafness) and figuratively (Teresa's spiritual deafness). The metaphor of deafness also grounds a series of allegorical paradoxes that pervade the text and are central to its theme: physical deafness/ spiritual hearing, physical illness/spiritual health, physical affliction/spiritual salvation. Loss of hearing is the pretext for Teresa's writing: while her deafness cuts her off from the world, it also provides her bond with the community of sufferers she addresses, for deafness authorizes Teresa's writing and occasions her exemplarity: "And she wrote this work in praise of God and for her own spiritual consolation and that of all those who suffer illness so that, forsaken of their physical health, they may place their desire in God who is true Health" (23). Finally, deafness is pivotal to how Teresa situates herself and her story in relation to prevailing gender ideologies and figures of selfhood, how she reads or interprets literary and cultural conventions, and how she reads or interprets herself.

In her attempt to constitute herself in her narrative, Teresa attends to two stories, those culturally constructed categories of male and female selfhood adumbrated in the Introduction (16–21 above):

> The mythologies of gender conflate human and male figures of selfhood, aligning male selfhood with culturally valued stories.
> . . . But the story of man is not exactly her story; and so her relationship to the empowering of male selfhood is inevitably problematic. To complicate matters further, she must also engage the fictions of selfhood that constitute the idea of woman and that specify the parameters of female subjectivity, including woman's problematic relationship to language, desire, power, and meaning.[16]

Marimón Llorca) to Teresa's Jewish background, but it may also respond to the isolation and paternal rejection suffered after the loss of her hearing (Teresa's mother was quite probably deceased at this time). What is extraordinary in her devotional text is the absolute lack of mention of the Virgin Mary, the loving maternal mediator markedly absent even in *Wonder at the Works of God*, where Teresa defends the possibility of women receiving acts of divine grace (the Virgin was a conventional presence in profeminist defenses in the late Middle Ages). This is all the more remarkable when we consider Teresa's family name (Cartagena/Santa María) and the tradition of her family coat of arms (see 4 n. 8). Although the Virgin is prominently cited in Pedro de Luna's consolatory treatise, her presence in *Grove* is restricted to the headliner preceding the title – possibly added by the copyist – quite outside the boundaries of Teresa's text, where affective religiosity is vested, instead, in the patriarchal Father and in Christ.

16 Smith, *A Poetics of Women's Autobiography*, 50. In negotiating maternal and paternal

Her deafness qualifies how she engages male and female figures of selfhood, Teresa's intertexts that shape her self-interpretation.

At the beginning of *Grove of the Infirm*, Teresa speaks of her loss of hearing, which probably occurred in her late teens or early twenties. She notes how involved she had been in the babble of worldly voices: "And thus enmeshed in the confusion of worldly chatter, with my understanding disordered and bound up in worldly cares, I could not hear the voices of holy doctrine that Scriptures teach us" (26). Indeed, Teresa's writing – even twenty years into her deafness – is steeped in orality, in formulaic language, repetitious style, rhetorical devices of popular sermons, proverbs, and popular wisdom (see Hutton, 29–31). Teresa continues: "But merciful God, who was with me in this din and with discreet observation saw my perdition and knew how important it was to my health to have the chatter cease so that I would better understand what was necessary for my salvation, signaled me with His hand to be quiet. And one may well say that this suffering is given to me by His hand" (26). The effect of Teresa's suffering is twofold: cloistered by her deafness, she turns inward; shut off from the physical voices of the world, she *reads*, tuning in to the spiritual voices of her "healthful books": "And since my suffering is of such a treacherous nature that it prevents me from hearing good as well as bad counsel, it is necessary that my consoling counsels be able to bring me to the cloister of their gracious and holy wisdom without shouting into my deaf ears; for this, I must recur to my books which have wondrous graftings from healthful groves" (24).

Susan Schibanoff has shown how increased female literacy in the late Middle Ages was an efficient means of immasculation, the process by which women learn "to think as men, to identify with a male point of view, and to accept as normal and legitimate a male system of values, one of whose central principles is misogyny."[17] Literate women, like Christine de Pizan and Teresa de Cartagena, confront the authoritative androcentric texts of their culture differently than their illiterate sisters. Oral cultures preserve literary and other "texts" through constant recitation; as texts are repeated, alterations occur according to current demands

---

narratives, the writer does not engage consciously the prevailing ideology of gender; rather, the double-voiced narrative of women's self-writing is inevitable, and this "situating of the autobiographer in two universes of discourse accounts for the poetics of women's autobiography and grounds its difference."

[17] Susan Schibanoff, "Taking the Gold Out of Egypt: The Art of Reading as a Woman," in *Gender and Reading: Essays on Readers, Texts, and Contexts*, ed. Elizabeth A. Flynn and Patrocinio P. Schweickart (Baltimore: The Johns Hopkins University Press, 1986), 83–106; the quote is from Judith Fetterley, *The Resisting Reader: A Feminist Approach to American Fiction* (Bloomington: Indiana University Press, 1978), xx.

of relevance and utility. Authority and tradition are readily altered or even eliminated to reflect the needs of a society's present cultural values and experience.[18] While, in the late Middle Ages, manuscript technology assured a uniformity and fixity of texts not possible in an oral culture, the means of textual dissemination and reception was predominantly oral/aural.[19] As Schibanoff notes, aural "readers" – like Chaucer's Wife of Bath – utilize the methodology and procedures of oral tradition: "She has no concept of the 'fixed' text of written tradition; unconsciously, she alters or destroys those authorities that conflict with her values or experiences. ... She resists immasculation because she instinctively rereads authority and tradition, a survival skill that does not come easily to the literate reader burdened by the immobile written records of the past" (89).[20]

Literacy, however, affords women readers no such freedom: the authority inscribed in "fixed" patriarchal texts triggers the reader's socialized inclination to adapt herself to the male viewpoint.[21] Teresa's deafness would make her even less resistant to this immasculation since it cuts her off from the alternative oral/aural subculture of other women and thrusts her, unmediated, into the dominant culture of male letters;[22] in the act of reading, Teresa tells us, she listens only to the voices of her texts.

What are these "voices" Teresa hears when she reads? Oliver Sacks emphasizes the crucial distinction between the postlingual deaf – the case

---

18 On orality in the Middle Ages and oral cultures, see Walter J. Ong, *Orality and Literacy: The Technologizing of the Word* (New York: Methuen, 1982); M.T. Clancy, *From Memory to Written Record: England, 1066–1307* (Cambridge, Mass.: Harvard University Press, 1979); and Franz H. Baüml, "Varieties and Consequences of Medieval Literacy and Illiteracy," *Speculum* 55 (1980): 237–65.

19 See, in addition to the works previously cited, Ruth Crosby, "Oral Delivery in the Middle Ages," *Speculum* 11 (1936): 88–110.

20 Thus Alisoun supports her argument for female supremacy in marriage by citing Paul's command that husbands love their wives (1 Corinthians 7:13), selectively forgetting the remaining command that wives obey their husbands; to justify her own multiple marriages, she offers the example of Old Testament patriarchs like Abraham and Jacob. As an aural reader, she remains relatively free to hear, remember, and reproduce texts according to her own concept of self and her own experience; unlike her literate counterparts, Christine and Teresa, Alisoun's rereadings are not inhibited by the fixity of words on a manuscript page.

21 See Judith Fetterley, *The Resisting Reader*; Elizabeth A. Flynn, "Gender and Reading," in *Gender and Reading*, 267–88; and Patrocinio P. Schweickart, "Reading Ourselves: Toward a Feminist Theory of Reading," in *Gender and Reading*, 31–62.

22 Schibanoff ("Taking the Gold Out of Egypt," 101) speculates that Christine de Pizan overcame her immasculation in part because of her private conversations with other women; these exchanges contradicted the misogyny of written male authorities and motivated her rewriting of patriarchal texts; the primary motivation for Christine's emasculation in *City of Women*, nevertheless, was her participation in the "Querelle des Femmes." Jane Chance's reading of the earlier *Letter of Othea* suggests that Christine's trajectory was not so linear, and that the *Othea* was not as traditional and patriarchal as Schibanoff maintains (*Christine de Pizan's Letter of Othea to Hector* [Newburyport: Focus Information Group, 1990]).

of Teresa de Cartagena – and the prelingual deaf (persons with congenital deafness or loss of hearing prior to the acquisition of language) in his exploration of the relation between language, thought, and culture.[23] Sacks refers to a male subject who had lost his hearing at the age of seven, at an age when he had already grasped the essentials of language and had mastered pronunciation, syntax, inflection, idiom, and a vocabulary which could be easily expanded by reading. This subject spoke of the phenomenon of "phantasmal voices" that he would hear when anyone spoke to him, provided that he could see the movement of lips and faces, of how he could "hear" the soughing of the wind whenever he saw trees or branches being stirred by a breeze. Although he knew these sounds to be illusory – "projections of habit and memory" – they remained intensely vivid for him throughout the decades of his deafness.

For those like Teresa de Cartagena, deafened after hearing is well established, the world may remain full of sounds even though these are "phantasmal." This hearing of phantasmal voices, when moving lips are perceived visually and visual signs are "heard," is quite characteristic of the postlingually deaf, for whom speech has once been an auditory experience. This is not "imagining" in the ordinary sense, but rather an instant and automatic "translation" of the visual experience into an auditory correlate, based on prior experience and association, a translation that probably has a neurological basis of experientially established visual/auditory connections, a transmodal transfer of knowledge from sight to sound.

When we recall that in the oral culture of the Middle Ages reading was almost invariably out loud,[24] we realize that when Teresa initiates a silent dialogue between herself and the phantasmal voices of her texts, the "voices" Teresa "hears" may well be the traces of her own voice, "projections of habit and memory" onto the written text. This would, in part, explain Teresa's remarkable capacity for interiorization, her in-

---

[23] *Seeing Voices: A Journey into the World of the Deaf* (Berkeley: University of California Press, 1989).

[24] Oral reading was characteristic of the individual reader in the Middle Ages and also of group readings; even professionals apparently processed meaning auditively rather than visually: "It was only in the late Empire that silent reading began to come into existence, and it seems to have remained an exceptional practice throughout the Middle Ages. There is abundant evidence that medieval *scriptoria* were noisy places filled with the sounds of the copyists reciting their texts. In addition, the character of medieval orthography clearly shows that the scribe's memory was auditory rather than visual" (Joseph Anthony Mazzeo, "St. Augustine's Rhetoric of Silence," *Journal of the History of Ideas* 23 [1962]: 190). See also Paul Zumthor, "Litteratus/illiteratus: Remarques sur le contexte vocal de l'écriture médiévale," *Romania* 106 (1985): 1–18; and Paul Saenger, "Silent Reading: Its Impact on Late Medieval Script and Society," *Viator* 13 (1982): 367–414.

tensely personal identification with literary texts, and, above all, her profound internalization of her male authorities; for if in one sense it is true that Teresa uses her personal experience to illustrate and gloss the *sententiae* of her devotional treatise, given her characteristic identification of self and text, she concomitantly uses literature to structure, define, dramatize, and give meaning to her own life.[25]

Teresa's deafness is also determinative to how she situates herself with regard to culturally constructed categories of women. Medieval gender ideologies established homologies between female sexuality, female speech, and female goodness predicated on the ideals of silence (closed mouth), virginity or chastity (closed womb), and enclosure in house or convent.[26] In her writing, Teresa figuratively associates her deafness with her entering the convent; God closed her ears to human voices, cloistering her hearing ("the cloisters of my ears") and enclosing her in a community of suffering ("the convent of affliction," "convent of the suffering," "convent of the infirm"). Although Teresa's figurative convent of suffering has more thematic presence in her work than her physical convent, medieval notions of the woman religious deeply inform her self-representation and her writing.

Both historically and theologically the celibate life of the woman religious is an empowering alternative to the life of inferiority and subordination outside the convent.[27] For the church fathers, virginity frees women from the malediction of Eve, from the sorrows of childbirth, and from subjection to male domination. Moreover, virginity and religious

---

[25]　Teresa's internalization of male literary analogues and authorities is so ingrained that although in *Wonder* she offers the story of Judith as an exemplum of blessings of grace conferred to women, she subsequently applies the blind man on the road to Jericho and an *imitatio Christi* as literary analogues in her self-writing.

[26]　Peter Stallybrass notes that control over woman's body in the early modern period concentrated on three specific areas – the mouth, chastity, and the domestic threshold – which were frequently collapsed into each other: "Silence, the closed mouth, is made a sign of chastity. And silence and chastity are, in turn, homologous to woman's enclosure within the house. ... The signs of the 'harlot' are her linguistic 'fullness' and her frequenting of public space" ("Patriarchal Territories: The Body Enclosed," in *Rewriting the Renaissance: The Discourses of Sexual Difference in Early Modern Europe*, ed. Margaret W. Ferguson, Maureen Quilligan, and Nancy J. Vickers [Chicago: University of Chicago Press, 1986], 126–27). These conventions are thoroughly internalized in Teresa's discourse; see, for example, the figure of the gadding woman applied to Teresa's wandering understanding (109–10).

[27]　See JoAnn McNamara and Suzanne Wemple, "Sanctity and Power: The Dual Pursuit of Medieval Women," in *Becoming Visible: Women in European History*, ed. Renate Bridenthal and Claudia Koonz (Boston: Houghton Mifflin, 1977), 90–118; McLaughlin, "Equality of Souls, Inequality of Sexes," 213–66, and "Women, Power, and the Pursuit of Holiness in Medieval Christianity," in *Women of Spirit: Female Leadership in the Jewish and Christian Traditions*, ed. Rosemary Ruether and Eleanor McLaughlin (New York: Simon & Schuster, 1979), 99–130.

profession can effectively immasculate a woman by freeing her of those "natural" female inferiorities of mind and body that would otherwise compromise her salvation. Several church fathers argue the transsexuality of religious devotion and virginity:

> She who does not believe is a woman and should be designated by the name of her bodily sex, whereas she who believes progresses to complete manhood, to the measure of the adulthood of Christ.[28]

> As long as woman is for birth and children, she is different from man as body is from soul. But if she wishes to serve Christ more than the world, then she will cease to be a woman and will be called a man.[29]

> [The virgin], forgetful of her natural feminine weakness, lives in manly vigor and has used virtue to give strength to her weak sex, nor has she become a slave to her body, which, by natural law, should have been subservient to a man.[30]

For the woman religious, virginity and religious profession are "not an affirmation of her being as a woman but an assumption of the nature of the male, which is identified with the truly human: rationality, strength, courage, steadfastness, loyalty."[31] Only the female, whose existence and finality are defined by her auxiliary procreative function, must deny what society has determined as her nature to follow the religious life; the male, constructed in terms of a superior rationality, realizes his "natural" potential upon entering the religious life, his celibacy suppressing what is external to his being (McLaughlin, "Equality of Souls, Inequality of Sexes," 234–35).

The imposition of Teresa's deafness initiates a process of cloistering (enclosure and reclusion) that rhetorically establishes her "goodness" by

[28] St. Ambrose, *Expositio evangelis secundum Lucam*; quoted by Vern L. Bullough, "Medieval Medical and Scientific Views of Women," *Viator: Medieval and Renaissance Studies* 4 (1973): 499.

[29] St. Jerome, *Commentariorum in Epistolam ad Ephesios Libri 3*; quoted by Bullough, "Medieval Medical and Scientific Views of Women," 499.

[30] Leander of Seville, *De Institutione Virginitatis*; quoted by Rosemary Radford Ruether, "Misogynism and Virginal Feminism in the Fathers of the Church," in *Religion and Sexism*, 159.

[31] McLaughlin, "Equality of Souls, Inequality of Sexes," 234. McLaughlin demonstrates, however, how Christianity's theoretical equivalence between male and female souls in the order of salvation and in religious life was from the first undercut by fundamentally androcentric conceptions.

distancing her from misogynous paradigms of "woman" and symbolically enables her assumption of masculinity, of human exemplarity. If, however, the closing of her ears is presented as an act of God, the subsequent closing of her mouth is presented as an act of Teresa. Her refusal to speak cloisters her from the outside public world (she refuses worldly conversations and visits [27]) and cloisters her desire: she rechannels her desire from the worldly to the spiritual ("for it would be of little profit to separate myself from these worldly things if my desire and care were still involved with them" [28]) and reconciles her desire with her suffering ("And I, who up until now desired but was not able to spend my time in worldly conversations, am no longer able nor inclined to have the power to fulfill such a harmful desire" [29]).[32] Teresa's own repression of speech completes the process initiated by her deafness by attaining full silence (ears and voice), full erasure from public life (no visits or conversations), full closure of the body (closed womb, closed ears, closed mouth), and full occlusion of worldly desire.

Teresa's exemplarity is compromised only in the transgressive act of breaking her silence and writing her story. Her awareness of this transgression is the source of her anxiety of authorship and the literary strategies applied to negotiate that anxiety (self-deprecating humility formulas, appropriation of male authorities, inscription of a female reader, oblique autobiography, figurative positioning of her self, double-voiced narrative structure). That her anxiety was well founded is evidenced in the prologue to *Wonder at the Works of God*, where she recounts the antagonistic reception of *Grove of the Infirm* by those prudent men who rejected a woman's access to writing and, more importantly, disputed Teresa's authorship of her own autobiographical and devotional text. In defending her right to write and asserting her authorship of *Grove*, Teresa thematizes some of the theoretical issues – the social construction of gender, the gendered conventions of medieval literature and literary authority – presented as background to her first work and ultimately offers her own exegesis of her text and her final interpretation of her self.

---

32 Teresa metaphorically casts worldly desire in terms of speech rather than sexuality. Her resistance to consider issues of sexuality is evident in her discussion of the seven sins; in her first catalogue (58), lust is the only deadly sin not directly named ("[suffering] extinguishes fires and promotes chastity") and is omitted altogether in the second (61). See Alan Deyermond, " 'El convento de dolençias': The Works of Teresa de Cartagena," *Journal of Hispanic Philology* 1 (1976): 27.

"And He Alone Read (to) Me": *Admiración operum Dey*[33]

> Women who do not challenge those gender
> ideologies and the boundaries they place
> around woman's proper life script, textual in-
> scription, and speaking voice do not write
> autobiography.[34]

Wonder at the Works of God is the product of a sustained critical rereading by Teresa of her previous text – and, therefore, of her self – and of the literary, social, and cultural conventions that provide the context for both her own writing and the hostility of her detractors. In addressing her right to read and write according to her experience and interests, Teresa becomes a more self-conscious and critical reader/writer in *Wonder at the Works of God*. This is not to infer a radical ideological shift between Teresa's earlier confessional and devotional writing and her subsequent profeminist defense.[35] The act of writing *Grove of the Infirm* – as the opening quote above reminds us – was in itself transgressive and a source of tension that I have examined as an anxiety of authorship. *Grove* is not a conservative or naive text but a problematic and ambitious work – somewhat schizophrenic – that halfway through (beginning with the

---

[33] Teresa's unusual bilingual title anticipates her arguments about the constructed tradition of male letters. In "Latin Language Study as a Renaissance Puberty Rite," *Studies in Philology* 56 (1959): 103–24, and *The Presence of the Word: Some Prolegomena for Cultural and Religious History* (Minneapolis: University of Minnesota Press, 1981), 249–52, Walter J. Ong discusses how in the Middle Ages, the mother tongue, the vernacular, was in large part the language of the illiterate while Latin became a sex-linked language, a badge of male identity, taught as a rite of passage in the schools. Josephine Donovan ("The Silence Is Broken," in *Women and Language in Literature and Society*, ed. Sally McConnell-Ginet, Ruth Borker, and Nelly Furman [New York: Praeger, 1980], 205–18) examines the effects of the masculinizing of Latin on early women writers.
In *Grove* Teresa intercalates Latin phrases to establish her knowledge of Latin and her authoritative status as a lettered person: "Oprobrium hominum et abiecio plebis" (23), "In camo et freno maxillas eorum constrinje, qui non aproximant ad te" (26), "Libenter gloriabor" (42), "façere et doçere" (74). The prominent situating of *operum Dey* in her title insistently flags her deliberate re-entry into the field of male letters.
[34] Smith, *A Poetics of Women's Autobiography*, 44; "Choosing to write autobiography, therefore, she unmasks her transgressive desire for cultural and literary authority" (50).
[35] I am not proposing for Teresa the kind of ideological conversion Schibanoff traces for Christine de Pizan from the immasculated reader who composed the *Letter of Othea to Hector* to the "woman reader" who presents feminist rereadings of women's history in *Book of the City of Women* (see 126 n. 22). Fetterley's idea of the immasculated reader is helpful in understanding Teresa's intensely personal identification with her male authorities, but an immasculated reader who has been indoctrinated to read like a man does not necessarily *write* like a man. Women's writing in the patriarchal literary culture of the fifteenth century is by definition transgressive and ridden with an anxiety of authorship; moreover, women's self-writing, as we have seen, involves a complex negotiation of both paternal and maternal narratives of selfhood.

discussion of patience, 47–85) abandons the transgressive autobiographical project. *Wonder* represents not a break but a deepening awareness by Teresa of what she had attempted and accomplished in *Grove*; there is considerable continuity between the two works, as we might expect in an apologetic defense that both thematizes and reaffirms the prior act of writing.

In defending and thematizing *Grove*, the anxiety of authorship characteristic of the earlier work is resolved in an assertiveness that is evident from the beginning of *Wonder*: "I remember, virtuous lady, that I offered to write at your discretion . . ." Gone is the pretext of the requested work, the oblique self-dramatization through literary analogues, and the figurative landscape to position that self; Teresa takes on responsibility for her writing and directly and literally positions herself in her text. The double-voiced structuring of content and rhetoric in *Grove* that proceeds from Teresa's negotiation of two universes of discourse – male and female – is replaced in *Wonder* with a pervasive irony that proceeds from her double audience and subtends the structure and rhetoric of her defense. In *Grove*, Teresa directs her confessional autobiography primarily to her inscribed reader, "virtuous lady," and secondarily to a more general audience of which "virtuous lady" is an extension. In *Wonder*, "virtuous lady" serves as the pretext for Teresa's writing ("And because they tell me, virtuous lady, that this abovementioned sheaf of rough draft papers has come to the attention of Señor Gómez Manrique and yourself, I do not know if these same doubts surrounding my treatise have occurred to you" [88]), but she is not identified with the secondary readership of Teresa's defense, those prudent men who are her detractors. Teresa's ironic commentary is thus aimed at a double audience: her defense is ostensibly addressed to the "virtuous lady" who acts more as an accomplice than a judge,[36] but rhetorical points are scored against her hostile but absent and silenced detractors.[37]

36 Because "virtuous lady" is an extension in *Grove* of a greater audience and because her principal rhetorical function is to initiate Teresa's writing, she is only directly addressed once in the earlier and much longer work. In contrast, she is invoked repeatedly in *Wonder* (eleven times) and her complicity is underscored in the affective formulas applied to her ("very discreet lady," "most discreet and beloved lady," "most virtuous lady," "my great lady," "most beloved lady").

37 Examples abound in the ironically exaggerated modesty formulas Teresa applies to herself and the equally exaggerated flattery she heaps on her critics ("And from this it follows that if a womanly text of little substance is worthy of reprehension among common men, with greater reason it would inspire consternation in exceptional and great men, for not without cause does the prudent man marvel when he sees that a fool can speak" [88]). Later, having noted that God created woman as a helpmeet to man, Teresa ironically comments: "And one could well argue here whether the helped or the helper has the greater strength, and you clearly see what reason would respond" (92). Having scored her point, she interjects an

As the basis of her defense, Teresa argues the social rather than divine construction of gender: "And thus, if it pleased God to make the male sex robust and valiant and the female weak and of little strength, one should not believe that He did this to confer more advantage or excellence to one condition than the other, but only, I believe, for the abovementioned purpose, so that with one helping the other, human nature might be preserved, and the marvelous works of His omnipotence and wisdom and goodness be noted" (155–56). While God invested the sexes with certain differences, these have been subsequently constructed into gender hierarchies of superiority and inferiority.

Literary conventions are likewise socially constructed, not divinely ordained: "For men have had the practice of writing books and learning and applying their learning since such ancient times that apparently this is assumed to be the natural course of things, and therefore no one wonders. But since women have not had this custom nor have acquired learning, and since their understanding is not as perfect as men's, it is considered a marvel" (92). Consequently, the institution of literature and learning has been passed down from male to male: "Yet if they were to consider it well, they would find that those who now are masters in another time were disciples, and those whose disciples they were were taught by yet another master. And thus by men teaching each other and learning, acquired knowledge came into the hands of its present male practitioners . . ." (99). Male letters is thus an example of the blessings of nature and of fortune, those sublunary blessings we often attribute to people here on earth although their ultimate source is God (95–96).

Women's writing, on the other hand, is a blessing of grace: "However, the greater and more exceptional blessings of grace He reserved for Himself, for these blessings we attain neither through the effort of nature, nor the good luck of fortune, nor through any human art or ingenuity, but only through the goodness and mercy and grace of God" (96). She lists

---

ironic disclaimer: "But these arguments and disputes make for worldly and vain arrogance [i.e., like the accusations of her detractors] and do not profit devotion and divert my intention from its purpose and end, which, may it please God, is not to offend the superior and honorable condition of prudent men nor to favor women but rather to praise the omnipotence and wisdom and greatness of God . . . " (92).

Not the least irony is the tautology of "prudent men" in the first part of Teresa's text, all the more striking in Spanish because of the position of the adjective (*prudentes varones* instead of *varones prudentes*). In the latter case, the descriptive adjective differentiates a group of men, but in Teresa's case – *prudentes varones* – the descriptive adjective becomes an epithet and precedes the noun, denoting an inherent characteristic of the noun taken as a whole. Thus the unnecessary repetition of *prudentes varones* while Teresa is demonstrating that their incredulity is, in fact, unwise ironically insinuates that their prudence is culturally assigned because of their maleness, not determined by their actions.

seven examples of blessings of grace, concluding "and if we see that women write treatises, we shall praise the gifts of His holy grace and divine generosity" (98). Moreover, Teresa strategically insists on the inscrutability of such blessings: "for with blessings of grace it is not fitting to scrutinize or judge the condition of the person – male or female – nor the disposition and ability of his intellect, whether very capable or totally insufficient, nor the merit of his deeds, whether he is righteous or a very great sinner. For divine grace surpasses and exceeds all this and more and abundantly fills the blank spaces of our defects" (96).

In refuting the socially constructed inferiority of women, Teresa also calls into question other literary conventions. To illustrate her point that God created differences between man and woman "so that each would be the preservation and adjunct of the other," Teresa offers a botanical example:

> And if you observe well the plants and trees, you will see how their outer bark or cortex is very robust and strong and resistant to the weather, to tempest and water and ice, and heat and cold. They are made in such a way that their firm and resilient bark protects the inner core or medulla enclosed within. And thus in this order the one works for the other, for the strength and hardness of the bark protects and preserves the medulla by resisting on the outside the inclemencies of the weather. The medulla, encased because it is weak and delicate, works inwardly and gives power and vigor to the bark; and thus the one preserves and helps the other and gives us each year the diversity and abundance of fruits that we see.

> And in this same way, I believe, our sovereign and powerful Lord wants these two opposites in human nature to operate: the masculine condition, strong and valiant, and the feminine, weak and delicate (91).

Teresa here inverts the gendering of allegorical reading which associates the outer, pleasurable, "lying" surface of the text, the cortex (*corteza*), the letter that appeals to the physical senses with sinful carnality (the flesh, the body) and with woman, and the hidden inner core of the text, the medulla (*meollo*), the spirit that appeals to the intellect with man. Woman in the traditional Pauline model of reading is the text's letter that must be passed through, stripped away, or penetrated to get to its truth, its spirit – its male spirit, as St. Ambrose and other church fathers suggest.[38] By

---

[38] See Dinshaw, *Chaucer's Sexual Poetics*, 19–22; the gendering of patristic heuristic models is ultimately traced to exegetical readings of the creation associating Eve with fallen language and Adam with its truth. See above, 18 n. 32.

homologizing male/*corteza* and female/*meollo*, Teresa subverts conventional patristic paradigms of allegorical reading and associates woman
with spirit and the higher truth, man with carnality and the letter.[39]
There is another tradition of gendered hermeneutics in the Middle
Ages that identifies acts of writing and related acts of signifying –
allegorizing, interpreting, glossing, translating – with the masculine and
the surfaces on which these acts are performed – the page, the text – with
the feminine.[40] Teresa invokes this hermeneutic paradigm in her beauti-
fully expressive reaffirmation of authorship of *Grove*:

> People marvel at what I wrote in the treatise and I marvel at
> what, in fact, I kept quiet, but I do not marvel doubting nor do I
> insist on my wonder. For my experience makes me sure, and the
> God of Truth knows that I had no other master nor consulted with
> any other learned authority nor translated from other books, as
> some people with malicious wonder are wont to say. Rather, this
> alone is the truth: that God of all knowledge, Lord of all virtues,
> Father of mercy, God of every consolation, He who consoles us
> in all our tribulation, He alone consoled me, He alone taught me,
> He alone read (to) me. He inclined His ear to me when I, besieged
> with great anguish and adrift in a deep sea of misfortunes, called
> upon Him with the Prophet, saying, "Save me, O God: for the
> waters are come in even unto my soul" [Psalm 68:2] (102–3).

The wonderfully enigmatic and suggestive image of God *reading* Teresa's
body as a text – her closed and silent body that has been imprinted with
her suffering[41] – recalls Teresa's identification of her self and her text in
Grove of the Infirm. Moreover, God's act of reading Teresa entails
listening to her inner voice just as Teresa when reading listens to the voices
of her books ("and He alone read me. He inclined His ear to me . . ."").
Teresa, then, positions herself as a (feminine) text that God reads and
interprets; as a consequence of His reading, He enlightens her under-

---

[39] The passage recalls an earlier subversive reading in *Grove* in Teresa's convoluted exegesis
of Psalm 44:11 ("Listen, O daughter, and behold, and incline thy ear: forget thy people and
the house of thy father"). There Teresa interpreted the source of sin as male rather than
female in homologizing father/bad desire: "for just as the father is the beginning and
engenderer of his children, so bad desire is the beginning and engenderer of sins" (32).

[40] Dinshaw, *Chaucer's Sexual Poetics*, 9. Masculine and feminine denote "roles, positions,
functions that can be taken up, occupied, or performed by either sex, male or female
(although not with equal ease or investment . . .)." Moreover, the significance and value of
the masculine and the feminine in such a model of gendered hermeneutics can constantly
shift and change in the exegetical tradition (9) and, as we shall see, in Teresa's defense.

[41] See Teresa's discussion of the third talent of mortification (63–68) made with the metal of
insinuation: "This mortification is like the stamp of our suffering, for just as a seal placed
over wax leaves its own impression, so afflictions with the stamp of mortification impress
on the body and face of the sufferer the seal of its own coat of arms" (63–64).

standing so that she acquires the knowledge to write her treatise – hence
the more conventional reading of "El solo me leyó" ("He alone read to
me").[42]

Yet Teresa would argue that this feminine position is, in fact, occupied
by all writers, male and female, and only the conventionality of male
authorship has diverted our recognition from God as the ultimate *Auctor*
who interprets, glosses, and authorizes meaning.[43] Teresa redefines patriarchal notions of male authorship by referring these to God, who then
authorizes the writing of texts by illuminating human understanding and
revealing His truth and knowledge. This is a remarkable strategy in
Teresa's defense: by femininizing both male and female writers with
regard to God, she rewrites and expands the androcentric perspective of
her detractors. This need for problematizing and redefinition remains a
challenge for contemporary feminists as well: "However, the posture of
resistance and combat that perforce she [the feminist reader/critic] adopts
imposes its own distortions. In particular, the female viewpoint becomes
defined negatively and thus remains a function of what it opposes."[44]
Teresa's strategy circumvents this negative definition of her viewpoint
and confounds stable and distinct binary categories of gender.

Teresa's defense is implemented through a variety of complementary
strategies. Initially in general terms she questions the conventionality and
constructedness of the tradition of male letters and learning; imbricated
in her discussion is her own personal experience of authoring *Grove of
the Infirm* and the subtle subversion of gendered medieval literary theory
and practices. The primary purpose of her defense, nevertheless, is to
reclaim the text her detractors have denied her. In the first half of *Wonder*,
Teresa reaffirms her authorship by arguing its possibility, the possibility
of women's writing as a blessing of grace (86–101); in the second half
she reaffirms her authorship by re-enacting its praxis (101–12). Here
Teresa reoccupies the interdicted (masculine) position of *auctor* and
writes – allegorizing, interpreting, glossing, and translating anew – re-
suming and ultimately completing the failed autobiographical project
initiated in *Grove of the Infirm.*

[42] Compare: "nor does our merciful Father disdain to sit in the seat of the understanding of the
simple and to read to them marvelous lessons" (99).

[43] "Yet no one marvels if men write books or compendious treatises, for this is attributed to
the very brain and sufficiency of understanding of the male author and to the great and
'natural' learning that he knows; and nothing is said about the glory of God, nor do I think
they remember whence came this 'natural' knowledge that men acquire in their studies . . .
[B]ut were we to inquire further, we would find that knowledge as well as the ingenuity and
grace to teach and learn all descended and descend from one Fount, for God alone is the
Lord of all knowledge" (98–99).

[44] Schweickart and Flynn, "Introduction," in *Gender and Reading*, xx.

The autobiographical account in *Grove* ends with Teresa's exegesis of the parable of the supper of the Lamb (Luke 14:16–24). The infirm are brought by their afflictions to a magnificent supper the Lord has prepared for them. Some enter willingly by calling at the door with their prayers; others – Teresa among them – linger in the streets outside, their desire and care bound up in the temporal plazas and marketplaces of this world (40–41). Yet recently Teresa experienced a sign of new spiritual life, a recognition of her own dangerous obstinacy and an appreciation of the great good of her suffering. She reacts by seeking the Lord with prayer, confessing her guilt, praising His mercy, glorying in her suffering.

In *Wonder at the Works of God*, Teresa resumes her autobiographical narrative with the parable of the blind man on the road to Jericho. The figurative landscape is one of spiritual conflict and struggle, for the road is crowded with residents from the worldly city of Jericho, "disordered thoughts and a great mob of temporal concerns" that try to silence Teresa's blind understanding as with secret voices it calls out to God.[45] The Lord responds to the request for spiritual vision – Teresa's fervent litany "may I see the light" (105) – by illuminating her understanding so that "it saw and followed its Savior, extolling God." Teresa immediately rebukes her critics: "Therefore, let those who wonder, doubting the treatise I composed, leave their doubt . . ." Not only does she rewrite her text but she also offers her own exegesis of her own text:

> And I wrote that treatise that deals with this intellectual light and
> the lesson I learned, which is: to praise God and to know God,
> and to know myself and to deny my will and conform it to His
> will; and to take in the hands of my inner understanding the cross
> of suffering I endure, and to follow my Savior in the footsteps of
> spiritual affliction; and to exalt God through the confession of
> my tongue, giving laud and praise to His holy name, recounting
> to the people the fairness of His justice, the greatness of His
> mercy, and His magnificence and glory (109).

Teresa reasserts her authorship and ultimately reclaims her text by completing the autobiographical project suspended halfway through *Grove of the Infirm* and by tracing her journey toward spiritual understanding ("to know God") and self-knowledge ("to know myself"), a journey that ends in Teresa's final biblical analogue, a daring *imitatio Christi* ("to take in the hands of my inner understanding the cross of the suffering I endure, and to follow my Savior in the footsteps of spiritual

---

[45] The parable of the blind man on the road to Jericho (103–6) in *Wonder* links up with the autobiographical narrative of *Grove* through the extensive interlacing of imagery documented in the notes to the text.

affliction") and in the writing of her texts "to exalt God through the confession of my tongue, giving laud and praise to His holy name, recounting to the people the fairness of His justice, the greatness of His mercy, and His magnificence and glory." In cataloguing the lessons she learned, sandwiched between the exaltation and knowledge of God and the abnegation and shaping of her will is Teresa's recognition of the self-knowledge she achieved in the writing of her autobiographical project ("to know myself"), the site of the quiet resolve and gentle irony of her defense as she establishes her text – and the self she constructs in her texts – as one of the admirable works of God.

Select Bibliography

Abel, Elizabeth. *Writing and Sexual Difference.* Chicago: University of Chicago Press, 1980–82.

Aers, David, ed. *Medieval Literature: Criticism, Ideology, and History.* Brighton: Harvester Press, 1986.

Alcalá, Angel, ed. *Inquisición española y mentalidad inquisitorial: Ponencias del Simposio Internacional sobre Inquisición, Nueva York, abril de 1983.* Barcelona: Ariel, 1983.

Allen, Prudence, R.S.M. *The Concept of Woman: The Aristotelian Revolution, 750 B.C. to 1250 A.D.* Montreal: Eden Press, 1985.

Amador de los Ríos, José. *Historia social, política y religiosa de los judíos de España y Portugal.* Biblioteca Histórica, 1. Buenos Aires: Bajel, 1943.

Arenal, Electa, and Stacey Schlau. *Untold Sisters: Hispanic Nuns in Their Own Works.* Albuquerque: University of New Mexico Press, 1989.

Ariès, Philippe, and Georges Duby, eds. *A History of Private Life: Revelations of the Medieval World.* Cambridge, Mass.: The Belknap Press of Harvard University Press, 1988.

Baer, Yitzhak. *Historia de los judíos en la España cristiana.* 2 vols. Madrid: Atalena, 1981.

Baüml, Franz H. "Varieties and Consequences of Medieval Literacy and Illiteracy." *Speculum* 55 (1980): 237–65.

Beinart, Haim. *Los conversos ante el tribunal de la Inquisición.* Barcelona: Riopiedras, 1983.

Benito Ruano, Eloy. *Toledo en el siglo XV: Vida política.* Madrid: Consejo Superior de Investigaciones Científicas, 1961.

———. *Los orígenes del problema converso.* Barcelona: El Albir, 1976.

Bennassar, Bartolomé. *L'Inquisition espagnole: XVe–XIXe siècle.* Paris: Hachette, 1979.

Benstock, Shari, ed. *The Private Self: Theory and Practice of Women's Autobiographical Writings.* Chapel Hill: University of North Carolina Press, 1988.

Blamires, Alcuin, ed. *Woman Defamed and Woman Defended: An Anthology of Medieval Texts.* Oxford: Clarendon Press, 1992.

Bloch, R. Howard. "Medieval Misogyny." In *Misogyny, Misandry, and Misanthropy,* eds. Bloch and Frances Ferguson, 1–24. Berkeley: University of California Press, 1989.

———. *Medieval Misogyny and the Invention of Western Romantic Love.* Chicago: University of Chicago Press, 1991.

Bloom, Harold. *The Anxiety of Influence.* New York: Oxford University Press, 1973.

Blumenfeld-Kosinski, Renate, and Timea Szell, eds. *Images of Sainthood in Medieval Europe.* Ithaca: Cornell University Press, 1991.

Boethius, Ancius Manliu Severinus. *Philosophiae Consolationis.* Loeb Classical Library. Cambridge, Mass: Harvard University Press, 1962.

Braunstein, Philippe. "Toward Intimacy: The Fourteenth and Fifteenth Centuries." In *Revelations of the Medieval World,* ed. Ariès and Duby, 535–630.

Bridenthal, Renate, and Claudia Koonz, eds. *Becoming Visible: Women in European History.* Boston: Houghton Mifflin, 1977.

Brodski, Bella, and Celeste Schenck, eds. *Life/Lines: Theorizing Women's Autobiography.* Ithaca: Cornell University Press, 1988.

Brownlee, Kevin, and Stephen G. Nichols, eds. *Images of Power: Medieval History/Discourse/Literature.* Yale French Studies, 70. New Haven: Yale University Press, 1986.

Brownlee, Kevin, and Walter Stephens, eds. *Discourses of Authority in Medieval and Renaissance Literature.* Hanover: University Press of New England, 1989.

Brownlee, Marina S., Kevin Brownlee, and Stephen G. Nichols, eds. *The New Medievalism.* Baltimore: The Johns Hopkins University Press, 1991.

Brundage, James A. *Law, Sex, and Christian Society in Medieval Europe.* Chicago: University of Chicago Press, 1987.

Bruss, Elizabeth. *Autobiographical Acts: The Changing Situation of a Literary Genre.* Baltimore: The Johns Hopkins University Press, 1976.

Bullough, Vern L. "Medieval Medical and Scientific Views of Women." *Viator: Medieval and Renaissance Studies* 4 (1973): 485–501.

Burrow, J.B. *The Ages of Man: A Study in Medieval Writing and Thought.* Oxford: Clarendon Press, 1986.

Bynum, Caroline Walker. *Jesus as Mother: Studies in the Spirituality of the High Middle Ages.* Berkeley: University of California Press, 1982.

———. *Holy Feast and Holy Fast: The Religious Significance of Food to Medieval Women.* Berkeley: University of California Press, 1987.

Cantera Burgos, Francisco. *Alvar García de Santa María y su familia de conversos: historia de la judería de Burgos y de sus conversos más egregios.* Madrid: Instituto Arias Montano, 1952.

Caro Baroja, Julio. *Las formas complejas de la vida religiosa (Religión, sociedad y carácter en la España de los siglos XVI y XVII).* Madrid: Akal, 1978.

Casagrande, Carla. "The Protected Woman." In *Silences of the Middle Ages,* ed. Klapisch-Zuber, 70–104.

Castro, Américo. *The Structure of Spanish History.* Princeton: Princeton University Press, 1954.

Certeau, Michel de. *The Practice of Everyday Life.* Berkeley: University of California Press, 1984.

Chance, Jane. *Christine de Pizan's Letter of Othea to Hector.* Translated with Introduction, Notes, and Interpretative Essay. Newburyport: Focus Information, 1990.

Chazan, Robert. *Daggers of Faith: Thirteenth-Century Christian Missionizing and Jewish Response.* Berkeley: University of California Press, 1989.

———. *Barcelona and Beyond: The Disputation of 1263 and Its Aftermath.* Berkeley: University of California Press, 1992.

Clanchy, M.T. *From Memory to Written Record: England, 1066–1307.* Cambridge, Mass.: Harvard University Press, 1979.

Clark, Elizabeth, and Herbert Richardson, eds. *Women and Religion: A Feminist Sourcebook of Christian Thought.* New York: Harper & Row, 1977.

Cohen, Jeremy. *The Friars and the Jews: The Evolution of Medieval Anti-Judaism.* Ithaca: Cornell University Press, 1982.

Correas, Gonzalo. *Vocabulario de refranes y frases coloquiales.* Madrid: Revista de Archivos, Bibliotecas y Museos, 1924.

Couser, G. Thomas. "Autopathography: Women, Illness, and Lifewriting." *A/B: Autobiography Studies* 6:2 (1991): 65–75.

Covarrubias, Sebastián de. *Tesoro de la lengua castellana o española.* Barcelona: Horta, 1943.

Crosby, Ruth. "Oral Delivery in the Middle Ages." *Speculum* 11 (1936): 88–110.

Culler, Jonathan D. "Reading Like a Woman." In *On Deconstruction: Theory and Criticism after Structuralism.* Ithaca: Cornell University Press, 1982.

Davis, Natalie Zemon. *Society and Culture in Early Modern France.* Stanford: Stanford University Press, 1975.

de Man, Paul. "Autobiography as De-facement." *Modern Language Notes* 94 (1979): 919–30.

Deyermond, Alan. " 'El convento de dolençias': The Works of Teresa de Cartagena." *Journal of Hispanic Philology* 1 (1976–77): 19–29.

———. "Spain's First Women Writers." In *Women in Hispanic Literature: Icons and Fallen Idols,* ed. Beth Miller, 27–52. Berkeley: University of California Press, 1983.

———. "Historia universal e ideología nacional en Pablo de Santa María." In *Homenaje a Alvaro Galmés de Fuentes,* 2: 313–24. Madrid: Gredos, 1985.

———. "Las autoras medievales castellanas a la luz de las últimas investigaciones." In *Medioevo y Literatura: Actas del V Congreso de la Asociación Hispánica de Literatura Medieval, I,* ed. Juan Paredes, 31–52. Granada: Universidad de Granada, 1995.

Diamond, Arlyn, and Lee R. Edwards, eds. *The Authority of Experience: Essays in Feminist Criticism.* Amherst: University of Massachusetts Press, 1977.

Di Camillo, Ottavio. *El humanismo castellano del siglo XV.* Valencia: Fernando Torres, 1976.

————. "Humanism in Spain." In *Renaissance Humanism: Foundations, Forms, and Legacy, 2: Humanism beyond Italy*, ed. Albert Rabil, Jr., 55–108. Philadelphia: University of Pennsylvania Press, 1988.

Dillard, Heath. *Daughters of the Reconquest: Women in Castilian Town Society, 1100–1300*. Cambridge: Cambridge University Press, 1985.

Dinshaw, Carolyn. *Chaucer's Sexual Poetics*. Madison: University of Wisconsin Press, 1989.

Donovan, Josephine. "The Silence is Broken." In *Women and Language in Literature and Society*, ed. McConnell-Ginet, Borker, and Furman, 205–18.

Dronke, Peter. *Women Writers of the Middle Ages: A Critical Study of Texts from Perpetua (+203) to Marguerite Porete (+1310)*. Cambridge: Cambridge University Press, 1984.

Eckenstein, Lina. *Women Under Monasticism: Chapters on Saint-Lore and Convent Life Between A.D. 500 and A.D. 1500*. Repr. New York: Russell and Russell, 1963.

Edwards, John. *The Jews in Christian Europe 1400–1700*. London: Routledge, 1988.

Ellis, Deborah S. "The Image of the Home in Early English and Spanish Literature." Ph.D. Diss. University of California, Berkeley, 1981.

————. "Unifying Imagery in the Works of Teresa de Cartagena: Home and the Dispossessed." Forthcoming, *Journal of Hispanic Philology*.

Erler, Mary, and Maryanne Kowaleski, eds. *Women and Power in the Middle Ages*. Athens: University of Georgia Press, 1988.

Faur, José. *In the Shadow of History: Jews and Conversos at the Dawn of Modernity*. Albany: State University of New York Press, 1992.

Féral, Josette. "Antigone or the Irony of the Tribe." *Diacritics* 8 (1978): 2–14.

Ferrante, Joan. *Woman as Image in Medieval Literature: From the Twelfth Century to Dante*. New York: Columbia University Press, 1975.

————. "The Education of Women in the Middle Ages in Theory, Fact, and Fantasy." In *Beyond Their Sex: Learned Women of the European Past*, ed. Patricia H. Labalme, 9–42. New York: New York University Press, 1980.

Fetterley, Judith. *The Resisting Reader: A Feminist Approach to American Fiction*. Bloomington: Indiana University Press, 1978.

Finke, Laurie A. *Feminist Theory, Women's Writing*. Ithaca: Cornell University Press, 1992.

Finke, Laurie A., and Martin B. Shichtman, eds. *Medieval Texts and Contemporary Readers*. Ithaca: Cornell University Press, 1987.

Fisher, Sheila, and Janet E. Halley, eds. *Seeking the Woman in Late Medieval and Renaissance Writings*. Knoxville: The University of Tennessee Press, 1989.

Flynn, Elizabeth. "Gender and Reading." In *Gender and Reading*, ed. Flynn and Schweickart, 267–88.

Flynn, Elizabeth, and Patrocinio P. Schweickart, eds. *Gender and Reading:*

Essays on Readers, Texts, and Contexts. Baltimore: The Johns Hopkins University Press, 1986.

Friedman, Susan Stanford. "Women's Autobiographical Selves: Theory and Practice." In *The Private Self,* ed. Benstock, 34–62.

Furman, Nelly. "Textual Feminism." In *Women and Language,* ed. McConnell-Ginet, Borker, and Furman, 45–54.

Gilbert, Sandra, and Susan Gubar. *The Madwoman in the Attic: The Woman Writer and the Nineteenth-Century Literary Imagination.* New Haven: Yale University Press, 1979.

Giles, Mary. *The Book of Prayer of Sor María of Santo Domingo: A Study and Translation.* Albany: State University of New York Press, 1990.

Gilligan, Carol. *In a Different Voice.* Cambridge, Mass.: Harvard University Press, 1982.

Gilman, Stephen. *The Spain of Fernando de Rojas: The Intellectual and Social Landscape of "La Celestina."* Princeton: Princeton University Press, 1972.

Gitlitz, David M., *Secrecy and Deceit: the Religion of the Crypto-Jews.* Philadelphia: The Jewish Publication Society, 1996.

Goldberg, Harriet. "Two Parallel Medieval Commonplaces: Antifeminism and Antisemitism in the Hispanic Literary Tradition." In *Aspects of Jewish Culture in the Middle Ages,* ed. Paul E. Szarmach, 85–119. Albany: State University of New York Press, 1974.

Graff, Harvey J. *The Legacies of Literacy: Continuities and Contradictions in Western Culture and Society.* Bloomington: Indiana University Press, 1987.

Greenberg, Caren. "Reading Reading: Echo's Abduction of Language." In *Women and Language,* ed. McConnell-Ginet, Borker, and Furman, 300–9.

Gunn, Janet Varner. *Autobiography: Toward a Poetics of Experience.* Philadelphia: University of Pennsylvania Press, 1982.

Homans, Margaret. *Women Writers and Poetic Identity: Dorothy Wordsworth, Emily Brontë, and Emily Dickinson.* Princeton: Princeton University Press, 1980.

Horowitz, Maryanne Cline. "Aristotle and Woman." *Journal of the History of Biology* 9 (Fall 1976): 183–213.

Howe, Elizabeth Teresa. "Sor Teresa de Cartagena and *Entendimiento.*" *Romanische Forschungen* 108 (1996): 133–45.

Jacquart, Danielle, and Claude Thomasset. *Sexuality and Medicine in the Middle Ages.* Princeton: Princeton University Press, 1988.

Jardine, Alice A. *Gynesis: Configurations of Woman and Modernity.* Ithaca: Cornell University Press, 1985.

Jelinek, Estelle C., ed. *Women's Autobiography: Essays in Criticism.* Bloomington: Indiana University Press, 1980.

———. *The Tradition of Women's Autobiography: From Antiquity to the Present.* Boston: Twayne, 1986.

Jordan, Constance. *Renaissance Feminism: Literary Texts and Political Models.* Ithaca: Cornell University Press, 1990.

Kamen, Henry. *Inquisition and Society in Spain in the Sixteenth and Seventeenth Centuries.* London: Weidenfeld and Nicolson, 1985.

Kamuf, Peggy. *Signature Pieces: On the Institution of Authorship.* Ithaca: Cornell University Press, 1988.

Kelly, Joan. *Women, History, and Theory: The Essays of Joan Kelly.* Chicago: University of Chicago Press, 1984.

Klapisch-Zuber, Christiane, ed. *A History of Women in the West, II: Silences of the Middle Ages.* Cambridge, Mass.: The Belknap Press of Harvard University Press, 1992.

Kolodny, Annette. "A Map for Rereading: Or, Gender and the Interpretation of Literary Texts." *New Literary History* 11 (1980): 451–67.

Laqueur, Thomas. *Making Sex: Body and Gender from the Greeks to Freud.* Cambridge, Mass.: Harvard University Press, 1990.

López Estrada, Francisco. "Las mujeres escritoras en la Edad Media castellana." In *La condición de la mujer en la edad media: Actas del Coloquio celebrado en la Casa de Velázquez del 5 al 7 de noviembre de 1984,* 9–38. Madrid: Editorial de la Universidad Complutense, 1986.

Lucas, Angela M. *Women in the Middle Ages: Religion, Marriage, and Letters.* Brighton: Harvester Press, 1983.

Luna, Pedro de. *Libro de las consolaciones de la vida humana.* In *Escritores en prosa anteriores al siglo XV,* ed. Pascual de Gayangos, 561–602. Biblioteca de Autores Españoles, 51. Madrid: Sucesores de Hernando, 1884.

Maccoby, Hyam. *Judaism on Trial: Jewish-Christian Disputations in the Middle Ages.* London: Associated University Presses, 1982.

Marichal, Juan. *Teoría e historia del ensayismo hispánico.* Madrid: Alianza, 1984.

Marimón Llorca, Carmen. *Prosistas castellanas medievales.* Alicante: Publicaciones de la Caja de Ahorros Provincial, 1990.

Márquez Villanueva, Francisco. "El problema de los conversos: cuatro puntos cardinales." In *Hispania Judaica: Studies on the History, Language, and Literature of the Jews in the Hispanic World, I,* ed. Josep Solà-Solé, Samuel G. Armistead, and Joseph H. Silverman, 51–75. Barcelona: Puvill, 1980.

Martínez Burgos, M. "Don Alonso de Cartagena, Obispo de Burgos: su testamento." *Revista de Archivos, Bibliotecas y Museos* 63 (1957): 81–110.

Mason, Mary. "The Other Voice: Autobiographies of Women Writers." In *Life/Lines,* ed. Brodski and Schenck, 19–44.

Mazzeo, Joseph Anthony. "St. Augustine's Rhetoric of Silence." *Journal of the History of Ideas* 23 (1962): 175–96.

McConnell-Ginet, Sally, Ruth Borker, and Nelly Furman, eds. *Women and Language in Literature and Society.* New York: Praeger, 1980.

McLaughlin, Eleanor Commo. "Equality of Souls, Inequality of Sexes: Women in Medieval Theology." In *Religion and Sexism,* ed. Ruether, 213–66.

———. "Women, Power, and the Pursuit of Holiness in Medieval Christianity." In *Women of Spirit,* ed. Ruether and McLaughlin, 99–130.

McNamara, JoAnn, and Suzanne F. Wemple. "Sanctity and Power: The Dual Pursuit of Medieval Women." In *Becoming Visible*, ed. Bridenthal and Koonz, 90–118.

Miller, Beth, ed. *Women in Hispanic Literature: Icons and Fallen Idols.* Berkeley: University of California Press, 1983.

Miller, Nancy K., ed. *The Poetics of Gender.* New York: Columbia University Press, 1986.

Minnis, A.J. *Medieval Theory of Authorship.* Philadelphia: University of Pennsylvania Press, 1988.

Mirrer, Louise. "Feminist Approaches to Medieval Spanish History and Literature." *Medieval Feminist Newsletter* 7 (Spring 1989): 2–7.

Molina, Irene Alejandra. "La *Arboleda de los enfermos* de Teresa de Cartagena: un sermón olvidado." Masters Thesis, University of Texas, Austin, December 1990.

Nader, Helen. *The Mendoza Family in the Spanish Renaissance, 1350–1550.* New Brunswick: Rutgers University Press, 1979.

Netanyahu, Benzion. *The Marranos of Spain From the Late XIVth to the Early XVIth Century According to Contemporary Hebrew Sources.* 1966; repr. Millwood: Kraus, 1973.

———. *The Origins of the Inquisition in Fifteenth Century Spain.* New York: Random House, 1995.

Nichols, John A., and Lillian Thomas Shank, eds. *Medieval Religious Women, I: Distant Echoes.* Kalamazoo: Cistercian Publications, 1984.

Nuevas perspectivas sobre la mujer: Actas de las Primeras Jornadas de Investigación Interdisciplinaria. Madrid: Seminario de Estudios de la Mujer de la Universidad Autónoma de Madrid, 1982.

Ong, Walter J. "Latin Language Study as a Renaissance Puberty Rite." *Studies in Philology* 56 (1959): 103–24.

———. *The Presence of the Word: Some Prolegomena for Cultural and Religious History.* Minneapolis: University of Minnesota Press, 1981.

———. *Orality and Literacy: The Technologizing of the Word.* New York: Methuen, 1982.

Patrologia cursus completus: Series latina, ed. J.P. Migne, 221 vols. Paris: Migne, etc., 1841–64.

Peters, Edward. *Inquisition.* Berkeley: University of California, 1989.

Power, Eileen. *Medieval Women*, ed. M.M. Postan. Cambridge: Cambridge University Press, 1975.

Quilligan, Maureen. *The Allegory of Female Authority: Christine de Pizan's "Cité des Dames."* Ithaca: Cornell University Press, 1991.

Rodríguez Rivas, Gregorio. "La *Arboleda de los enfermos* de Teresa de Cartagena, literatura ascética en el siglo XV." *Entemu* (Centro Asociado de Asturias) 3 (1991): 117–30.

Rose, Mary Beth, ed. *Women in the Middle Ages and the Renaissance: Literary and Historical Perspectives.* Syracuse: Syracuse University Press, 1986.

Rosenthal, Joel T. *Medieval Women and the Sources of Medieval History*. Athens: University of Georgia Press, 1990.

Roth, Norman. *Conversos, Inquisition, and the Expulsion of the Jews from Spain*. Madison: University of Wisconsin Press, 1995.

Round, Nicholas G. "Renaissance Culture and Its Opponents in Fifteenth-Century Castile." *Modern Language Review* 57 (1967): 204–15.

————. "Five Magicians, or the Uses of Literacy." *Modern Language Review* 64 (1969): 793–805.

Ruether, Rosemary Radford. "Misogynism and Virginal Feminism in the Fathers of the Church." In *Religion and Sexism*, ed. Ruether, 150–83.

Ruether, Rosemary Radford, ed. *Religion and Sexism: Images of Woman in the Jewish and Christian Traditions*. New York: Simon & Schuster, 1974.

Ruether, Rosemary, and Eleanor McLaughlin, eds. *Women of Spirit: Female Leadership in the Jewish and Christian Traditions*. New York: Simon and Schuster, 1979.

Sacks, Oliver. *Seeing Voices: A Journey into the World of the Deaf*. Berkeley: University of California Press, 1989.

Saenger, Paul. "Silent Reading: Its Impact on late Medieval Script and Society." *Viator* 13 (1982): 367–414.

Saperstein, Marc. *Jewish Preaching 1200–1800: An Anthology*. New Haven: Yale University Press, 1989.

Schibanoff, Susan. "Taking the Gold Out of Egypt: The Art of Reading as a Woman." In *Gender and Reading*, ed. Flynn and Schweickart, 83–106.

Schmitt Pantel, Pauline, ed. *A History of Women in the West, I: From Ancient Goddesses to Christian Saints*. Cambridge, Mass.: The Belknap Press of Harvard University Press, 1992.

Schweickart, Patrocinio P. "Reading Ourselves: Toward a Feminist Theory of Reading." In *Gender and Reading*, ed. Flynn and Schweickart, 31–62.

Sconza, M. Jean. "A Reevaluation of the *Siete Edades del Mundo*." *La Corónica* 16 (1987–88): 94–112.

Sears, Elizabeth. *The Ages of Man: Medieval Interpretations of the Life Cycle*. Princeton: Princeton University Press, 1986.

Seidenspinner-Núñez, Dayle. " 'El solo me leyó': Gendered Hermeneutics and Subversive Poetics in *Admiración operum Dey* of Teresa de Cartagena." *Medievalia* 15 (1993): 14–23. .

————. " 'But I Suffer Not a Woman to Speak': Two Women Writers in Late Medieval Spain." In *Hers Ancient and Modern: Women Writing in Spain and Brazil*, ed. Catherine Davies and Jane Whetnall. London: Department of Hispanic Studies, Queen Mary and Westfield College, in press.

Serrano y Sanz, Manuel. *Apuntes para una biblioteca de escritoras españolas desde el año 1410 al 1833*. 2 vols. Madrid: Sucesores de Rivadeneyra, 1903–5.

Shahar, Shulamith. *The Fourth Estate: A History of Women in the Middle Ages*. London: Methuen, 1983.

Shank, Lillian Thomas, and John A. Nichols, eds. *Medieval Religious Women, II: Peaceweavers*. Kalamazoo: Cistercian Publications, Inc., 1987.

Sicroff, Albert A. *Les Controverses des statuts de pureté de sang en Espagne de XVe au XVIIe siècle.* Paris: Librairie Marcel Didier, 1960.

Sissa, Giulia. "The Sexual Philosophies of Plato and Aristotle." In *A History of Women in the West, I: From Ancient Goddesses to Christian Saints,* ed. Pauline Schmitt Pantel, 46–81. Cambridge, Mass.: The Belknap Press of Harvard University Press, 1992.

Smith, Sidonie. *A Poetics of Women's Autobiography: Marginality and the Fictions of Self-Representation.* Bloomington: Indiana University Press, 1987.

Solà-Solé, Josep M. *Sobre árabes, judíos y marranos y su impacto en la lengua y literatura españolas.* Barcelona: Puvill, 1983.

Sprinker, Michael. "Fictions of the Self: The End of Autobiography." In *Autobiography: Essays Theoretical and Critical,* ed. James Olney, 321–42. Princeton: Princeton University Press, 1980.

Stallybrass, Peter. "Patriarchal Territories: The Body Enclosed." In *Rewriting the Renaissance: The Discourses of Sexual Difference in Early Modern Europe,* eds. Margaret W. Ferguson, Maureen Quilligan, and Nancy J. Vickers, 123–42. Chicago: University of Chicago Press, 1986.

Stanton, Domna, ed. *The Female Autograph.* Chicago: University of Chicago Press, 1987.

Storm, Melvin. "Alisoun's Ear." *Modern Language Quarterly* 42 (1981): 219–26.

Stuard, Susan Mosher, ed. *Women in Medieval Society.* Philadelphia: University of Pennsylvania Press, 1976.

———. *Women in Medieval History and Historiography.* Philadelphia: University of Pennsylvania Press, 1987.

Surtz, Ronald E. "Image Patterns in Teresa de Cartagena's *Arboleda de los enfermos.*" In *La Chispa '87: Selected Proceedings,* ed. Gilbert Paolini, 297–304. New Orleans: Tulane University, 1987.

———. *The Guitar of God: Gender, Power, and Authority in the Visionary World of Mother Juana de la Cruz (1481–1534).* Philadelphia: University of Pennsylvania Press, 1990.

———. *Writing Women in Late Medieval and Early Modern Spain: The Mothers of Saint Teresa of Avila.* Philadelphia: University of Pennsylvania Press, 1995.

Teresa de Cartagena. *Arboleda de los enfermos y Admiraçión operum Dey,* ed. Lewis Joseph Hutton. Anejos del Boletín de la Real Academia Española, 16. Madrid: Real Academia Española, 1967.

Thiébaux, Marcelle, ed. *The Writings of Medieval Women.* New York: Garland, 1987.

Thomasset, Claude. "The Nature of Woman." In *Silences of the Middle Ages,* ed. Klapisch-Zuber, 43–69.

Valdeón Baruque, Julio. *Los judíos de Castilla y la revolución Trastámara.* Valladolid: Universidad de Valladolid, 1968.

Vicente García, Luis Miguel. "La defensa de la mujer como intelectual en Teresa de Cartagena y Sor Juana Inés de la Cruz." *Mester* 18:2 (Fall 1989): 95–103.

Warner, Marina. *Alone of All Her Sex: The Myth and the Cult of the Virgin Mary*. New York: Vintage Books, 1976.

Wilson, Katharina M., ed. *Medieval Women Writers*. Athens: University of Georgia Press, 1984.

Zumthor, Paul. "Litteratus/Illiteratus: Remarques sur le contexte vocal de l'écriture médiévale." *Romania* 106 (1985): 1–18.

Index

abstinence, 14, 58, 61
Adam, 17, 18, 121
admiración (see wonder)
affliction(s) (see also suffering), 13, 14, 29,
35, 36, 38–40, 41, 43, 49, 50, 51, 52, 53,
57–63, 64, 68, 74, 83, 112
allegory, 21, 119, 120, 134–35
Amador de los Ríos, José, 6
Ambrose, Saint, 38, 116, 129, 134
anger (see ire)
Antequera, Fernando de, 7
antifeminism (see also misogyny), 2, 17
anti-Semitism, 3, 5, 6
anxiety of authorship, 20, 21, 113–14, 130,
132
Aquinas, Thomas, 16, 17
Aristotle, 7, 16, 17
Augustine, Saint, 16, 48, 67, 81, 89, 104, 116
authority, 20
autobiography, 1, 19, 20, 117–23, 136–38
avarice, 14, 58, 61, 82
Avignon, 5, 6

Baer, Yitzhak, 6
Benedict XIII, Pope (see also Pedro de Luna),
4, 6
Bernard, Saint, 57, 62
blessings of grace, 15, 95, 96–98, 133–34,
136
blessings of nature and fortune, 15, 60,
95–96, 97, 133
blind man on the road to Jericho, 15,
103–06, 123, 137
Bloom, Harold, 114
Boccaccio, 7
Boethius, 42, 116
Bruni, Leonardo, 7
Burgos, 4, 5, 6, 7, 9, 10, 11

cancionero poetry, 2, 116
Cantera Burgos, Francisco, 6, 7, 8
Cárcel de amor, 2
Cartagena, 4
Cartagena, Alonso de (uncle of Teresa), 5, 6,
7, 8
Cartagena, Alonso de (brother of Teresa), 5,
9
Cartagena, Alvaro de, 5, 9

Cartagena, Juana de, 5, 9
Cartagena, Paulo de, 5
Cartagena, Pedro de (father of Teresa), 5, 7,
9
Cartagena, Pedro de (half-brother of
Teresa), 5
Cartagena, Teresa de, ix, 1–5, 8–15, 19–21,
23, 86, 113–38
allegory, 119, 120
anxiety of authorship, 113–14, 132
convent, 11, 128–30
deafness, 1, 3, 9, 10–11, 12, 23, 113,
124–30
family, 2, 4–8, 11
humility formulas, 114–15
life, 8–11
University of Salamanca, 9, 10
Cartagena/Santa María family, 4–8
Castelloza, 3
Castile, 4, 8
Castro, Américo, 6
Catherine of Lancaster, 7
Catherine of Siena, 3
Catholic Monarchs (also Fernando and
Isabel), 5, 8
charity, 14, 28, 36, 37, 42, 58, 61, 62, 63,
84, 85, 95, 100, 102, 104, 112
chastity, 14, 58
Chaucer, 126
Christine de Pizan, 3, 125
Cicero, 7
convent of afflictions (also convent of the
infirm, convent of the sick), 13, 40, 42,
128
conversos, 3, 4, 7, 8
anti-converso riots, 3
Coplas de las calidades de las donas, 2
*Coplas en vituperio delas malas hembras y
en loor delas buenas mugeres*, 2
Corbacho, 2
Council of Basel, 5, 8
Council of Constance, 6
custom, 14, 89–90

David (also the Prophet, the Psalmist), 12,
24, 32, 35–36, 38, 44, 45, 49, 50, 55, 62,
67, 70, 76, 84, 92, 96, 97, 98, 101, 102,
103, 104, 107, 108, 109, 111, 114, 123

CPSIA information can be obtained
at www.ICGtesting.com
Printed in the USA
BVHW04s2012140918
527324BV00006B/41/P